D1066178

HALLS OF THE MIGHTY

HALLS
of the
MIGHTY

My 47 Years at the Senate

Richard Langham Riedel

ROBERT B. LUCE, Inc. WASHINGTON–NEW YORK

copyright © 1969 by Richard Langham Riedel

All rights reserved, including the right to reproduce this book, or parts thereof, in any form, except for the inclusion of brief quotations in a review.

Library of Congress Catalog Card Number 70–76375

328.73
R551

DEDICATION

To my wife and coauthor Angela Bachman Riedel,
without whom this book could not have been written,

To our daughters Angela Lynn and Kathleen Cody,
for whom it was written

In the spirit of the venerable Mix.

FOREWORD

I could name no person who could better write of the *Halls of the Mighty* after forty-seven years of service to the Senate than Richard Langham Riedel.

It was his responsibility to serve as liaison between Senators and the press, radio, and television reporters; and to say the least it was a labor that required infinite patience.

When Dick, as he was affectionately called, came to see a Senator on the Floor of the Senate and told him who would like to see him in the President's Room, more often than not that particular Senator was quite busy and did not want to be disturbed at the moment. This did not offend Dick Riedel nor did it in the least shadow his patience as he waited for an interminable time if necessary in order to bring the Senator and the Reporter together.

This not only required patience but a sense of diplomacy since on occasion it involved matters of considerable delicacy. There were many occasions when a Senator could not leave the Floor so that reporters resorted to the technique of sending in a verbal or written question with Dick Riedel and asking that he submit it and wait for an answer. This also was sometimes a delicate operation but he exercised it with skill and meticulous accuracy.

Hundreds of newspapermen along with radio and television reporters moved through the press gallery of the Senate in the almost half century that Dick Riedel served.

He was serving the Senate when Woodrow Wilson occupied the White House. Then came President Harding followed by President Coolidge. Then came President Hoover and in 1933 came President Roosevelt and then President Truman. Following him came Eisenhower, Kennedy, and Johnson. So it might be said that Dick Riedel served this branch of our government under nine Presidents.

That indeed is a long record and is surely the basis for his observations on the *Halls of the Mighty*. I am personally delighted to know that he was willing to devote so much time to his reminiscences because they will serve as interesting postscripts to Senatorial history.

Everett McKinley Dirksen
United States Senate

CONTENTS

October 6, 1965

Dear Richard:

I hear you are about to begin a new life. Yet, I can't
imagine what the Senate will be like without you.

You have served so long and so faithfully that for me--
and for so many of your friends--you seemed as much
a part of the Senate as its marbled halls.

I well recall the many times when, as majority leader,
I could not leave the floor, and you relayed questions
and answers for reporters. You always served honestly
and with good common sense.

In a historic setting--that of the United States Senate--
you wrote a history of your own. I believe that my good
friend Gould Lincoln is the only member of the Senate
Press Gallery who was a member when you came to the
Senate in 1918.

You can be proud of having served as liaison between
the press and the senators longer than any other person
in the history of the United States Senate.

Good luck in your new life, and in all your undertakings.
When you go camping in the wilderness, don't forget to
come back.

Meanwhile, your friends will remember you.

Sincerely,

Lyndon B. Johnson

Mr. Richard Langham Riedel
14027 Braddock Road
Centreville, Virginia   22020

THE YOUNGEST PAGE

On September 27, 1918, I climbed the steps of the United States Capitol to become the youngest Senate page. That first morning I was carefully decked out in the style then required for the well-dressed page: white shirt, blue serge suit with knickers, long black stockings, and white tennis shoes. I had said good-bye to my fourth grade classmates the week before. To our young minds becoming a page was almost comparable to being appointed a Senator of the United States. It created the illusion of graduating from the school world of preparation into the adult world of participation.

A sense of pride and a mirage of achievement was strong within me as I left home alone to walk across the familiar Capitol grounds. I lived with my parents and maternal grandparents at 123 A Street, Northeast, where the Supreme Court building now stands. We were so close to the Capitol that I later discovered I could be on the Senate Floor in three minutes, ready for the duties of a page.

Once inside the Senate wing, I easily found the austere office of Colonel Charles P. Higgins. He had been Sergeant at Arms of the Senate for many years but never before had he administered the oath of office to a nine-year-old. The old gentleman was reassuring as he asked me to raise my right hand while he recited the oath.

11

Standing erect with eyes straight ahead, I did solemnly swear to "support and defend the Constitution of the United States against all enemies, foreign and domestic." With all the earnestness of my full nine years, I assured the world that I would "bear true faith and allegiance to the same," that I took "this obligation freely, without any mental reservations or purpose of evasion," and that I would "well and faithfully discharge the duties of the office" on which I was about to enter, so help me God!

The formalities over, I eagerly walked onto the Senate Floor for the first time. The Chamber was impressive in its stateliness. The neatly curving rows of desks elevated on tiers were like a stage set awaiting the Senatorial actors. Galleries floated in a separate world above, presided over by dignified doorkeepers, and a glass-paneled roof illuminated the entire scene with the clarity of daylight. Immediately my fellow pages introduced themselves and introduced me to the legislative routine.

The duties of a page, then as now, were more than enough to keep any young man hopping all day, beginning at 9:30 A.M. when we reported to the Chamber. Before the Senate convened there were many details to attend to. Each page was responsible for the desks of six Senators. Each desk had a file of the *Congressional Record* to be added to daily and a Calendar File of the bills to be acted upon. Now, the bills come from the Government Printing Office with holes neatly punched, ready for each Senator's Calendar File. In my day, however, we had to punch the holes by hand with a sharp awl. It was a feat of strength and skill to tackle a pack of a few hundred bills, taking pains to keep the edges even. With our knees we braced the stack of bills on the then green-carpeted floor of the Senate and punched two holes in the proper places. Keen rivalry existed to see who could keep the file with the neatest edges. Tuesday after "Calendar Monday" the job had to be redone; and the entire stack of bills would be gone through to remove those that had been acted upon.

In addition, I distributed stationery supplies for the Lobby, Marble Room, cloakrooms, and the Senate Floor. Dating from quill-pen days, Senators are still supplied with lead-colored sand

Senator "Cotton Ed" Ellison D. Smith of South Carolina takes a pinch of snuff from the lacquer box on the rostrum.—photo: Herbert French Collection, Library of Congress

The Senate Chamber had a glass roof before the 1947 remodeling. On the rostrum the flag marks the Vice President's Chair directly beneath the Press Gallery.—photo: Library of Congress

that is kept in a square bottle on each desk. Those who have experimented with it have found dusting sand to dry the ink a decidedly messy process. How does one dispose of the sand? Shake it or blow it into a wastebasket and grains still cling to the ink. It was one of man's least successful solutions to a problem. Even in my early days the sand duster was simply a historic curiosity, but at the Senate, traditions never die or even fade away.

In niches on the wall near the rostrum are two other curiosities, the lacquer snuff boxes, one on the Democratic and one on the Republican side. I had to keep these filled with snuff. No one uses that form of tobacco today, but fifty years ago there were those who would come by for a pinch, such as Senators Ellison D. "Cotton Ed" Smith of South Carolina and Lee Overman of North Carolina. Overman with his silky white hair and black morning coat would inhale a pinch of snuff ceremoniously with a little twist of the wrist, while Cotton Ed was less fastidious. It must have helped clear their noses, for occasionally we page boys would sniff a little snuff just for the fun of inducing a sneeze.

Cuspidors were taken for granted and were strategically located throughout the Chamber so that a tobacco-chewing Senator could find one in transit as well as beside his own desk. The House of Representatives had shiny brass ones everywhere, reminiscent of a county courthouse. But the Senate in its refinement had only the best china of the proper shade of green to blend in with the carpet.

Before the Senate convened we would take turns unlocking the Vice President's desk to bring out the original ivory gavel which every Vice President, including John Adams and Thomas Jefferson, has used while presiding over the Senate. Shaped like an hourglass, it conveniently fits the hand. In the 1930's one Senator whiled away his hours in the Chair by carving on the ivory with his penknife, making it necessary to cover the ends with silver caps. Now the original gavel that called Henry Clay and Daniel Webster to order resides in a special wooden box. Beside it is the working gavel used today, a modern ivory piece given by India. Together they are brought daily to the Chamber by a page from the office of the Sergeant at Arms, where they are locked up for safekeeping.

By the time the Senate met at noon, we had already given our all with only a twenty-minute break for lunch. The life of contemporary pages has been improved by having a half-hour for lunch and two ten-minute breaks during the day. With the convening of the Senate the principal duty of serving on the rostrum begins. A page sits on the steps of the rostrum below the Vice President's desk, knees bent, ready to spring into action.

At the snap of a Senator's fingers one of us jumped up and ran to his desk for the errand he commanded: to take his newly-introduced bill or amendment to the rostrum, to carry documents to his office, or even to get a drink of water for him from the cloakroom. I had not been sitting on the rostrum long before Charles McNary of Oregon snapped for me. Always friendly with pages, McNary's delight was a special initiation for new boys which I unwittingly followed to the letter. In a serious Senatorial voice he instructed the novice to find "Senator Sorghum" for him immediately, said statesman having last been seen in the Senate restaurant. The waiters, elevator operators, and clerks were all in on the joke and sent the unsuspecting page to every corner of the Capitol on hearing that "Senator McNary wants to find Senator Sorghum." Eventually the page had to report back to McNary empty-handed. Another day, he would send a gullible new page to the Document Room for a nonexistent bill stretcher, but McNary failed to trick me the second time.

One compensation of being sent to the Senate Office Building was the breezy ride on the subway. Built primarily to enable Senators to reach the Capitol quickly to answer roll calls, the Senate subway has been the only free ride in Washington for over half a century. Long before I became a page, I rode in the early Studebaker wagons which were battery-driven and steered by the driver. They were high like circus bandwagons with big wheels and hard-rubber tires. To replace these wagons, the Washington Navy Yard built two monorail cars in 1915. They looked like giant wicker baskets full of Senators, but they were sturdy enough to operate for forty-six years. Since 1961, when the new Senate Office Building required a new subway system to serve both buildings,

four sleek metal cars have swished over in seconds. Most important, the subway ride is still breezy and still free.

If a Senator requests a book, a page dashes up to the Senate
Library in the old center part of the Capitol under the shoulders of
the dome. Here, where the Library of Congress was originally
housed, can be found almost everything in the legislative field.
Within minutes the book will be in the Senator's hands.

When more extensive or specialized knowledge is needed, a
quick request to the Library of Congress will bring a volume
immediately by way of the "library chute," a small tunnel under
the Capitol grounds through which books come on a conveyor
cable in large suitcase-like containers. Pages pick them up at the
little alcove behind the patriarchs of Statuary Hall and rush them
to the Senator waiting on the Floor.

The most enjoyable task in my page days was leading Senator
Thomas P. Gore about the Chamber or through the subway to his
office. One of Oklahoma's first Senators, Gore had been blind since
boyhood but he became an able lawyer and served four terms as
Senator. He knew me instantly by my voice, and through the years
he would comment on my rapid growth as we walked along arm in
arm. With his quick mind and infinite patience, Thomas Gore had
more perception than many sighted Senators.

How many errands does a page run? Senator George H.
Moses of New Hampshire once called me over to his desk to ask
that question. This inspired me to keep a record, and for the six
days of the week that ended February 22, 1919, I counted 310
errands. Without doubt, pages earn their salaries.

Several days after the swearing-in ceremony with the Sergeant
at Arms, my next official act was to collect my first pay in the
southwest corner of the Senate wing, now occupied by the Secretary of the Senate. It was necessary to sign the payroll slip, but the
Disbursing Officer saw that I was too small to reach the counter.
He had to bring me inside the office to a desk so I could sign my
name and collect my pay of $11.33 for the closing days of Septem-
ber. My full page's salary of $97.50 per month was paid when the
Senate was in session but not during long adjournments. Now

pages receive $450 each month.

On days when the Senate did not meet, pages had to report to the Chamber to attend to the desks and be ready to answer calls from Senators' offices. When work slackened, we held mock sessions while sitting at Senators' desks. We introduced bills, made speeches, and took roll call votes. Being boys, we found other pursuits totally unrelated to Senate procedure and decorum, such as sending paper darts flying up into the gallery. Or we would see who could launch a paper clip with a rubber band hard enough to hit the glass ceiling. A champion launcher could make the old roof ring or hit a paddle arm on one of the electric fans that were suspended from the ceiling before the era of air conditioning.

When the Senate was not in session, my favorite sport was to sprint to the top of the dome, up stairs so narrow that they have been closed for years. I could make the trip up in less than three minutes. Once above the ceiling of the Rotunda, among the curving iron girders of the dome's inner and outer shells, it is like climbing in the hull of a ship. It is a heady sensation to stand alone out on the small balcony with only the statue of Freedom above. The dome leaps away in all directions, the Senate and House spread like the wings of an eagle on each side and the avenues of the city lead to the Maryland and Virginia hills beyond. To see Washington from the top of the dome is to understand the Congressional point of view: the center of government, if not the universe, can only be Capitol Hill!

The Capitol and its surroundings have been more to me than a historic shrine and an interesting place to work. I grew up on Capitol Hill, roller-skating over the shaded walks and sledding down the west slope in winter. Our A Street neighborhood, which was razed to make way for the Supreme Court building in 1930, included the Old Capitol, a blocky structure that housed Congress from 1815–19 after the British burned the new nation's Capitol.

Our narrow, three-story row house was ample for the five of

us, including my mother's parents. My father, Richard Reinhold
Riedel, was a Baptist minister and a skilled artist cut in the
vigorous mold of a Teddy Roosevelt. He was one of the seven
students with whom Russell Conwell founded Temple University
in Philadelphia, and he was graduated from Temple as well as
from Crozier Theological Seminary. My mother, Carrie Edna Langham Riedel, had taught school and music in her younger days in
western Pennsylvania before becoming a minister's wife.

The family rarely missed an important event in our home-
town. When the cornerstone of the Lincoln Memorial was laid on
February 12, 1915, one of the architects invited me to spread
mortar on the stone after the ceremony, a proud moment for a
six-year-old. Later that year I marched down Pennsylvania Avenue
in the last large parade of the Grand Army of the Republic,
walking beside my grandfather, Joseph L. Langham, who was a
commander in the veterans' organization of the Union Army. Two
years later I joined my mother and grandmother Elizabeth Johnston Langham in a suffragette parade to the White House where
Woodrow Wilson welcomed us at a reception. In those early days
before World War I, the national capital had the mellow atmosphere of a small college town.

When we moved to Washington in 1913, from Chicago where
I was born in 1908, we brought with us a little toy automobile
which my father had fashioned from an enormous tin can and
other pieces of cast-off metal. In this tin "touring car" I would
meet our neighbor Senator George Chamberlain as he walked
home across the Capitol grounds after a weighty day as Chairman
of the old Senate Military Affairs Committee. The stately Oregonian was the first United States Senator I knew. It surprised him
when I became a page not too long after I had pedaled down the
street beside him. Neither of us realized that before my service at
the Senate would come to a close, I would know 558 Senators
from every state.

It is a fair question to ask how I became a page at all, much
less the youngest in the twentieth century. By Senate tradition,
Henry Clay is said to have appointed the first page in the early

nineteenth century, a boy who was also nine years old. The age limit for pages today is fourteen to seventeen; in 1918 it was twelve to sixteen. How did a nine-year-old get in?

Senators in those days could waive rules and customs just as grandly as they could wave the flag. Boies Penrose, the czar of Pennsylvania politics who personally had to approve a generation of Republican presidential candidates, could have put a toddler on the rostrum if he had wanted to. Senator Penrose sent his secretary Layton Taylor to our home in the summer of 1918 with the news that there was a vacancy among the Senate pages. "Will you let Richard take it?" Taylor asked. My parents, though not active in politics, thought that it would be an unusual opportunity for me to have a year or two at the Senate and then return to school. After we had accepted this unsolicited offer, Taylor asked for a letter requesting my appointment from my uncle Judge J. N. Langham of Indiana, Pennsylvania, who sent the letter immediately. When Uncle Nick had represented the old 27th Congressional District of Pennsylvania from 1908–15, he had taken me with him on the Floor of the House of Representatives. He was a good friend of Boies Penrose and considered it an honor for me to be on the Senator's patronage.

In this way the door of the Senate was opened to a youngster who even then looked forward to returning to school and a normal boyhood. When my father died suddenly not long after my eleventh birthday and within two years after the death of my grandparents, it became necessary for me to support my mother whose health was impaired. Being a page was no longer a luxurious opportunity; it became our means of survival.

There was no page school until the 1930's, long after I had been a page. Though I tried several times from 1919–35 to continue schooling at night, the irregularity of Senate sessions made it impossible to complete a standard program. However, I did learn touch typing at the age of ten. To be at the Senate itself was a liberal education, though the curriculum was always unplanned and completely unpredictable.

The life of a page seems glamorous on the surface. Twenty-five boys have the rare opportunity of an inside look at the Senate. But in exchange for the honor and the experience, the boys lead an irregular life totally unsuited to their mid-teen years. While the Capitol Page School begins classes at six A.M. in the Library of Congress and continues until Floor duties start at nine, uncertain Senate hours sometimes extend far into the night, leaving no time for study and recreation. Instead of playing on athletic fields, the boys pound marble corridors. The exhausting pace would be better suited to the late teens during an interlude between high school and college. Senate pages have gone on to succeed in many fields, but only Arthur P. Gorman of Maryland, a page in the 1860's, returned as a Senator. Though not a preparation for a specific career, starting out as a page is an industrious beginning.

IN SEARCH OF SENATORS

For six years I was a page. During a routine two-week assignment to work with the members of the press, I achieved a special rapport with the newsmen who asked that I be permanently assigned to them. For a while there were so few newsmen that my time could be divided between them and my duties on the rostrum. After ceasing to be a page, I continued my work with the press through the years. As the number of correspondents multiplied, so did their needs and the scope of my job. Eventually I was given the title of Press Liaison to describe my work, the first such title to be granted by the Senate. I grew up with the job and the job grew up with me.

Until 1919 the Senate Lobby adjacent to the Chamber was open to anyone who wished to talk with a Senator. Washington correspondents, lobbyists, and constituents all converged in the long picturesque room with its row of dazzling chandeliers. Comfortable leather sofas and writing desks line the walls today where Senators may telephone, dictate and sign correspondence, or read the latest bulletins from the Associated Press and United Press International tickers that click away in glass-covered cabinets. But the Lobby had no furniture when I went to the Senate.

Senators would take their guests into the Marble Room where they could be seated. Colorful marble walls and a high ceiling supported by white marble columns give the room its name. Now

In pre-page days, Richard Riedel grew up on Capitol Hill.

At thirteen, the author had been a Senate page four years.—photo: UPI

Vice President Thomas R. Marshall being cheered after his annual Christmas dinner for pages.—photo: Underwood & Underwood

the Senators' exclusive reading room, it is an inner sanctum closed to everyone else. Newspapers from all states line the tables, ready to keep legislators informed of grass-root opinion. A giant weather map lets Senators know the national weather scene before they fly home. The tile floor is carpeted to soften sounds in this secluded haven. Of all corners of the Senate wing, the classical Marble Room with its sofas and lounges is the best place to snatch a Senatorial nap on a quiet afternoon or during a late night session.

In contrast, the two L-shaped cloakrooms, one Democratic and one Republican, that hug the opposite side of the Chamber are usually bustling with activity. Pages, Senators, and staff members continually pop in and out to the tune of ringing phones and laughter. Until the late 1930's they were actually cloakrooms where each member had a mahogany cabinet with his name in gold on a glass plate affixed to the door. If a Senator arrived in the Chamber with hat in hand and overcoat over his arm, before he could walk two steps a page would rush to take his coat and put it away in his locker. Ten large telephone booths in each cloakroom have since replaced the lockers, so that now pages must take a Senator's hat and coat all the way to his office or hang them on an ordinary rack near the Chamber. With sofas, desks, and telephone booths, the cloakrooms are private conversation centers a step away from the Floor.

As a new page boy circulating in and out of the Chamber, I found that my daily associates were the most notable statesmen of the day: Henry Cabot Lodge, Sr., Oscar Underwood, Frank B. Kellogg, Warren G. Harding, William E. Borah, Hiram Johnson, George W. Norris, Bob LaFollette, and many others. I would speak shyly with them, calling them out to see the correspondents waiting in the Lobby.

Five of the newsmen who were covering Capitol Hill in 1918 remained members of the Press Gallery throughout my half century. Gould Lincoln, with the *Washington Star* since 1909, is now the dean of the press corps. Bascom Timmons had just begun to build his nationwide news bureau. David Lawrence, a reporter for the *New York Evening Post,* went on to found his own publishing

empire, including *U.S. News and World Report*. Arthur Sears
Henning was already Washington bureau chief of the *Chicago
Tribune* and Jay Hayden was chief of the *Detroit News* Washing-
ton bureau.

My first lesson in tact and diplomacy came from the only
woman member of the Press Gallery at that time, Mrs. Myra
Richards of Exeter, New Hampshire. Mrs. Richards had taken her
late husband's place as correspondent for papers throughout New
England. She was a very precise Victorian, both in dress and
manner, and her trademark was a black turban nestled securely
upon red-tinted hair. When Mrs. Richards asked me to go in the
Chamber, I faithfully reported her exact words to John Wingate
Weeks of Massachusetts, who was later to become Secretary of
War in President Harding's cabinet. Emphatically I said, "Senator,
Mrs. Richards is very anxious to see you." "Well," he replied with
a hint of the subtle humor that dwelt within his great bald head,
"you tell Mrs. Richards that I am *not* very anxious to see her."

Blissfully unaware that anything but verbatim replies were in
order, I carefully repeated the message to Mrs. Richards, word for
word. Suddenly this diminutive old lady was a spectacle terrifying
enough to make any little page tremble as she began shaking with
rage and embarrassment. I was afraid that the wig she was reputed
to wear would fly right off her head. In the aftermath of the storm I
was introduced to the useful and peaceful art of diplomacy. Forever after I would prudently notify Mrs. Richards' Senators that
she would like to see them "if it were convenient." In time her ire
subsided, and Mrs. Richards and I became friends.

With the arrival of the 66th Congress in March, 1919, the
Senate closed the doors of the Lobby to all but Senators and staff
members. Constituents and lobbyists had to await Senators in the
more remote Senate Reception Room, while news correspondents
were allotted the President's Room, hitherto reserved for rare visits
of the Chief Executive to the Capitol. This room had received the
full attention of Constantino Brumidi whose beautiful frescoes on
walls and ceiling portray George Washington, his first cabinet, and
various figures in early American history. The full-length pair of

wall mirrors, elaborately trimmed in gold, face each other across the room to give the effect of an endless corridor. A large oval table in the center of the room was used by President Lincoln when he signed bills at the Senate. The colorful English tile on the floor and the costly gold chandelier made a sumptuous setting for the press. The newsmen rather liked its exclusiveness, and I began my base of operations in the square anteroom just outside.

The location of the President's Room adjacent to the Senators' private men's room has had a practical advantage to newsmen. The only access Senators have to their facilities is by the President's Room, where they almost always encounter correspondents. It is a fact that many of the best news sources have been Senators with weak bladders and strong minds!

Guarding the entrance to the Lobby outside the President's Room, a giant French vase stands like a sentinel while its mate adorns the other end of the Lobby. In 1918 Marshal Joffre presented them to the Senate and another pair to the House in gratitude for our victorious role in World War I. With France's unpaid war debt in mind, the perennial joke about the vases has been, "These are what we got for winning the war."

With larger areas of the Senate wing now inaccessible to newsmen, my search for Senators became more extensive. The new orbit not only contained my customary loop around the Floor and through the two cloakrooms, but included the Reception Room, the Lobby, and the Marble Room as well. It would have been a staggering thought to me when a young boy to realize that during the next half century I would ultimately travel approximately 30,000 miles within this same circuit.

The only members of the press who were still permitted past the President's Room were a representative of each of the four wire services: Associated Press, United Press and International News Service which later merged to become United Press International, and the now extinct Universal Service. Since most of the country's newspapers relied on the wire services for spot-news coverage, these correspondents served as a kind of news pool. They enjoyed the privilege of the Floor where one of the long tables in the well of the Senate was reserved for them and they were permitted to circulate in the back of the Chamber.

When the Senate withdrew their Floor privileges in May, 1929, my work increased tenfold. The wire-service men, accustomed to nabbing their own Senators on the Floor, were now doubly anxious that I cover the Floor constantly for each one of them, not only asking Senators to come out to see them but asking spot-news questions for them as well. With the keen competition and split-second deadlines of the wire service correspondents, I had to rush around the Chamber at full speed, taking care that I did not knock down some aged Senator on my daily dash through history.

It was from this turn of events that the first stages of the metamorphosis from page to Press Liaison took place. At this time I was first assigned an assistant, that cherished Washington status symbol. In 1929 Dick Oyster of Maryland and Arthur Caldwell of Arkansas became the first of many assistants; the last was my successor, Tom Pellikaan of Missouri.

However, there is more to working for the Senate than filling one's job; there is a political system to combat at every turn. A long road stretched ahead before my position as Press Liaison would be secure.

PATRONAGE PIE

As a place to experience the dramatic unfolding of history, the Senate is unsurpassed. As a place to build a lifetime career of service in a staff position, it is deficient in the extreme. The great United States Senate is cheapened by a patronage system under which all jobs are controlled by political appointment. Instead of a career based on ability, at the Senate it is based on patronage, on the whim of one's superiors, on the heartbeat of one's Senator. When a Senator goes, whether through defeat, retirement, or death, everyone on his patronage is automatically subject to dismissal unless salvaged by another Senator. The question is not, "Does this staff member do a good job?" Instead the patronage system asks, "Who is this person's Senator? How much patronage does he have? Can this person or some of his relatives or friends deliver the votes?"

My own battles for survival amid the shifting sands of Capitol life illustrate how inept and unfair a system which ignores dedication and ability can be. For the first three years I had been secure under the broad mantle of Senator Penrose, so busy with the duties of a page that I was all but oblivious to the political basis of my job. On the last day of 1921 death removed the ample figure of Boies Penrose from the Senate, suddenly exposing me to the cold, biting winds of a world without patronage. Had my father's death not made me the family wage earner, I would have quietly returned

27

to school at this point, but to continue to be a page was to continue to eat. I had to find more patronage without delay!

The natural person to look to was the man appointed to take Penrose's seat, George Wharton Pepper, a Philadelphia lawyer. Pepper was to become the best personal friend of all the Senators I have known, but at first he was just a busy new Senator who had no chance to get to know one little page boy. Therefore, I was forced to go through the regular channels of his office. The Senator had inherited, but did not long retain, Penrose's last secretary Charles P. Swope. This beer-barrel-shaped politician who sat like an impenetrable wall in Pepper's outer office was the one through whom I had to make my appeal to save my job. Swope scarcely glanced at the impressive collection of letters which had been given to me by Senators and newsmen, attesting to my efficiency as a page. Slouching at his desk, Swope answered with the flat, cold creed of political pragmatism, "Merit don't count in Pennsylvania politics." My job was saved when a short time later, the mail brought another letter from my uncle Judge Langham, proving again the old saw, "It is not *what* you know but *who* you know . . ." a perfect description of the patronage system.

Luckily for me, Swope did not succeed in dampening my idealism. Any skill and initiative that I have shown has been acknowledged by the always grateful members of the press and frequently by appreciative Senators. George Wharton Pepper proved to be the foremost of the latter group, but unfortunately he was not to stay in the Senate long. His defeat in 1926 because of a three way race was a loss to the country and to me.

Once more I was adrift without a Senator. Again I was at the mercy of the system, personified by the Senate Sergeant at Arms David S. Barry, a small man whose trademarks were a large mustache and ever-present derby hat and cane. To secure a year-round salary for me, Senator Pepper had me assigned to clerical work in Barry's office during adjournments when there were no duties with the press. Vacations were brief and rare. At one point my salary was cut to $80 a month, but it eventually reached $1500 a year. After Pepper's defeat, Barry slashed it back to $1100 before he would allow me to take three weeks away from the Senate in 1927 to enjoy a western trip I had earned through a religious organization.

During his tenure of office as Sergeant at Arms David Barry was a tyrant to many of the employees under his supervision. On one occasion I heard him abuse and unjustly discharge a dignified old Civil War veteran. Barry pushed his arrogant ways too far when he wrote an indiscreet magazine article in which he inferred that some Senators were dishonest. This article, which appeared in a national publication early in 1933, resulted in his being summarily brought before the "bar of the Senate" and discharged by a roll-call vote.

Aside from an autocratic official now and then, the Senate community as a whole can be magnanimous during a time of emergency. After my sudden appendectomy in 1926, a number of Senators were inspired by Colonel Chesley Jurney, later Sergeant at Arms, to contribute money to cover the hospital and medical bills. It was as though I had never left the Floor when the nurse asked how I felt after the operation. Still groggy from the anesthetic I answered, "Senator, the pain is still in session!"

The ups and downs of a job at the Senate can illustrate one thing, the vicissitudes of a career based solely on personal relationships rather than on efficient performance. It has always amused me how I became a good friend of "Genial" Jim Watson, the powerful Majority Leader during the Hoover administration. It was not hard work primarily that won his approval. He first took special notice of me on the steps of the Capitol one evening during a little pageant in which I participated. I had dressed up in my father's top hat and frock coat to impersonate Henry Clay. I spoke no word; it required no talent; and I did not look at *all* like Henry Clay. But from that moment on, Senator Watson considered me above the ordinary. He began to take more notice of my frequent hurried trips about the Chamber. Upon hearing of my ridiculously low salary, he simply picked up a telephone and ordered Barry, who was still Sergeant at Arms, to correct the situation saying, "After all these years of good faithful service, Richard should have had his salary *raised* instead of lowered." With the approval of Senator Hiram Bingham of Connecticut, Chairman of the Majority Patronage Committee, my salary was almost doubled by 1928.

For the next five years security seemed to be in my grasp at last. I was on the Permanent Efficiency Roll along with the clerks at the rostrum and other rare individuals who seemed to be above the patronage struggle. But with the overwhelming shift in political control of the Senate brought about by the change of administration in 1933, my cherished Permanent Efficiency Roll quickly faded into history. Ahead loomed the gravest crisis yet in my Senate career.

I was not then and never have been a politician, despite having grown up at the political center of the nation. I had done no partisan favors, helped in no campaigns, secured no votes. My only claim on the Senate was fifteen years of hard work, dedicated to the better press relations of all Senators. In the midst of the New Deal blitz I soon found that my labors were appreciated by one group, the press. Word that I had been left on the battlefield brought forth the newsmen in a figurative rescue mission in the form of a petition. Signed by the members of the Press Gallery, including foreign correspondents such as Sir Wilmot Lewis of the *London Times,* this document eloquently stated that I was indispensible to the press and that they wanted me to stay. The petition was presented to that artful Minority Leader Charles McNary who used it to pursuade Chairman Carl Hayden of the Democratic Patronage Committee to save my position.

This rescue operation by the press placed me beyond the reach of partisan politics once and for all. In a very real sense the newsmen became my sponsors. Where in the past I had tried to do the best I could, now I would exert twice the effort if it meant a newsman would get his story and meet his deadline. A certain independence and personal perspective came with this new status that would never have been possible under the yoke of ordinary patronage.

At the request of the press, Senator James F. Byrnes in 1938 elevated my job to an individual status by designating me the first Press Liaison of the Senate. The pay was never luxurious, but the footing was secure at last. Like a guaranteed annual wage, I received the same salary regardless of all-night and year-round sessions, while adjournments evened the score now and then by providing long vacations. Automatically retained regardless of which party was in the majority, I had reached that nonpartisan Valhalla that only a fortunate few Senate employees achieve.

It is only on Capitol Hill where patronage holds sway. Within the giant apparatus of the rest of the federal government, most employees are classified, hired, and protected by the Civil Service Commission. Those working for the legislative branch of the government, however, are all hired and promoted under the patronage system, from the most responsible position to the least skilled.

Within a salary spread of $5,000 to $28,000, the range of Capitol jobs is vast, covering not only the obvious administrative functions but the many tasks of protecting, operating, and maintaining the building itself. Senate personnel fall into three categories: committee experts, Senators' office staffs, and employees who serve the entire Senate. It is in the latter group where, all too frequently, patronage alone is what counts. There is no set rule as to how much patronage of this type one Senator can control. The majority members have more say; because it is the majority party that divides the greater part of the patronage pie after slicing off a modest portion for the minority. The available salaries are then totaled and divided by the number of majority Senators in order to arrive at the amount that theoretically belongs to each.

Despite this attempt at equality, the use of patronage is an individual matter. One Senator will want a single large salary for a favored employee. Others prefer to control none, believing in the old axiom that a political job serves only to create nine enemies and one ingrate. The jobs are assigned according to supply and demand, with the current patronage committee laying down rules that tomorrow could be changed arbitrarily by a new committee.

Several Senators began their careers as Capitol employees, including President Lyndon Johnson who was secretary to Congressman Richard Kleberg and Bobby Kennedy, counsel for the Government Operations Committee. Alan Bible of Nevada ran an elevator and worked in the Sergeant at Arms' office while a student. New York's James Mead was once a Capitol policeman and Dennis Chavez of New Mexico served his apprenticeship as a clerk in the office of the Secretary. Joseph O'Mahoney was secretary and then successor to John B. Kendrick of Wyoming, while New Hampshire's Norris Cotton began as secretary to George H. Moses. Senators who give patronage jobs never know where they will lead.

The nearest thing to altruism in the political world is the commendable type of office position known as an "internship," which is awarded to a few fortunate college students by Senators who want to encourage and train young people in government. It is refreshing to see any standard other than mundane patronage.

The one area in which a personal basis for employment will always be justified is a Senator's own office staff where loyalty to him is paramount. The available patronage in this category has increased over the past half century from a staff of three to as many as fifty for Senators from the larger states. The difference in size and cost of a Senator's staff is one of the best illustrations of the growth of government during that period.

In my early days the federal government had little contact with a citizen's daily life beyond delivering his mail. A western Senator in the 1920's did well to receive a dozen letters a day, and the Senator's secretary saw to it that each farmer got his free packages of seed from the Department of Agriculture. Now a vast staff carries on a network of activities, virtually lobbying for constituents throughout the government. Veterans and the recipi-

ents of Social Security alone have countless problems for their
Senators to solve each day. The key post in any staff is the
well-paid administrative assistant who is actually an assistant Senator and complementary alter ego. Legislative assistants devour and
interpret the Senator's work load and often put speeches in his
hand for him to deliver on the Floor or at a banquet halfway
across the country. Besides a battery of stenographers and clerks,
there is a press relations expert who fortifies the Senator's public
image. Operating a Senator's office today is far more complicated
and costly than any of the old-timers would have thought possible.

To staff the committees, Senators are compelled to seek
experts with coveted technical knowledge, frequently drawing
upon college faculties. But all of an expert's diplomas and experience are not worth the ink with which he signs the payroll without
the lifeblood of patronage. Through both coincidence and good
fortune, a large number of people with real ability have been able
to survive and serve the Senate well. On the other hand, the Senate
and thereby the nation have been deprived of many fine employees
of the upper echelon because of their lack of the vital patronage.

A system based on personal favor rather than merit breeds
insecurity. It is as though a staff member had one hundred bosses,
because the animosity of even a single Senator could mean the loss
of one's job if there were no other Senator sufficiently powerful or
interested to come to the rescue. This autocratic off-with-his-head
feature of the system can only be described as unsettling to the
employee.

On the other hand, the patronage of a strong Senator can be
a protective umbrella under which a person of questionable compe-
tence or integrity can rise to a position of power. I have never been
able to fathom how any Senator could allow himself to become
deeply indebted to a political henchman who is abysmally inferior
to himself. Discouraging as it may be, this phenomenon has occurred repeatedly. Some of the best Senators brought the lowest
hacks to roost on Capitol Hill. Happily for the Senate and the employees, these despotic types have been the exception rather than
the rule throughout the years. Most of the thousands of Capitol

Hill employees are hardworking servants of government.

Considering the complete freedom of choice given Senators in selecting men to serve the Senate on their patronage, the high caliber of the staff and officials is a credit to the office holders and the Senators themselves. Some of the finest men I have ever known have served the Senate in an official capacity. At the top of the list would go Charlie Watkins of Arkansas who was Parliamentarian for sixty years. His parliamentary rulings were made under trying circumstances at the nerve center of Senate proceedings, and yet he was always kindly, patient, and fair.

It must be admitted that politicians are no more likely to give up the juicy patronage pie than a gourmet would turn down exotic foods. Taking care of one's friends would seem to be built into the very core of our political beings. But perhaps in some enlightened tomorrow, the archaic system of personal patronage will pass into history along with other forms of privilege and arbitrary power. In the meantime, individual patronage battles must be resolved before the actual work for the Senate can begin.

PRESS LIAISON

Behind the scenes there has never been the air of calm deliberation that the usually quiet Chamber imparts to visitors. Off the Floor the atmosphere has crackled with tense alertness. Senators have always considered their needs immediate. Newsmen have always struggled against their impending deadlines to unearth fresh ideas. Anyone serving these two poles of interest has found himself stretched taut as a wire between them, jumping first at one signal, then at another.

The field of gathering, interpreting, and dispensing news was comparatively limited in 1918; but as the century progressed, the technological developments of the teletype, wire photo, radio, and television combined to create the big business of news. The press corps has grown steadily in numbers and diversity of news coverage. The press photographers, the radio and television correspondents, and the periodical press each has its own gallery. Interpreting our government's activities to the people has become so complex an undertaking that the sheer numbers of newsmen and women have increased nearly tenfold during my years at the Senate, from 210 members of the solitary Press Gallery in 1918 to over 1800 members of the combined four galleries when I retired. At the same time the foreign correspondents have multiplied from eleven to 112, illustrating the growth of Washington as a world news center. Unfortunately, very few foreign newsmen have covered

35

Congress regularly, as Oscar Reschke of the Deutsche Presse
Agentur did in the 1950's and as Maarten Bolle represents Dutch
and Belgian papers today. Nevertheless, a steadily growing stream
of correspondents converges on the Senate to engage in the only
large-scale private enterprise at the Capitol.

A typical day at the Senate began in a mood of deceptive
tranquillity. No one seemed in a hurry to push the appropriation
bill that was currently dragging along, least of all the Senator who
was picking it apart, item by item, in a long speech on the Floor.
Most Senators were either working in committee meetings or in
their offices. Half a dozen were napping in the cloakrooms and
Marble Room, some with their faces tactfully covered by their
home-state papers.

In the Press Gallery above, a few newsmen were pounding
out their stories on typewriters while Gallery Superintendent Joe
Wills and his alert staff kept a watchful eye on the network of
complicated Capitol proceedings. At such an hour you would have
found me walking steadily on my appointed rounds, now arranging
an interview for television commentators Joseph McCaffrey or
Robert McCormick, now asking the Alabama Senators to see Jim
Free of the *Birmingham News* and questioning midwest Senators
for Ken Scheibel.

A Senator who was watching the Floor for the Majority
Leader gave me a verbal answer: "Yes, the administration did
contact several members of the committee. Tell them I agree with
what the Secretary of State said as he originally presented it, but I
cannot go along with the opinion he expressed today. I am still
looking out for the Americas."

Another Senator, while waiting to take the Floor, gave a
crusty reply to my next question: "I think that witness' testimony
was erroneous. Tell them I am not changing my position one iota,
and you can tell them further that the hearings will reopen next
Tuesday at 10:00 A.M. We are going to get to the bottom of this

with some facts!" Even as I turned to leave, he jumped up and said, "Mr. President, will the Senator yield?"

The Floor debate was beginning to pick up when unexpected ·news broke with the abruptness of an alarm clock. The President sent up a surprise request for an increase in income taxes and instantly the place came alive as the tempo quickened. Some of the members of the press rushed out into the Gallery to hear any comments that were forthcoming from the Senators who were gradually coming in on the Floor. Most of the newsmen shot downstairs on the west elevator to cluster about the door to the President's Room.

What had been a steady routine changed to a fever pitch. Tensions rose to an acute stage as newsmen scrambled not to be scooped. My assistants and I would tackle the legion of correspondents together, but luck would more often produce a great news crisis when one or all of my assistants had been called away to their Senators' offices. Then I faced the surging tide alone and, like an earthbound relay satellite, rushed into the Chamber for as many as ten newsmen at a time. Among other requests, Chuck Bailey of the *Minneapolis Star and Tribune* wanted me to ask Majority Leader Mike Mansfield a question concerning the President's new plan. Several correspondents were waiting until Minority Leader Everett Dirksen could leave the Chamber and come out for an interview. Pete Brandt of the *St. Louis Post-Dispatch* wanted to see the Chairman of the Finance Committee who would consider the President's proposal that started the pot boiling in the first place.

The newsmen watched anxiously as I disappeared around the corner, past the French vase into the Lobby and headed toward the swinging doors into the Chamber. First I had to locate and close in discreetly on a Senator, waiting until he looked up from his work and gave me the sign that he was ready to hear about my mission. In low tones I spoke carefully into his "good" ear. Usually I made immediate contact for the newsmen, ticking off Leaders and other Senators right and left. But there were frequent snags. One Senator was in the sanctity of a cloakroom telephone booth, momentarily unapproachable. Knowing that the correspondents in the President's Room were chaffing at the bit and were being joined by new ones all the time, I did not wait for the phone call to end but made a dignified dash to relay what information I had been able to gather: the Majority Leader's answer was repeated verbatim; one newsman's Senator was on the way to see him; another would have to wait five minutes for his Senator.

Now I found that a dozen correspondents were waiting in the President's Room to interview the Minority Leader as soon as he could leave the Floor, while Ollie Atkins of the *Saturday Evening Post* had his camera ready to photograph the group. Representatives of the major television networks waited to escort both Leaders up to the Radio-Television Gallery with them to comment on the President's request.

While asking other Senators questions for still more newsmen who were constantly coming and going, I rushed back to the cloakroom to determine the status of the prolonged telephone call, hoping that the Senator had not flown the booth to his office. With luck, I intercepted him as he left and he agreed to come out immediately to see his correspondent.

Another Senator had been in the Senate Reception Room, cornered by a lobbyist or greeting constituents with unhurried charm. Such conversations were not to be interrupted but to be watched from afar, perhaps during several discreet trips. The trick was to capture the Senator just after the farewells and just before he could become overwhelmed by more visitors.

On one of these breathless journeys with not a second to spare, when just on the brink of closing in on a Senator, I heard the urgent voice of another Senator saying, "Richard, will you call Bill Theis [of UPI] and John Chadwick [of AP] right away before they file their stories? Tell them that my amendment to the Education Bill cuts the expenditure by fifteen million instead of ten million and that the states must match the funds before they can be used." Everything stopped without question for the request of a Senator. I grabbed a phone in the Lobby and tried to locate Chad and Bill in the Press Gallery, all the while keeping one eye on the first Senator, hoping that he would not get away.

Meanwhile back at the President's Room, the newsmen were growing in numbers and tenseness. John Steele of *Time,* Sam Shaffer of *Newsweek,* and Don Irwin of the *Los Angeles Times* joined a cluster awaiting the Chairman of the Finance Committee. Anxious to interview a North Carolina Senator was Bruce Jolly of the *Greensboro Daily News,* while Sarah McClendon asked for either Senator from Texas. Florence Lowe of Metromedia needed two Senators to videotape a panel discussion, while Ted Granik telephoned about a Senator for *Youth Wants to Know.*

The representatives of radio recording syndicates, whom Senator George Aiken has nicknamed the "beepers," swarmed in, packing their tape recorders over their shoulders, and for the next few hours tried to cut tapes of almost all one hundred Senators. Their small hand microphones with the cables dragging in all directions filled the President's Room like a network of spider webs. Even a sneeze or a cough by a Senator seemed welcome to the beepers who had to meet a daily quota of voices for the independent radio stations among their clientele.

During the rush Charlie Gorry, AP photographer, was making new headshots of all one hundred Senators for the AP files. Simultaneously George Tames was shooting up a whole roll of film to illustrate a feature story for the *New York Times Sunday Magazine,* taking pictures of one Senator from every conceivable angle. For *Time*'s coverage of the tax story, Wally Bennett wanted me to get together the Leaders and the Chairman and ranking minority member of the Finance Committee. At that point in dashed Frank Cancellare of UPI Newspictures, assigned by bureau chief George Gaylin to photograph the key figures in the tax story. "Cancy" was soon joined by the other photographers for a group picture of half a dozen Senators on the committee.

The highest diplomacy was called for in assembling several Senators for one picture. First I approached the most sensitive ones to see if they had objections, political or personal, to posing

with the others. While not divulging the names of those who did
not want to pose, I found substitutes who would agree to come,
ever keeping in mind the photographers' deadline.

Such were the hectic mechanics of a day's journey through
the halls of the mighty. It was a world where momentous decisions
affecting millions of people were part of the very air one breathed.
One sensed power flowing all about, not in thunderous bolts, but in
the quiet nod of the Majority Leader and the inscrutable expression of the Chairman of the Appropriations Committee. All the
while within the crowded President's Room, the frescoed occupants of memorial niches looked down in cold serenity. The Senate
scene never failed to fascinate.

SENATORS AND THE PRESS

When Senators come out to meet the press in the President's Room, they may be making the most important move of that day. If the Senator is a good news source, willing to talk about his committee activities and share his insights, he may be rewarded with a front-page story that will accomplish more than a dozen speeches to win public support. It is to a legislator's advantage to treat news correspondents well. With notable exceptions, most Senators go out of their way to help the press.

A private interview in the President's Room does not put Senators on the spot as television panels are known to do. It is apt to be a relaxed, respectful encounter between two knowledgeable friends who open up and share information because they trust each other. The Senator can give valuable off-the-record leads because he knows that he will never be quoted without his permission. Or he can caution the correspondent in the manner of North Carolina's Sam Ervin who sometimes says with a cherubic smile, "Just say you got it from a source nearest the truth!"

Longtime friendships between Senators and newsmen are mutually beneficial, but are the friendly exchanges in the President's Room suspect because they might stifle the independence

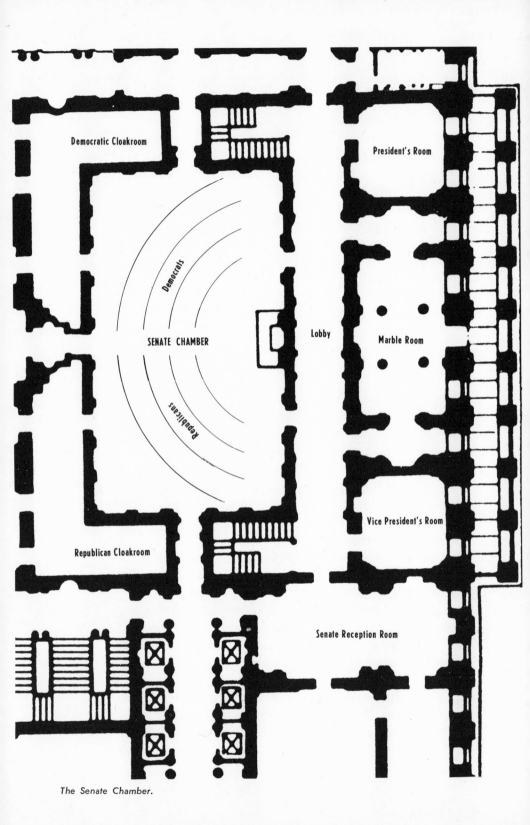

The Senate Chamber.

and objectivity of the press? Would we be better informed if all newsmen were bloodhounds, sniffing out trouble and treeing Senators right and left? On the contrary, the public gains from the mutual trust between Senator and correspondent. The informed Senator can supply background information that will define the issues and personalities. Who supports and who opposes a bill and why? In what way is a bill likely to be amended? Which pressure group is most active in trying to influence Senatorial thinking? The public has a far more thorough analysis from a free flow of information among friends than it would have from the guarded comments of Senators who are suspicious lest a newsman violate his confidence.

There can be the other extreme. While all established correspondents have their main sources of information, William K. Hutchinson had two or three veritable pipelines on both the Democratic and Republican sides. Chief of the Senate staff of Hearst's International News Service for twenty years, Hutch would come to the President's Room with fire in his eyes and in a snarling undertone, ask for his Senator to meet him at the south door to the Chamber. Upon hearing who wanted him, the Senator would never refuse but go immediately to the rendezvous like a trained seal.

If a correspondent bites the hand that feeds him news, he may have severed that news source forever. It is human for a newsman to cast a better light on his Senatorial friends, but it does not follow that he must always agree with them or cover up for them. Most Senators have a healthy tolerance for dissent. Like Senator Richard Russell of Georgia, they ask only that their own position be stated fairly and not distorted. Russell's committee work and leadership of the Southern Senators gave him few spare moments for an interview, but he would always come, sometimes explaining to me, "I don't have time, but that man has been so honest in his reporting, I just must go to see him." Another time he would go out reluctantly to a different newsman, saying, "That fellow! No matter what I say, he'll twist it around to mean something else. Oh well, here we go!"

Objectivity in a newsman leads to genuine respect from Senators. The two Democratic Senators from Connecticut welcomed veteran Bob Byrnes of the Republican *Hartford Courant*. More important than politics is the fact that Bob has always been scrupulously fair.

Very few Senators go as far as Wayne Morse of Oregon in defining a fair article as a favorable one. Senator Morse became so incensed by a story written by Milt Kelly of AP that it was years before he would see anyone from the Associated Press. However, Morse would open up graciously to the correspondent of a certain conservative paper even though the newsman began by saying, "Senator, you know my paper will never compliment you, but I have to know the background of the education bill you are sponsoring." Out of respect for the newsman's honesty and his own devotion to education bills, Senator Morse gladly supplied his information.

Those of us who knew Senators through daily contact came to regard them as human beings more than as public figures. It is not unusual for a newsman to take a liking to a Senator whose beliefs are at odds with his paper's policy. Warren Francis, who with his wife Lorania covered Washington for the *Los Angeles Times* for over twenty years, found himself an admirer of the tireless Sheridan Downey of California, though the *Times* criticized the Senator severely for his welfare ideas. Not until the paper and Downey united to fight for California's share in the water rights of the Colorado River did the Senator realize what a valuable friend he had in Francis. Senators would do well to consider newsmen as individuals, not solely as spokesmen of their papers.

Tensions frequently reach heroic proportions at the Capitol, one of the world's most sensitive news beats. Senators under the strain of work and worry have momentarily blown their tops when I approached them for newsmen, responding in this key, "I don't ever want to see that stupid fellow again! He couldn't write a story straight if he wanted to!" In these darker moments I would go back to the newsman with a soothing story that the Senator was tied up or that he could not answer at that time, with never a hint at the verbal attack. In this way many of the feelings directed at the press

have been ventilated in my presence and have evaporated harm-
lessly into the air.

Many Senators have realized and appreciated my protection.
It could even have international implications if the newsman were
the correspondent of a foreign paper. An influential Senator ex-
ploded one day when I asked him to see the representative of a
paper in a Balkan country, "Tell him I don't give a damn about
him or his government and I don't want to talk to him, period." I
simply told the newsman that the Senator was busy, which was true
enough. Later the Senator approached me anxiously to ask, "You
didn't tell that foreign correspondent what I really said, did you?"
With great relief he thanked me for smoothing over a situation
which could have been embarrassing to him and to the United
States.

Senator Barry Goldwater's reaction to the press was not
limited to an occasional eruption. He was the one Senator who
nursed an increasingly bitter attitude toward most of the newsmen.
When any correspondent wanted to see him, Goldwater waved me
away with an oath and said, "You know I don't want to see those
damn newsmen! Can't you see I'm busy?" Some days he issued a
general order that he would not come out for anyone. When
correspondents had a question for him, I found it necessary to
perform a flanking maneuver, knowing that even speaking to him
would bring forth his wrath. Coming up behind him abruptly, I
had to fire the question at him point-blank without any amenities.
Often in sheer surprise he gave an answer in spite of himself.

For some time I gave him the cover-up treatment I always
reserved for Senators with momentary frustrations, but the months
of hostility grew into years of antagonism. As Senator Goldwater
continued to spurn my every effort to smooth his press relations,
the situation became more disillusioning and untenable every day.
Finally he made it impossible for me to give bland excuses for him,
leaving me no alternative but to tell the press exactly what the
Senator had said. As his attacks reached their mark, noticeably his
press invitations began to drop off.

Senator Goldwater left no illusions, but he does present a
study in what might have been had he not been so belligerent. He

cut a trim and dashing figure with his bronze, Arizona-desert tan, his dark-rimmed glasses, and his crisp, executive manner. It should have been a press agent's dream to cast him in the image of the Great Zorro, not astride a black steed but zooming away from Capitol Plaza in his Thunderbird or swooping down a canyon in his jet plane. There is about him a distant air of the fabulous man of wealth, accustomed to instant command and response. As a skilled photographer and a general in the Air Force Reserve, Goldwater possesses many possibilities for building up a legend of glamour. That he chose instead to build a wall between himself and the public's eyes and ears, the press, is beyond explanation.

Another conservative Republican took the opposite view. Though fatally ill, Eugene Millikin of Colorado would come out whenever a newsman asked for him. The portly Senator might be settled on a comfortable cloakroom sofa when I approached, but Millikin would smile wanly, stretch out both hands and say, "If you can help me out of here, I can make it!" I would hoist his heavy frame to a standing position and uncomplainingly he would go to the waiting correspondent. Senator Millikin's powerful brain and key position on the Finance Committee made him a valuable source of information while his graciousness endeared him to the entire press corps. He considered it an obligation to come, despite his infirmities, to enlighten the press and thereby the country.

While no Senator has been as antagonistic toward the press as Barry Goldwater, few have been as selfless as Eugene Millikin. The majority are caught in the revolving door of Senatorial urgencies. Somehow they must find time for their committee work, study, hearings, and meetings, and to appear on the Floor to answer quorum calls, to debate, and to vote. In hundreds of letters and scores of telephone calls and visits each day, Senators "run the maze of bureaucracy for their constituents," as Abraham Ribicoff of Connecticut puts it. There are also flying trips around the country on speaking dates. Altogether the Senatorial pace is almost inhuman.

Understandably a Senator cannot do everything. By a process of natural selection he responds more quickly to those correspondents who will give him the best return on his time: his home-state papers, the wire services who represent legions of newspapers, a national radio or television network, and the syndicated columnist whose words are widely read. The names of Ralph McGill or Marquis Childs, Eric Sevareid, Bob Novak or Rowland Evans impress even the most prominent Senators. "I'll be right out!" is their instant response.

When Allen Drury first came to the Capitol in 1943 with the United Press, Senators came out readily enough to see the lanky young reporter. By the time he had moved from *Pathfinder Magazine* to the *Washington Star* and on to the *New York Times* and *Reader's Digest,* Al had become a legend around the Senate as the author of the Pulitzer Prize winning novel *Advise and Consent.* He continued to come with the same modest smile, listening to and mentally recording every word of an interview in order to translate it into the trenchant language of his articles and books.

When Joseph Alsop appeared at the Senate, he might well have left the tents of the Arabs the day before on one of the self-assignments that have taken him all over the globe. "What's on the menu, Rit-chard?" Joe would ask as he jauntily seated himself on the bench outside the President's Room, whipped out his advance copy of *Time* or the latest book to read until I found his Senator. No one devours the printed word of others more avidly than the working press.

When his Senator hurried out to greet him, Alsop's reading material disappeared under his arm. He strode across the English tiles, thrust forward his hand and boomed out, "Sen-ah-tah!" As he literally propelled the legislator into the President's Room, Joe Alsop's exurberance was as intriguing as his sophistication was sobering. Perhaps the world's only effervescent cynic, he was more than a match for an intellectual like Senator William Fulbright.

Awe is not the only reaction columnists arouse among Senators. A reserved caution is the general mood when confronting Drew Pearson or his presently more active assistant Jack Anderson, who have dedicated themselves to finding the splinter in the official eye. Occasionally Jack Anderson would be seated on a sofa discussing the downfall of one Senator while on the opposite side of the room, columnist and Pulitzer Prize winning author William S. White would be seeking to build up another. Bill White has devoted himself so consistently to the Senate scene since hitting the Normandy beaches and covering the European theatre in World War II that he seems a part of the Senate itself.

Freewheeling columnists gravitate to independent Senators. The mere sight of Robert S. Allen barrelling from the west elevator would send me on a search for Senators Gruening, Morse, and Cooper who are solitary thinkers on many issues. Drew Pearson's one-time partner Bob Allen has given Capitol corridors a fast-paced beating for forty years with time out to serve as aide to General George Patton during the war. Patton was probably the only man who could match Bob Allen in determination and color-ful vocabulary. Bob's loss of his right arm during the Battle of the Bulge has not deterred him in the least. With his jutting jaw and low boiling point, Bob Allen continues to be a symbol of the most vigorous and unrestrained nature of the working press.

Women correspondents, particularly a columnist like Doris Fleeson or Mary McGrory, inspire a certain courtliness in the majority of Senators that enables the correspondent to get away with more pointed questions. With a mind as sharp as her tongue, Doris Fleeson produced one of the most memorable moments to occur in the anteroom outside the President's Room. A young Senator John F. Kennedy of Massachusetts stood for many long minutes listening to a pithy lecture from Doris in which she vehemently reproached him for following the Establishment. Ken-nedy took it all with patient good nature and no visible strain. He went on seemingly to follow Doris' advice as he began to strike out more on his own. Proving his regard for her, President Kennedy once closed his press conference with the quip, "Now I must go read what Doris Fleeson has to say!"

The first woman to blaze a trail in the Press Gallery was a Mrs. Briggs who, the records show, represented the *Philadelphia Press* in 1870 during the 44th Congress. It took an aggressive amazon like Isabel Worrell Ball of the *Lawrence* [Kansas] *Journal* and the *Arkansas City Traveller* to invade the all-male domain for any length of time, from 1900–03. She was greeted with the enthusiasm of a case of smallpox, according to veteran newsmen who noted that the cussing and hairy chests on a hot day disappeared when she arrived.

From the time of Myra Richards and May Craig, two New England ladies, the place of the newswoman in Washington has been secure. The 1920's brought Ruth Finney and Bess Furman to the Gallery while Ruby Black joined in 1933 when Eleanor Roosevelt admitted only women correspondents to her press conferences. Each of these early members was married to a newspaperman. Today there are over 250 women members of the combined press galleries.

Perhaps the most glamorous correspondent ever to come to the Senate was a young reporter from the *Washington Times-Herald* Jacqueline Bouvier. The President's Room played its part in furthering one of the world's best known romances when an early meeting between Senator Jack Kennedy and Miss Bouvier took place amid the heroic frescoes.

Recently returned from the Sorbonne after two years at Vassar, she was very shy and ill at ease in the legislative setting. With a gracious smile Miss Bouvier introduced herself in the breathless whisper that would become world famous. It was all I could do to catch the words "Jackie Boo-vhay." I had such difficulty deciphering her French pronunciation that I would inform the Senators almost under *my* breath that they were wanted by the *Times-Herald*'s Jackie "Boovvvvay," skimming lightly over her name.

The future Mrs. Kennedy would wait for her Senators, as all correspondents do, sitting on the bench outside the President's Room. Reserved as she was, she must have been aware of the effect she had upon my young assistants. They were totally overcome by her glamour, tittering in her presence to the point where I finally suggested that they walk away into the Lobby to spare her embarrassment. John Kennedy was only one of several Senators Miss Bouvier interviewed during her intermittent visits to the Capitol.

Senators can be naive about the press, but the opposite is rarely true. The freshman lawmaker, whose new nameplate is barely fastened to his desk, can be tempted to rattle off answers without first learning the questions. If he does, he gets a reputation for glibness or a narrow party outlook that may take him years to live down.

Then there is the grandstander who prefers to make an occasional nationwide splash as man of the day. A wise old-timer like Walter F. George understood the long-term value of complete coverage on the grass-roots level. He would always come for wire service and local correspondents whose stories reached every paper in Georgia.

It takes more than wanting headlines to get them. Even the best-prepared press releases do not help if they lack substance or timeliness. I have watched Senators read mediocre speeches that called for a revolutionary solution like a "meeting of the minds," after which they would glance up longingly at the Press Gallery to see if some newsman were dashing out to write it up. They would hurry out to the news tickers in the Lobby, searching vainly for word of their speech.

To be newsworthy, Senators must work hard on legislation, know their facts, and keep themselves available to the press. They must answer questions with directness instead of campaign oratory, and when they have no answer, admit it. Experienced correspondents are worldly-wise and well-informed individuals who expect a lot of a Senator. Empty clichés do not fool them.

On the other side of the interview, inexperienced newsmen can be exasperating unless they have studied enough to ask intelligent questions. Many Senators would echo Russell Long's ruffled comment about an uninformed reporter, "Why should I write his story for him? He needs to do his own homework!"

Directness is a key virtue for newsmen as well as Senators. I feel sorry for the new reporter whose shy introduction goes on ad infinitum, "How do you do, Senator? I don't want to take your time. I know you are a busy man, but could you answer a question for me? It won't take long." The correspondent has already taken the Senator's time merely by calling him off the Floor and now he has drowned the Senator's interest in a flood of unnecessary apologies. The best approach is a smile, one word of greeting, and an immediate question to the point. "How are you, Senator! What action do you expect your committee to take on the Housing Bill this week?"

Unfortunately, hard work alone does not guarantee good publicity. Senators can work for months on constructive legislation, and newsmen may cover them well, but their efforts often result in a small story on an inside page. The hint of a scandal is shouted from page one, but many valuable Senators and their finest accomplishments rarely make the headlines.

Several Senators have had the rapport that clicks with newsmen as well as the nourishing information on which the press thrives. In first place would come William E. Borah who will be described later. Homer T. Bone of Washington rated high in press popularity, along with Joseph O'Mahoney, Homer Ferguson, H. Alexander Smith, and Leverett Saltonstall.

Today it is the inner calm of Eugene McCarthy of Minnesota that attracts the press. He is welcomed to the Press Table in the Senate Restaurant where he comes to share opinions over a morning cup of coffee. As Senator McCarthy makes off-the-record comments, he is doing his own news gathering. The questions asked him by the correspondents are an excellent gauge of the important undercurrents of the day.

McCarthy is more than a likeable friend and a droll scholar. He is a phenomenon of relaxation in a world of hypertension, the quiet conscience expressed with a take-it-or-leave-it shrug of the shoulders. Hidden within his underplayed tone is a surprising depth of analysis that envelops the listener instead of attacking him as more vociferous speakers do. Perhaps Senator McCarthy's disarming calmness, so contrary to the hectic pace of Washington, can be traced back to the year he spent as a Benedictine novice. Whether he is with the press, campaigning for the presidency, or simply visiting as a friend, Gene McCarthy takes everything in stride better than any Senator I have ever known.

Senator Alexander Wiley, one-time Chairman of the Foreign Relations Committee, did not wait to be asked. He would come out unannounced to josh the newsmen with a friendly, "What do you fellows know?" Pale and paunchy with his pockets full of packets of cheese, Senator Wiley was a walking Chamber of Commerce for the State of Wisconsin. Once he interrupted Bob Barr of Fairchild Publications to thrust a piece of cheese candy into the Press Gallery telephone booth where Bob was calling in his story. The Capitol parties given by the Senator and Mrs. Wiley were a delight to any lover of cheese.

While not the deepest thinker, Senator Wiley was one of the friendliest men ever to serve in the Senate. He often went out of his way to provide the comedy relief during a weary day. Stopping by the President's Room, he would say, "Let's get some pep out here, young fellows!" Then he would go into a remarkable tap dance with all his pounds pounding on the tile floor while we clapped in time to keep his rhythm. Like a perennial Santa Claus, Senator Wiley emitted a continual ha-ha-ha. He kept people from taking themselves too seriously, ribbing Senators and newsmen.

Senators who have been newsmen themselves have the special advantage of seeing both points of view. They anticipate the questions before they are asked and answer first things first in the factual language of the press. At least one-tenth of the Senators I have known have had some experience in the news world. Half of these were publishers in their pre-Senatorial days, such as Medill McCormack of the *Chicago Tribune* and William Benton of the *Encyclopaedia Britannica*. Others were reporters like Arthur Capper of Kansas who came to the Press Gallery in the 1890's. He went home to build a political career upon the broad base of his agricultural news empire which reached millions of readers throughout farming communities in the Midwest.

Blair Moody was the only one to step down immediately from the Gallery onto the Senate Floor when he was appointed in 1951 to fill the Michigan seat vacated by the death of Senator Arthur

Vandenberg, another newspaperman. Well-known as Washington correspondent of the *Detroit News* for eighteen years, Blair caused a sensation among his press colleagues who proudly applauded him when he took the oath of office. Thereafter newsmen took delight in leaning over the gallery railing and occasionally dropping spitballs whenever Blair occupied the Chair as presiding officer. Handsome and youthful, Blair Moody was the first Senator I have called by his first name. He remained unchanged, the same hyper-tense individual searching for facts with hard-driving impatience. Though Blair continued his television appearances and fully utilized his press experience, he did not win the election following his appointment and suffered a fatal heart attack during his second try for the Senate in 1954.

The one member of the Press Gallery to make a second career of politics was Louis Ludlow, amiable Washington correspondent, author, and Member of Congress from Indiana. He had covered Washington for almost thirty years when he was elected to the House in 1929. A Democrat from a strong Republican district, Louie Ludlow was an untiring worker who served his people like a devoted minister. They responded by returning him to Congress for twenty years, where he never lost his sense of brotherhood for the press.

Mike Monroney first wrote of the political world for the *Oklahoma News* before coming to the House and later to the Senate. Intent and nervous, like so many newsmen, Monroney was always on the move and one of the most capable legislators. He translated his energies into constructive legislation such as the improvement of aviation and the measure for which he is best known, the LaFollette-Monroney Act of 1946 providing for the reorganization of Congress. Three years before Mike Monroney came to the House, his fellow reporter from Oklahoma City Jack Bell came to Washington to cover the Capitol. As chief of the Senate staff of the Associated Press, Jack is the one who looks and acts like the arrived Senator, while Senator Monroney has retained the unaffected manner of the press corps.

Henry Cabot Lodge, Jr. stands out as the Senator whose

previous ten years of newspaper work may well have been responsible for the breadth of his outlook as a legislator. The sheltered
but unspoiled grandson of Henry Cabot Lodge became a reporter
after being graduated from Harvard. When I first met him, he was
with the Washington bureau of the *New York Herald Tribune*. His
experiences with the press gave Lodge a taste of life that made him
plainspoken and understanding of the needs of the average citizen.
When he came to the Senate in 1937, no one was more concerned
with the problems of unemployment and old-age insurance than
the handsome young man from Massachusetts.

The press greeted Cabot Lodge as one of their own, a factual
man of action who could shoot back answers as quickly as they
were asked. I was amazed at the quality of his press interviews that
approached Borah's in sharp perception. The twinkle in his eyes
and tilt of the head had all the charm of his grandfather without
the reserve and scholarly preciseness. However, I could sometimes
sense a struggle between the plainer side of his personality and his
aristocratic heritage. In times of extreme pressure a touch of the
frosty aristocrat would crop up in Lodge when he would say to me,
"I haven't time to go out there to see anyone. I'm here to make
history!"

Once during a dull day in the late 1930's, Senator Lodge
replaced Vice President Garner in the Chair. The young Senator
leaned back a little too far until his chair upended noisily, hitting
the flag behind him. The next moment Lodge found himself
literally wrapped up in the American flag. When Ed Haakinson of
AP came dashing down to find out what happened, Senator Lodge
reluctantly agreed to see him. Knowing that the mishap would not
add to the dignity of either the Cabots or the Lodges, he had to be
convinced that the story was newsworthy. Finally Lodge agreed to
its publication saying, "All right, but be sure to say it must have
been a Democratic chair!" That was one of the few times Senator
Lodge forgot his newspaperman's sense of values.

Cabot Lodge is one of those men who has followed conscience rather than expediency. When he made the difficult choice
of going into active combat during World War II rather than

remaining as one of the Senate's military experts, he met his sense
of duty, winning admiration and service medals, but losing his
seniority when he returned to the Senate in 1947. While his
grandfather played a major role in shaping the earlier postwar
world as a partisan figure of deep conviction, the younger Lodge
joined Arthur Vandenberg in pushing the bipartisan Marshall Plan
through the Senate. In seeking to moderate his party's policies, he
lost the support of conservative Republicans by opposing Robert
Taft for the leadership. Lodge helped convince General Eisenhower to accept the presidential candidacy. In the end he lost his
Senate seat to John Kennedy by working harder for Eisenhower
than for his own reelection. As vice presidential candidate with
Richard Nixon in 1960, Cabot Lodge lost another close race with
Kennedy.

Going on to serve as ambassador to the United Nations and
to Viet Nam, he has made the most of each difficult assignment
with the spirit of a good soldier tackling his job without regard to
glory. By considering himself the servant of the nation rather than
first promoting Henry Cabot Lodge, he has made his career the
very essence of statesmanship.

Being a Capitol correspondent can have its element of danger
as Charles Stevenson, then of the United Press, proved in the
spring of 1933. In that budget-minded era he wrote an article for
Liberty Magazine detailing what the government furnished to various officials. The Senate Disbursing Officer Charles F. Pace was
enraged by the article, for while it did not mention him by name,
his car and chauffeur were included as unnecessary expenditures.

Early one morning Pace charged into the Press Gallery in an
excited state. A nervous man at best, he began waving a gun
around and demanding to see Stevenson. Fortunately Charlie had
not yet arrived. Joe Wills and others in the Gallery calmed Mr.
Pace down until he pocketed the gun and went on his solemn way.

The incident was the sensation of the day. Charlie Stevenson
heard about it while covering a hearing on the House side when he
was warned to watch out for Pace. The other Stevenson in
the Gallery, known as "Stevie", was chief of the Senate staff of the

Associated Press. To make the distinction clear, Stevie posted the following notice on the Gallery bulletin board, "My name is Francis Xavier Stevenson. Henceforth will my friends please call me Mr. Smultz?" When the Rules Committee investigated, it was found that Pace's revolver was an old Army .45 automatic that was too rusty to shoot in any case.

A decade later after years of otherwise peaceful service, Mr. Pace asked his chauffer to drive him down to Haines Point. There he stepped out of his official limousine and disappeared into the muddy waters of the Potomac in a successful suicide. A very healthy Charles Stevenson now heads the Washington bureau of *Reader's Digest*.

The atmosphere at the President's Room might bristle occasionally but only once did press relations come close to physical combat. One day in the 1930's I brought Senator Kenneth McKellar of Tennessee out to see Bob Horton of Scripps-Howard without realizing that the Senator was angered by an article Horton had written. He no sooner caught sight of the newsman than he began to tell him off as only the volatile McKellar could. In a chain reaction the Senator grew more and more excited, shaking his clenched fists in Bob's face. Suddenly he stepped back and started to swing at Horton with his right fist. I had been watching the entire show, and when I saw that McKellar was actually going to hit Bob, I stepped between them and said, "Please!" That was all that was necessary. They both walked away, McKellar to cool off in the Chamber and Bob Horton to tell his colleagues in the Press Gallery about his close call. The interview was ended permanently for they never spoke again. Later Senator McKellar thanked me for saving him from an embarrassing situation.

A decade earlier Senator McKellar was being interviewed by a newsman on the far side of the President's Room while another Senator and correspondent occupied a sofa nearby. I was in the anteroom outside when suddenly there was a tremendous crash mixed with the sound of breaking glass. Simultaneously a great cloud of dust came rolling out the door. Knowing that McKellar was in there, I wondered what he had done this time! So much dust filled the room that it was impossible to see inside. Immediately two very shaken Senators and the newsmen emerged, stepping through the debris of broken glass and plaster. Luckily they were uninjured. No one knew what had happened until the dust settled and we could inspect the damage.

Like the tale of Chicken Little who spread the word that the sky was falling, the story went out that the huge chandelier had fallen. Actually only the center panel of thick plaster immediately over the chandelier had broken loose, but its shattering descent had stripped off most of the lovely etched globes and the crystal pendants. The whole imbroglio had struck the Lincoln table below with a hollow boom.

Constantino Brumidi had covered every inch of the President's Room with his elaborate frescoes, so that nothing could fall without damaging his work, but only three cherubs met disaster. Though another artist endeavored to replace them later, the new cherubs do not have Brumidi's vivid three-dimensional quality. With carefully regulated humidity and plaster preservatives, none of the painter's work has toppled since.

With all of its overwhelming ornateness, the President's Room does capture and hold a sense of history. And well it might, for history has been made within its four walls. Each President since Abraham Lincoln has used the room briefly. Until Franklin Roosevelt's first administration it was thought essential that a President sign bills before Congress actually adjourned. I have watched Presidents Wilson, Harding, Coolidge, and Hoover sit at the large table with its green felt padding to sign the last-minute legislation passed by an outgoing Congress. A dramatic restoration of the custom came on August 6, 1965, when Lyndon Johnson chose to come to the President's Room to sign the Voting Rights Act upon an ancient desk. It was said to be the one Lincoln had used when he signed a bill on the same date in 1861 to free slaves who had been drafted into serving the Confederate Army.

Thousands of news stories have originated from interviews in the President's Room. Fortunately the news is not often as sensational as it was the summer day in 1947 when I brought a very pale Senator John Bricker of Ohio out to tell the press about his brush with death only moments before. The Senator had been walking to the subway car in the Senate Office Building when a disgruntled constituent fired two shots at him that luckily missed their target, taking some chips out of the wall. The sound of the gun going off in the tunnel was deafening but Senator Bricker had the presence of mind to run forward and jump on the subway car. The operator gave the electric vehicle full power and they sped away toward the Capitol and safety. Within minutes the police nabbed the man with the gun and took him away for observation, correspondents had *the* Capitol story of the day and photographers caught a shaken Senator Bricker telling me about it in the President's Room.

Since the advent of the flashbulb around 1930, more Senators have been photographed in the President's Room than in any other part of the Capitol. In the old days, pictures were almost always made outdoors in daylight, but occasionally an early photographer, such as Herbert French or Buck May, would be granted special permission to use powder-flash equipment in the Reception Room. The photographer crouched under the black cloth thrown over the camera. His feet protruded while he held the flashpan above his head in a Statue of Liberty manner. Counting to himself, "Ready-open-boom!" he uncovered the lens as a cap detonated the powder. Like a miniature atomic mushroom, a cloud of smoke would puff to the ceiling and descend to envelope everyone in a dense haze. Groping their way out, Senators were usually able to get back to the Chamber before the smoke had drifted out an open window. When they discovered the white dusty "fallout" all over their clothes, Senators vowed never to allow a powder flash in the Capitol again—until the next time.

Flashbulbs and then strobe lights made later photographers more popular with the Senate and they were allowed to use the President's Room like other newsmen. For a while they were

Senator John Bricker of Ohio tells author Riedel of narrowly escaping assassination in the Senate subway minutes before the picture was taken.—photo: UPI

Arthur Vandenberg (right) comments on the United Nation's Charter to newsman Blair Moody in the President's Room. Moody later succeeded him as Senator from Michigan.—photo: Library of Congress

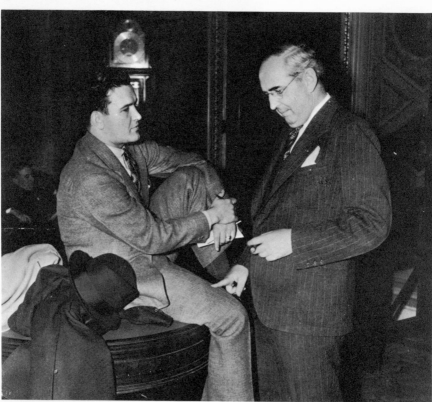

permitted to photograph the Senate in session from the Gallery and, by special permission, to take pictures on the Floor after the session had ended. But because some pictures were taken showing an almost empty Chamber and were published with captions which implied that Senators were not on the job, the privilege was withdrawn. Only one picture has been taken in recent years: the National Geographic Society photographed the full Chamber on September 24, 1963, at the time of the atomic test ban treaty vote.

The exacting life of a news photographer has produced the most lively members of the press corps. Beyond the technical mastery of their equipment and an intuitive sense of what is newsworthy, they are professional artists with a gift for composition. Every photographer is continually on the lookout for that rare shot that will win a prize in the annual contest of the White House News Photographers Association, the organization of those who cover the national scene from Washington. So valuable are good photographs to politicians that both parties now have acquired permanent staffs. Longtime White House photographers Arthur Scott and Clyde Wilkinson focus on the GOP for the Republican Senatorial Campaign Committee, while brothers Al and Frank Muto photograph their Democratic counterparts. Veteran White House photographer Bill Forsythe has been the only superintendent of the Senate Photographers Gallery. There he keeps his World War II helmet ready for whatever comes. The rugged career of news photographer has never been and never will be for the faint of heart.

Radio was an infant in crystal sets and headphones during my page days. Electronic technology grew with such speed, however, that on March 4, 1925, Calvin Coolidge's inauguration was broadcast nationwide.

The pioneer radio men serving the Senate in the late 1920's were a hearty trio: Bob Trout of WJSV [WTOP] of the Columbia Broadcasting Company, Hurlif Provensen of WMAL which joined the American Broadcasting Company, and Graham McNamee of WRC of the National Broadcasting Company. They had to drag their heavy equipment with them for not until 1939 was the Senate Radio Gallery established.

As the only staff member assigned to the press at the Senate Floor, I became the first person to help these pioneers make contact with Senators for their live broadcasts. In those early days not many legislators grasped the political possibilities of radio. Very few had ever broadcast before doing so at the Senate, and most were leery of speaking before microphones, not knowing how they would sound on the air. I would try to persuade them with a "Really, Senator, the microphone won't bite!" Even then some refused point-blank and others would tremble as they came out to confront the mikes for the first time.

Newsreel photographers came soon after the radio correspondents, giving the moviegoers of the nation their first sight of Senators in motion. Early newsreel men would escort their Senators outside to make daylight pictures. When sunlight failed, they would burn flares to supplement the lighting. The first newsreels, like the first feature movies, were shown with titles, but eventually sound was added which made the Senatorial image complete. Paramount newsmen used sound for the first time during President Roosevelt's second inauguration in 1937 when ten-ton trucks were needed to haul the equipment around. In the rain Bob Denton's camera shorted out and knocked him twenty feet. When the finished production was put together, each camera had recorded the inaugural address in a different sound level. One moment Roosevelt's voice would be a tenor while the next shot would send him down to a bass or up to a high squeak. Today with the technical difficulties long since solved, television has replaced newsreels.

Television came to Washington first as a demonstration in the 1930's. Senators and staff people were driven down the Mall to a location in front of the Department of Agriculture where we were interviewed by Bryson Rash, then a young announcer for NBC. Later at the National Press Club not far away, we could watch others broadcasting with Bryson on the Mall. To recognize the image of a Senator almost a mile away seemed an amazing achievement to me that day.

Thirty years later on November 22, 1963, the combined television networks asked me to broadcast from the studio in the Senate Radio-TV Gallery. Before the largest audience in history, I sadly told of the Senate's reaction to the tragedy of President Kennedy's assassination, relating how I had broken the news to Senator Teddy Kennedy who was presiding in the Chair that afternoon. A hundred million people could share the sorrow simultaneously.

In less than two generations we have progressed from the novelty of hearing a Senator's voice on early radio amid a shower of static to the familiarity of seeing legislators in our homes by way of television. Whether broadcast through the immediacy of TV and news photos or the written words that pour out over the wires of the Press Gallery, most of the nation's news of the Senate begins in a quiet meeting between correspondent and Senator in the President's Room.

CEREMONIES AND SPECIAL OCCASIONS

The Senate abounds in idiosyncrasies of custom and language that make it a world of its own. In contrast to the informality of the cloakrooms, the public facade of Senators on the Floor has the ceremonial quality of a historical pageant. Senators on stage must work within the framework of parliamentary language. "Hello, John!" in the cloakroom becomes "I would say to the Senator from Texas" on the Floor. It may sound formal, even pompous, but I have found that beneath the surface, even the most solemn ceremony at the Capitol has its human side.

Of all occasions the most naturally exuberant is the first day of a session when the cloakroom camaraderie spills over onto the Floor. Every other year a new Congress convenes on the third day of January unless a later date has been designated. In the carnival spirit of a reunion Senators pour into the Chamber from all directions, bombarding each other in the politician's way with belated New Year's greetings, genial shakes of the hand and slaps on the back.

Florida and West Indian sunburns are everywhere. There are Senators who have just dashed in from the airport to the Senate Floor. Many have completed trips abroad during adjournment and compare notes on places like Saigon, Berlin, and Nairobi. Allen Ellender of Louisiana returns from his one-man investigating trips with 16 mm. movies. Others come from their committees which

63

have met throughout adjournment or from their offices where the work of staff members has never stopped. Ahead is the long pull of lengthy investigations, dull office chores, and long hours of tension over baffling problems of legislation. But the first day is freely given to the jovial ceremony of reunion.

The uproar on the Floor is matched in the galleries where Senators' families join delegations of loyal campaign workers who have come to see their Senator take the oath of office. They point out one Senator and then another whom they recognize. The hum and buzz of their conversation rises in a crescendo as the hour of noon approaches.

Press galleries are filled. There are a few new correspondents intrigued by the scene before them along with the old pros who take it all in stride. Even the old-timers catch the spirit of a new beginning and exude restrained enthusiasm. Each morning before convening, members of the press, radio, and television galleries are permitted to come in on the Floor for a few minutes. Usually about fifteen attend, but the first day the delegation is doubled. They gather around the empty Minority and Majority Leaders' desks to gain a good vantage point, anticipating that the Leaders will speak in their usual low tones, every word of which can be important to a story in the making.

Everett Dirksen, with his capable assistant Oliver Dompierre, is usually the first Leader to enter the Chamber, greeting colleagues and settling back in his chair with the calm joviality of an old sage. Newsmen mix their banter with respectful questions, but Senator Dirksen is an old hand at saying exactly what he wants to say and no more. While he is generally the best news source, an anecdote or a colorful phrase may be his entire fare the first morning. "We are all working for a nonprofit organization known as the United States," he has been known to comment. "At least it hasn't made any profit since I came along." If a newsman should say that he could not hear, Senator Dirksen might answer facetiously, "I didn't mean that you should!"

Majority Leader Mike Mansfield, by careful design, comes in quickly five minutes before the convening. Correspondents flock across the aisle to his desk, the urgency of their questions masked by genial greetings. What bills will be given top priority this session? Mansfield's answers are friendly but crisp. He feels little need to elaborate for the year is young, many press conferences stretch ahead and he is above all a patient Leader.

The bells ring throughout the Capitol and Office Buildings announcing the convening. The Vice President enters the Chamber by the northeast door to the Lobby followed by the Chaplain and the Secretary of the Senate, as newsmen scurry out the other side like so many Cinderellas at the stroke of twelve. In minutes most of them are looking down on the Floor from their own world in the Press Gallery, the only observers of the Congressional scene who can make notes during an actual session.

When the gavel falls at last in the crowded Chamber, the gallery occupants rise as the Senators quietly stand. The Vice President, standing at his desk, says, "The Senate will come to order and the Chaplain will offer prayer!" Dr. Frederick Brown Harris, Senate Chaplain for twenty-five years, offers prayer in the silent, waiting Chamber, expressing the general sense of renewed dedication and reminding the legislators of a Universal Power far greater than their own.

The only order of business on this ceremonial occasion is administering the oath of office to new Senators and newly re-elected members. Though Senators are elected for a six-year term, only one-third of them face the voters in any given election year. It is that third that must be sworn in with each new Congress.

As the roll is called, they come to the rostrum in groups of four. The Vice President reads the same oath that was given to me as a page, to which the Senators answer, "I do!" Since each Senator is customarily escorted down the aisle by the colleague from his state, much is made when this tradition is broken. Margaret Chase Smith of Maine asked Maurine Neuberger of Oregon to accompany her, pointing up the historic fact that two women were serving in the Senate at that moment. Bad feelings over the past election cause an occasional Senator to refuse to go forward with his colleague. Huey Long chose to go with Democratic Leader Joseph T. Robinson instead of Louisiana's senior Senator Edwin Broussard, who had declined to support Long's candidacy.

When the swearing-in ceremony is completed, the Vice President recognizes the Majority Leader who arranges in parliamentary fashion for the Senate to meet next to hear the President's State of the Union message. Upon a motion for adjournment, the Vice President pounds the gavel and announces, "The Senate stands adjourned until twelve o'clock noon tomorrow."

Since no pictures are allowed in the Chamber itself, all the Senators who have just been sworn in are rounded up and escorted to the Vice President's Room. There they are photographed with right hands upraised in reenactments of the oath of office. Immediately the pictures are taken to be developed and sent over the wires to make the evening edition of the home-state papers.

For the senior Senators who are nearing their last roll call, the appreciation of the scene is the keenest of all. Many have spent a lifetime making the Senate what they thought it should be. They survey the freshmen with curiosity. What will the Senate make of that young fellow, and what will he make of the Senate? The new Senators fresh from the electorate display much enthusiasm and some humility. Which ones will retain their vision for the country and which will smother it in their own self-interests?

Despite the doubts and fears, the clean pages of a new calendar work their magic. There is another chance to right the wrongs that an old and tired Congress had left unresolved upon last year's adjournment. The spirit of a new Congress, springing from energies renewed, is definitely optomistic.

In the same spirit a new presidential term begins every four years on January 20 when the President is inaugurated outside the Capitol's East Front. An elaborate wooden structure of Greek Revival design is built anew for each inauguration with special seats for honored guests on the platform and throughout the Plaza. The crowd that gathers inside the Capitol that day is not composed of sightseers but the greater part of national and international officialdom, waiting to take their places on the platform.

Swathed in overcoats for the bitter January weather, Senators are seated on the north side of the platform and members of the House on the south. Beginning with Woodrow Wilson's second in 1917, I have witnessed fourteen inaugurations from every conceivable angle: located two rows behind Warren Harding, standing on the base of a pillar above Dwight Eisenhower's head, and facing Franklin Roosevelt from the photographers' stand.

The preparations for inaugurations begin months in advance; the earliest, even before the November elections determine who will be inaugurated. Harry F. Byrd, Sr., as Chairman of the Senate Rules Committee was in charge of Roosevelt's fourth inaugural ceremony. When the Senator announced that $100,000 had been appropriated for the occasion, the President countered with a statement calculated to put the budget-minded Virginian on the spot. "We don't need to spend so much; a fourth of that will do," smiled the confident man in the White House. Senator Byrd readily agreed to the President's figure, knowing full well that no inauguration could be executed for such a paltry sum.

It was not long before Roosevelt found it out for himself and began asking the Senator to up the appropriation. "I will be glad to do it if you will write me a letter requesting it," answered the cagey advocate of fiscal responsibility. When the President protested that he was afraid the Senator would make his letter public, Harry Byrd assured him that that was exactly what he intended to do. Roosevelt stubbornly refused to write the letter and Senator Byrd refused to budge. It was this impasse, according to Harry Byrd, Jr., now Virginia's senior Senator, that forced the President to have his fourth inauguration in 1945 at the White House instead of the Capitol. Since the ceremony cost a mere $526.02, economy won the day.

Aside from presidential inaugurations, a joint session of Congress is the foremost state occasion in our government. It is comparable in its formalities to a high ecclesiastical ceremony. When the President addresses Congress, the Senate meets in joint session with the House of Representatives in the larger House Chamber. On television it appears to be a staid affair. Actually there is far more animation surrounding a joint session than a telephoto lens can convey.

For any large ceremony the logistics require careful preparation. Admission cards to the House galleries are specially printed for the occasion and are in great demand. It becomes a privilege just to sit on a gallery step. Each official group gathers in a predesignated room, ready for its moment of entrance.

The Senators meet first in their own Chamber where they take the proper parliamentary steps to meet with the House of Representatives. They line up in pairs down the center aisle, ready to walk through the Capitol in a stately procession. At the head of the line are the Senate's two highest staff members, elected at the beginning of each Congress, the Secretary of the Senate and the Sergeant at Arms. Next comes the Vice President of the United States and the Senator who is also the President Pro Tempore. Side by side the Senators follow, speculating about the President's address.

The route through the center of the Capitol is guarded by watchful statues from our past. The procession passes by William E. Borah who seems to be reminding us not to involve ourselves overseas. Abraham Lincoln and Andrew Jackson watch as they cross the spacious Rotunda under the dome. If they glance up, Senators might meet the eerie eyes of Pat McCarran whose whole stance demands that we guard the gates against immigrants like his own parents. In the old House Chamber that is now Statuary Hall they pass an unthinkably silent Huey Long, William Jennings Bryan, and Robert M. LaFollette, Sr. The Senators then proceed straight ahead toward the House Chamber where their fellow legislators have already assembled.

With the pageantry of a royal herald at court, the Chief Doorkeeper of the House announces their arrival. "Fishbait" Miller, whose proper name of William is rarely used, booms out in his deepest Mississippi drawl, "Mis-tah Speee-kaaah, the Vice President and members of the United States Senate!"

House members and officials rise courteously until the Vice President takes his place on the rostrum beside the Speaker of the House and the Senators are seated in the front rows.

Each official group enters in a similar fashion, proudly announced in Fishbait's authoritative style:

"Mis-tah Speee-kaaah, the Ambassadors and Ministers Charge d'Affaires of foreign governments!

"Mis-tah Speee-kaaah, the Chief Justice of the United States and Associate Justices of the Supreme Court!

"Mis-tah Speee-kaaah, the members of the President's cabinet!" and finally,

"Mis-tah Speee-kaaah, the President of the United States!"

Television cameras have brought the President's annual State of the Union Message into every home, but cameras cannot duplicate the atmosphere on the Floor. Reactions would be easy to predict. If I sat on the minority side, I would be surrounded by a stoney silence unless the President gave a plea to "Save the Flag!" on which both parties could agree. If I sat on the majority side, assuming the President were of the majority party, the cheers would abound to almost every proposal. Nods and smiles of approval would be everywhere, while across the aisle there would be satirical comments throughout the opposition. The cameras may sweep around from the galleries, but microphones scattered around the Floor would spice up the coverage considerably.

When Members of Congress become the audience for a guest speaker other than the President of the United States, the event is called a joint *meeting* rather than a session. It takes a king, an astronaut, a poet, a prime minister, or a noted general to catch the attention of these legislators. No one who was there will forget Carl Sandburg's reading of his poetry to celebrate the sesquicentennial of Abraham Lincoln's birth. His voice had the mellow tones of a guitar and gripped the entire Congress with his ringing refrain, "Lincoln said . . . this is what Lincoln said . . ."

A spirit of jubilant victory greeted John Glenn who addressed a joint meeting and his fellow astronauts who have spoken before the Senate and House separately. Congress has reacted like proud parents viewing the results of years of appropriations for the space program. As President Kennedy said, "Space is the new ocean and we must sail upon it," to which one could add, the moon is our first port of call on the new ocean, and we must make safe harbor there. No one Senator has cheered our astronauts more enthusiastically than Spessard Holland of Florida who was an aerial observer in France during World War I. Senator Holland has intently followed each flight on a cloakroom radio, never relaxing until our spacemen were safely back on earth.

The single moment of greatest emotion, however, was the farewell of General Douglas MacArthur in 1951. Everyone whom I observed was affected by the pathos of his speech and the controversial events surrounding it. Even a seasoned newsman like Joseph Farrington, then Delegate from Hawaii, had tears rolling down his face by the close of the address. In a hushed Chamber, General MacArthur dropped his voice for his now-famous climax, "Old soldiers never die; they just fade away." Whether the General was right or wrong in his defiance of President Truman's policies, that day he gained an oratorical victory.

The spacious Rotunda beneath the dome has been the scene of Capitol ceremonies since its completion in 1822 in time for the triumphant visit of the Marquis de Lafayette. In the most solemn of all national pageants, eighteen Americans have lain in state here on the same catafalque built for Abraham Lincoln in 1865. The Unknown Soldiers of World Wars I and II and the Korean War have lain here before being buried in Arlington Cemetery. Mourners lined up for blocks to pay honor to Warren Harding, General John J. Pershing, and Robert Taft. They filed in the East door and out the West Front, as they did past John Kennedy's flag-draped bier.

The Rotunda has reverberated to the music of the Marine Band on those interesting occasions when a statue is presented to the Capitol. Each state has been permitted to send images of two of its noted citizens. Among the busts and full-length figures are seventeen men, Presidents, Vice Presidents, and Senators, that I have known in life and now encounter in stone, as though I were walking down corridors of time.

Perhaps the most lifelike statue of all is the bronze Will Rogers presented by Oklahoma. Though never a member of Congress, in the 1930's he was often called the ninety-seventh Senator because of his commentaries on politics and politicians. The statue of the humorist is standing in the corridor on the House side, contemplating the stream of visitors who pass before him. The tousled forelock, the broad grin, and even the humor in the eyes is so natural, I expect him to drawl out a dry observation at any moment. Will would have had the perfect comment for the tourists who waddle past in backyard shorts. With his left hand in his pocket he leans slightly to one side as though he were ready to start down the corridor to visit the Senate.

When Will Rogers came, at least once each session, a holiday spirit prevailed. His daily newspaper column would have made him eligible to be a member of the Press Gallery, and he was always a welcome guest there as anywhere in the Capitol. But the public galleries were his delight. I would watch him take a seat, sandwiching himself between the plainest visitors he could find. Soon they would be exchanging whispered comments while Will turned his grinning face from side to side in animated conversation. He was at ease with everyone at all times.

When Will Rogers came around to the President's Room, a circle of Senators would gather immediately. Will's contagious humor would trigger off a session of repartee that would outrival the cloakroom storytelling fests during a filibuster. His wisecracks on current events would roll out as naturally as he breathed or worked on his inevitable chewing gum.

On one visit he was glad to find that Jim Preston, superintendent of the Press Gallery for twenty-five years, had returned to the Senate to become Librarian after a stint at the National Archives. Will slapped me on the chest as he exclaimed, "Ya know, they got ole Jim Preston stuck up there in the Senate

Library, asweepin' cobwebs off the books!" Jim, who came as close as anyone to being the historian of the Senate, actually did uncover long lost documents, several with George Washington's signature.

Senator Pat Harrison of Mississippi was the best match for Will Roger's wit. Harrison with his cigar and Rogers with his gum were like tennis players sending quips back and forth at an eye-batting speed. After the Democrats swept the Senate in 1932 and gained more seats in 1934, Will had to tease the Leader of the dwindling Republicans, "Charlie McNary here is gettin' to be one of a rare breed. We gotta do somethin' about this. We gotta preserve the Republican Party like the bison and the whooping crane!"

The dedication of Will Rogers' statue after his untimely death in 1935 was the most poignant ceremony I have seen in the Rotunda. After the speeches that accompanied the unveiling, the usual martial airs and patriotic songs were not in evidence. Instead, the Marine Band began to softly unfold a medley of cowboy ballads that reverberated under the Dome as though we were inside a great bass viol. The easygoing gait of "Home on the Range" and "The Last Roundup" described Will Rogers as no words could. It was a fitting tribute to the homespun humorist, a genuine cowboy as much at home in the halls of the mighty as on the western range.

TWILIGHT OF ELEGANCE

My generation, born in the early part of the century, arrived in time to know two worlds: the fading glow of early America and the blazing dawn of the twentieth century. Fortunately, I went to work at the Capitol in time to know the Senate's own remnants of a bygone age of elegance.

As a little boy I thought the shoulder-length hair of James K. Vardaman of Mississippi gave him the appearance of Benjamin Franklin. Beneath this eccentricity was a very mild and gentle man.

Another vision of the eighteenth century, like a courtier of Louis XV, was the debonair person of James Hamilton Lewis of Illinois. He not only spoke French with all the Gallic gestures but also could bow halfway to the floor like an archduke when greeting lady visitors under the glittering chandeliers of the Reception Room. When Senator Lewis took the Floor, his pronunciation was precise with delicate intonations. The flowery phrases rolled in a succession of scintillating rhythms. His chin whiskers danced with every phrase. No one could equal his grand exit from the Senate wing as he twirled his cane with the dexterity of a drum major.

Ham Lewis' distinctive tastes centered around brown suits, gray vests, and spats with buttoned patent-leather shoes. What immortalized him was the splendor of his wavy pink toupee which matched his whiskers and his elaborate mustache. Dustlike specks frequently seen on his coat were suspected to be artificial dandruff to further the illusion of natural hair.

One day he was interviewed by a newsman while sitting on a bench next to the upper railing of the Senators' private staircase.

73

Before air conditioning, during summer sessions the windows were always wide open. A strong gust of wind began playing tinkling, chimelike sounds on the crystal pendants of the chandeliers as I saw the front of Senator Lewis' pink toupee start to lift, about to become airborne. Just before its actual takeoff, the Senator slapped his hand firmly on the top of his head and saved himself great embarrassment. I could imagine myself rushing down the stairs to retrieve the toupee from the floor below, but who could have retrieved the Senator's equanimity after such a startling change in his appearance?

Ham Lewis never lacked an outlet for his polished demeanor, from his days in Cuba as a dashing Inspector General during the Spanish American War to the various foreign assignments that led to his being decorated by the kings of Belgium and Greece. When he died in 1939 while a Senator, his state funeral in the Chamber had a somber elegance most befitting the discriminating spirit of J. Hamilton Lewis of Illinois.

One Senator in the 1920's looked as though he could have gone back far enough to have voted on the Louisiana Purchase. Senator J. Thomas Heflin of Alabama was a rotund man towering six feet. Within his huge oval face, his owlish eyes and hanging jowls were framed by iron-gray hair. He was always immaculately groomed in a high collar, white vest with pearl buttons, and black cravat, all in harmonious accord with his dark frock coat, striped trousers, and gray spats. In summer he wore Senatorial white.

When deep rumblings were heard out in the Lobby, I knew that inside the Chamber Senator Heflin had taken the Floor and was holding forth in the thunderous tradition of the old school. Heflin always roared. His face got red, his neck would go down, and his collar would come up making his eyes bulge. He would emphasize his points by great sweeps of his arms in an arc from the back forward, ending in a clap of the palms, resoundingly punctuating his remarks. In another favorite gesture, Heflin raised his clenched fists overhead and lowered them to pound on his desk for accent with his huge French cuffs flashing around him.

Senatorial elegance was epitomized by the pink whiskers of J. Hamilton Lewis of Illinois.—photo: Underwood & Underwood

Alabama's J. Thomas Heflin fulfilled the cartoonist's image of a Senator.—photo: Underwood & Underwood

Tom Heflin could be inspired to poetry upon a moment's notice. He once jeered at the Republicans who opposed continuing an investigation into campaigns that were embarrassing to them:

"You are opposed to this committee's work, and you are saying in your hearts,

'Committee, spare that campaign boodle tree,

Touch not a single bow;

In election times it shelters me,

You must not harm it now.' "

Senator Heflin's most vehement speeches were against what he termed "the hungry wolves of Wall Street, taking the milk out of the mouths of babes." Once as Heflin's almost daily campaign against the financial interests of the country was reaching a high crescendo, Henry Cabot Lodge, Sr., opened the door to the Chamber and listened for a moment. Then with a flip of his little white goatee, Lodge turned around and in an unusually frank comment said to me, "Just listen to that big bag of wind!"

With all of his bluster, Senator Heflin was not an arrogant man. He was affable, considerate, and intelligent. A born dramatist, he could have been a successful actor. Certainly he was the most skillful Senate storyteller of all time, regaling his cloakroom audiences with hilarious stories of the Old South. His listeners were fascinated, not so much by the stories themselves, as by Heflin's vivid dramatizations with rolling eyes, accented voice, and the total use of his giant frame in synchronized gestures. Though a teetotler himself, Senator Heflin caught the full flavor of the language when he described the effect of a mint julep on a willing imbiber in one of his stories. Heflin closed his eyes and purred, "The amber-colored liquid flowed over the velvet folds of his stomach like a dewdrop sinking into the heart of a rose." Even to his colleagues, J. Thomas Heflin fulfilled the cartoon stereotype of a Senator.

The last of the picturesquely dressed Senators was North Carolina's Clyde Hoey, unfortunately pronounced hoo-ee. His frock coat and aquiline nose produced a silhouette like that of an eagle with folded wings. The picture of his tall frame bent forward with a slight stoop was complete from the wing collar to the high buttoned shoes with spats. His flowing gray locks were swept back in the style of antebellum statesmen.

In general, old-fashioned dress and oratory went together, but not in the case of Senator Hoey whose rapid speech was remarkably clipped and to the point. Though keenly aware of the twentieth century, Hoey apparently had set out to look the part of those statesmen who had inspired his youthful dreams. With characteristic verve his attire was perfected each day by a red rose carefully placed in his lapel, a striking accent in an elegant portrait in Confederate gray.

One morning in March, 1954, the Senate heard with "profound sorrow of the death of the Honorable Clyde Hoey, late a Senator from the State of North Carolina," as the formal announcement goes. Someone in a kindred spirit of nostalgia placed on his desk that day a solitary red rose as a silent memorial to the last remnant of a bygone age.

When I first went to the Senate, the sure harbinger of spring was Senator Charles Thomas of Colorado. He wore a very neat toupee, cleverly built to taper down and blend with the natural gray hair remaining on the sides of his head. It matched so well that no one would have guessed its presence until the weather warmed in the spring. Then suddenly Senator Thomas would appear minus his toupee with his bald head gleaming. Come autumn, just as unexpectedly he would appear again in full head gear. The transformation took place so magically that it was as though the Senator had grown an extra head of hair overnight.

It has not been many years since at least two-thirds of the Senate used to announce the change of season with white suits, presenting a dazzling view from the galleries. One of the best-looking and most expensive wardrobes belonged to Huey Long who was reputed to own a hundred white suits. Senator Arthur Vandenberg became so fascinated by Huey Long's attire that he inquired of Long as to his tailor, material, and cost. Shortly afterward

Vandenberg himself made a grand entrance into the Senate Chamber arrayed in some of the most elegant and ample yardage of the double-breasted era. His spotless white raiment did for the Republican side what his sartorial inspiration, Huey Long, accomplished on the Democratic side.

But the white suits that used to blossom in the summer are no more. Harry F. Byrd, Sr., wore one of the last. Today Senator Norris Cotton of New Hampshire with his white attire courageously clings to and thereby preserves one of the last vestiges of summer charm left in the Senate.

Elegance was not limited to Senators alone. On the rostrum from 1908–47 sat Reading Clerk "Uncle John" Crockett whose stentorian voice added color and tone to the entire procedure of the Senate. Uncle John wore a gray ensemble specially tailored for him in England. The style was a hybrid, combining a morning coat and a Prince Albert with tails that did not fork enough to be swallow-tailed but enough to be distinctive.

Uncle John had gotten his early voice training by calling hogs in Iowa and then came to Washington to call Senators for the rest of his life. He could put more drama into a roll call than most Senators could inject into their best speeches. His penetrating voice reverberated to every corner of the Chamber, sometimes with such speed that a Senator would call him down. Crockett's showmanship spiced up the reading of the dullest amendment.

For simple amusement the pages would look ahead on the printed Calendar of Bills to see if any funny titles were due for consideration. On Calendar Monday we would watch Uncle John closely as he read down the list, pausing only for the presiding officer to say, "Without objection, agreed to," or "Over," if there were one objection to a bill's consideration. With great dignity, Uncle John would roll out the most unpronounceable names. A claim bill entitled "For the relief of Konstantinos Dionysiou Antiopos" might slow him down or cause him to stop and spell it out. Others granting a pension to Annie E. Laurie, Running Grouse, or Amos Red Owl brought a faint smile. What drew the biggest laugh of all was the bill "For the relief of Winnie Left Her Behind."

There was no one in the Chamber who did not wish for the full history behind that remarkable Indian name. Whether the occasion was sublime, ridiculous, or mundane, no one could match the style of Uncle John Crockett.

Echoes from an ornate past, archaic habits of speech are continually heard in the Senate Chamber today. Open the *Congressional Record* at random and the words "distinguished" and "eminent" will leap up from almost every page.

Senate tradition dictates that a Senator must address the chair as "Mr. President" and refer to a colleague as "the Senator from the State of __," rather than by name. Embellishing the latter has been an ancient sport handed down from past generations, until it is no time at all until even the newest Senators begin to play the game of lavish epithets.

In the midst of a space age debate a Senator will glibly roll off a phrase that should have gone out with Prince Albert coats. The dialogue goes something like this, "Mr. President, will the eminent and distinguished Senator yield to me?" "I am delighted to yield to my good friend, the distinguished Senator for whom I have always had the highest esteem and utmost regard for his integrity . . ."

These flowery echoes from a bygone age are more than quaint curiosities. They are useful as a stalling measure to fill in the moments until a Senator can think of something to say. When a slow warm-up with "Mr. President" is not sufficient, then to add, "May I say in answer to the distinguished and eminent Senator . . ." can often give a Senator time to marshal a salvo upon the verbal firing line. Senatorial language was so sticky that Kenneth Wherry would sometimes get enmeshed in it and refer to himself as "the distinguished Senator from Nebraska."

An innoculation which might grant immunity from the habit could be given at the beginning of each session of Congress. The Senate could set aside a day when each Senator could tell how eminent, distinguished, and full of integrity every other Senator was. If they let it go at that, thoroughly convinced that they all had a sufficient measure of integrity and eminence to last throughout the rest of the session, thus encouraged, they could proceed with the business at hand.

The real heyday of the flowery, embroidered eulogy was in full bloom when I came to the Senate. Those were the days when the death of a colleague opened up the floodgate of cascading emotional fervor, with overtones and undertones colliding together and producing tear-jerking reminiscences about the departed Senator. The old eulogies were given in memorial sessions on Sunday afternoons. That was when new pages were told by the older ones that "chocolate eulogies" would be served on Sunday. Sometimes it proved to be an apt description.

Sincere tributes inspired by genuine sorrow were usually delivered, but occasionally, a eulogy would succeed in completely remodeling a dour Senator. With the skill of a retouch artist, the speaker would paint him as a man who had loved flowers and children, sunsets and evening stars. As the last tribute faded away, one could believe that the deceased had actually resembled St. Francis of Assisi talking with the animals.

Those Senators whose style resembled the preaching in an old-time revival meeting, sent the stereotyped eulogy soaring to its crowning height. After hearing this type of tribute repeated so often, I could predict exactly when the Senator's voice was going to break, when he would choke up, pause a moment, wipe a tear from his eye, gather himself together and plow on through the eulogy with chest heaving under his white pearl-buttoned vest.

The orator might soar into phrases like these which capture the spirit rather than the letter of any particular eulogy, "Our departed colleague fought on the Senate Floor with his face uplifted into the sharp, wintry gale and his feet firmly gripping the ground as he moved one step at a time toward his shining goals. He had to cross glaciers of difficulty and crevasses of defeat to overcome the avalanches of political annihilation and persecution. Nevertheless, he fought here beside us steadfastly, as long as there was any breath in him. We shall miss him. Ah yes, we try to move forward without him, but we shall never see his like in the Senate again!"

Years ago there were instances in which two Senators had been bitter opponents for years. When one of them died, the surviving antagonist began paying glowing tributes to him, possibly the first nice things he had ever said about his departed adversary. Perhaps the reason for this phenomenon was that he liked his deceased colleague much better in his new state of tranquility.

Today when a Senator dies, two or three hours are set aside from a regular business session to pay tributes to him. Most are appropriate to the deceased; a few are as stereotyped as ever.

A happier custom has grown more frequent in the last several years, that of giving meaningful testimonials to a Senator on his birthday or in recognition of various honors he has received. It contributes cheer and warmth to routine sessions while a Senator is living to sit back and enjoy his own eulogies.

A contemporary tribute of note was paid to the very much alive Republican dean of the Senate George Aiken of Vermont, whose unpretentious manner has placed him among the most beloved Senators of all time. After Majority Leader Mike Mansfield and Minority Whip Thomas Kuchel had seriously expressed their gratitude that Senator Aiken was a colleague, Frank Lausche of Ohio took the Floor with a mischievous smile on his broad countenance. An independent thinker who is equally free from affectation, Senator Lausche is a long-time Aiken admirer, but he chose to entertain the Senate by relating the precarious beginnings of their friendship.

"Mr. Lausche: Mr. President, I fully subscribe to what the Senator from California has just said. However, I wish that I could erase from my mind the initial contact I had with the Senator from Vermont when I was the Governor of Ohio and came to Washington to testify before a committee of the Senate over which the Senator from Vermont presided. With me was a union labor leader. Remember, I was the Governor. We came into the room and the Senator from Vermont went right by me—the Governor—and shook hands with the labor leader and said to him, 'I am glad you are here, Mr. Governor.'

"I could not judge what was wrong; but, the next time I met the Senator from Vermont was when I went to the White House, shortly after I became a U.S. Senator. I was wearing my tuxedo or—

"Mr. Aiken: They were tails.

"Mr. Lausche: Yes, they were tails. So was the Senator from Vermont in tails.

"Mr. Mansfield: The Senator from Ohio does not know the difference between a tuxedo and tails.

"Mr. Aiken: He does not know.

"Mr. Lausche: I have not had them on since.

"To continue my story, I left the White House later and walked to the porch to hand my automobile ticket to the man who would get my car. I stood there waiting, when out came the Senator from Vermont and handed me his automobile ticket to get his automobile for him. (Laughter)

"Mr. President, the distinguished senior Senator from Vermont (Mr. Aiken) is a worthy gentleman. I am glad that this colloquy will be placed in the Record. You are a great citizen and a great Senator.

"Let me close by saying, "I forgive you, George."

Congressional Record, 89th Congress, 1st session, 1965, p. 22207

As the outward trappings of elegance have faded away, the modern Senate more readily turns to real human values.

FILIBUSTERS

If one custom is unique to the Senate, it is the rule of unlimited debate which leads to those doleful words "night session" and "filibuster." They bring forth images of one Senator droning away on the Floor while others snore on and off key in the cloakrooms. Official reporters ply their weary way through page after page; doorkeepers drink black coffee to keep awake; page boys slump on the rostrum and I would slow down to a footsore limp.

Over it all like a demon beacon shines the bright electric lantern in the top of the dome. Though the entire dome is illuminated every evening at dusk, a special lantern in the uppermost colonade is lighted whenever the House or Senate session stretches beyond the hour of eight. Since the early days of gaslight long before the telephone, it has beckoned to legislators throughout the city to let them know when they are needed at a night session.

Working late into the night can be justified to meet an emergency. Perhaps a law is about to expire, the life of an agency depends on renewal legislation or an appropriation bill needs to be passed before the fiscal year closes at the end of June. But can one justify a filibuster, that last-ditch stand by a minority desperate enough to create its own emergency?

I have seen the Senate caught in the grip of many such blizzards in which words pile up like snowflakes day after day after day. It becomes a grim sort of madness. Brains are dulled from

weariness. Judgment wavers, and the United States Senate is reduced in the public eye to a seemingly helpless body, trapped in its
own rules and unable to offer leadership or solutions. Is it a
reasonable price to pay in order to protect the rights of the
minority? Is the Senate's unique system of unlimited debate the
essence of, or a travesty on, justice?

An orthodox filibuster is an attempt to kill a bill by talking it
to death with the avowed intention of never allowing the Senate to
vote the legislation up or down. The word itself does not exist in
parliamentary language. It is a pirate term that comes from "vrij-
buiter," the Dutch word for freebooter or buccaneer, though "free
mouther" would seem more appropriate. A filibustering Senator,
then, is a swashbuckling adventurer with the word instead of the
sword. Depending on one's point of view, he is either plundering
the time and efficiency of the Senate or fighting to salvage a sinking
cause.

In my early days Progressives like the senior Bob LaFollette
considered the filibuster a noble course of action for a minority to
take. It was especially effective before the old March adjournments
which took place every other year. Anyone who could talk until
the hour of noon on the fourth of March automatically killed
unenacted legislation of the dying Congress. Since the Lame Duck
Amendment to the Constitution in 1933 shifted the convening of
Congress to January 3, the outgoing body adjourns less dramatically in the fall of the preceding year. But the threat of a filibuster
at any time is still disquieting.

In our fast-moving age any long delay is labeled obstructionist, so very few Senators will admit that they are filibustering these
days. Some Southern members still announce their intentions to
talk indefinitely to block civil rights legislation. The publicity they
gain lets the folks back home know that their man is in there
fighting for the values of the status quo. They stick to debating the
bill, however, and no longer read aloud recipes for Louisiana
potlikker as Huey Long did.

There are more refined terms for filibustering now; they are
called extended argumentation and educational debates. An extended debate is not obstruction, the defenders argue. It can

instruct the public as to the dangers of the majority's bill and possibly force the drafting of a better bill. Though their social views were poles apart, both Wayne Morse of Oregon and Sam Ervin of North Carolina have defended the necessity of listening to the whole story a minority has to tell. The conservative Senator Ervin in the 1964 Civil Rights controversy pointed out:

"There is a fundamental distinction between an educational debate in which participating Senators seek converts to what they conceive to be the truth in respect to pending legislative proposals and a filibuster which is merely the use of extreme dilatory tactics—as speaking merely to consume time—by an individual or group in an attempt to delay or prevent action by a majority in a legislative or deliberative assembly."

Congressional Record, 88th Congress, 2nd Session, 1964, p. 5040.

Liberal Wayne Morse justified his record-breaking filibuster against the Submerged Lands Bill of 1953 which gave the states title to offshore oil rights:

"This debate, in my judgment, had to go on for a long period of time if we were going to make the record we needed for the use of the court in the future litigation which is bound to arise under this measure . . .

"It is perfectly legitimate to prolong a debate for whatever period of time may be necessary to give some assurance that the parties to the dispute will have an opportunity to negotiate . . .

"Sometimes we get a thunder of silence from the press . . . One who reads the newspapers knows that practically nothing is being said about the subject now before the Senate. If there is a little drama or a little conflict, . . . (the) press in competition with radio, television and other media of public information, cannot ignore the drama of conflict . . ."

Congressional Record, 83rd Congress, 1st Session, 1953, p. 3769.

Extended debates can accomplish all of these things, but the question still remains: when has the debate ceased to educate and when, by repetition, has it begun to obstruct the vote? Unless the Senate comes to a vote eventually, the charge of "Filibuster!" is justified.

Filibusters do not break out suddenly as a rule. If the subject is civil rights, one can be forecast with certainty. Even so, there is usually a long, slow warm up of debate rumbling along for two weeks or more of daily sessions until it becomes obvious that the participants are going to prevent a vote at all costs. When the consensus is that the principles and alternatives have been thoroughly explored, the Majority Leader will rise at his desk one day to sternly announce that he believes there has been a reasonable amount of debate. "Therefore, we are going to stay here until we vote if it takes all night or all week!" Then the storm that has been building up breaks in full fury. From the Leader's announcement everyone knows that behind-the-scenes peace negotiations have failed. Open hostilities have been declared on the Floor.

How can one member or a small group of members hold up the entire Senate as a buccaneer would detain a whole ship? What rules give a minority such power? Senate Rule XIX does limit the number of speeches by requiring that ". . . no Senator shall speak more than twice upon any one question in debate on the same day without leave of the Senate." Like *Alice in Wonderland,* this does not mean a real calendar day; it means a *legislative* day. Under a technicality, if the Senate "recesses" each evening, the same legislative day continues sometimes for weeks, as though time were standing still. Usually not until the filibuster has ended does the Senate use the word "adjourn," and a new legislative day begins at the next meeting.

But in the same way that Senate days have no limit, a Senate speech knows no bounds. Unless there is unanimous consent to limit the time of speaking, a Senator can continue with one speech as long as he can stand on his feet and talk. If he has used up his two speeches, he can introduce an amendment and make two new speeches on it, unless the opposition succeeds in tabling his amendment. Every rule seems to have its loopholes. It takes teamwork to keep a filibuster going, with one team member keeping the Floor until another speaker is ready to relieve him, like long-distance relay runners.

The opening night spectacle begins like a Roman holiday with galleries packed and Senators joking in the Lobby. A filibuster presents unusual difficulties for the leadership and the speaker who must hold the Floor all night, but the rest of the Senators have only to remain on call. The real human toll of a long session can be counted in the weariness of staff people who cannot nap and leave the Chamber at will, as Senators can. The clerks on the rostrum have a red-eyed, hopeless look as they contemplate the long vigil ahead. Even a tolerant Kentucky gentleman like Emery Frazier, who was Clerk for thirty-three years before becoming Secretary of the Senate in 1966, has been known to wear a "Let's go home!" look as the clock creeps on.

The Senator in the Chair has only to listen to the low voice of the Parliamentarian sitting in front of him. Like a ventriloquist, Floyd Riddick leans back to advise the presiding officer, telling him word for word what to say. Even the most knowledgeable Senators appreciate Riddick's advice in a delicate situation.

When the speaker takes a thirty-second gulp of water, the pause gives the official reporter a moment to flex his fingers. These skilled reporters take verbatim notes in shorthand, each man serving ten minutes of each hour. He dictates his notes immediately to a recorder from which an expert transcriber prepares the manuscript for the Senator to edit before his speech appears in the *Congressional Record* next day. Though every word is taken down as spoken on the Floor, the published *Record* is polished up a bit with accurate literary quotes and perfected grammar.

Minority Leader Dirksen once eulogized the reporters:

"It baffles me when I think of the readability of the *Congressional Record,* because, when all is said and done, I think it will be agreed that Congress is really the home of the split infinitive where it finds its finest fruition; this is the place where the dangling participle is certainly nourished; this is the home of the broken sentence; and if there were no dashes I do not know what our distinguished Official Reporters would do. This is the home where, with impunity, we can ignore the comma and the period, we can ignore the colon and the semicolon, we can ignore the exclamation mark and the question mark; and yet,

somehow, out of this great funnel it all comes out all right, and
it is always readable . . . and the reason why it is readable, Mr.
President, is to be found in the endeavors of the distinguished
group who are the Official Reporters of Senate debates."
Congressional Record, 88th Congress, 1st Session, 1963, p. 13746.

As the reporters record history around the clock, word by
droning word, the galleries gradually become empty, for nothing is
so dull as an all-night speech. The members of the press go home,
leaving only a skeleton crew. By midnight the lights are dimmed in
the cloakrooms as Senators drop off to sleep one by one. The
elegant Marble Room is cluttered with cots, army blankets, and
shoeless Senators. Some members straggle down to have a midnight snack in the Restaurant which never closes as long as the
Senate is in session. Others take refuge in their offices, riding on
the subway cars that never stop running during a night session. Still
others take a long chance and go home, knowing full well that they
may have to come right back if needed to make a quorum or to
vote. Throughout the night the overworked Leaders and their staffs
keep worried checks on the whereabouts of Senators.

The monotony of an all-night session is shattered as the bells
signaling a quorum call ring out like a fire alarm over the Capitol.
Members roll off cots and pile onto the Floor in wrinkled coats and
baggy pants. They look like anything but United States Senators
with their eyes red and their ties askew, their hair tousled and their
shoes untied. Some are unsteady on their feet, depending on the
type of refreshment they have had that evening. A sprightly figure
in dinner jacket or white tie may arrive from a party. He strides
across the Chamber, kidding his sleepy colleagues who admire his
dapper attire. Above all, he is welcomed as a live body needed to
answer "Here!" to his name when the roll is called.

The quorum call is one of the chief weapons in the minority's
arsenal of delay. If at any time the filibustering few can catch the
leadership without a majority on hand to answer the roll, the
Senate must adjourn, which lets the speakers rest up for a longer
tomorrow. But if the Majority Leader is to break the back of the

filibuster, he must use the full power of the Senate rules to produce his quorum and stay in session. He makes a motion that the Sergeant at Arms be directed to *request* the attendance of absent Senators. When such motion is agreed to, the Sergeant at Arms and his staff enforce it, as Legal Counsel Bill Cheatham makes discreet calls to Senators' offices and homes. In recent times this has always produced sufficient results, but a generation ago, it occasionally became necessary to resort to a motion which *compelled* the attendance of absent Senators. A subpoena was prepared for each missing member, whereupon the Sergeant at Arms' staff began seeking out Senators who were known to be in the city.

When Secretary of the Minority Mark Trice was Deputy Sergeant at Arms in the 1930's, he once manned a rowboat at four in the morning to reach the palatial yacht of Senator Jesse Metcalf of Rhode Island. The spacious craft on which the wealthy textile manufacturer lived was riding at anchor in the middle of the Potomac, silhouetted against the lights along the shore. When the Senator was awakened, Mark informed him that he was needed on the Senate Floor to make a quorum. Senator Metcalf obligingly came ashore immediately.

A greater challenge for Mark Trice came late one evening in 1943 when Majority Leader Alben Barkley was determined to get a quorum, come what may. "Do you mean Senator McKellar, too?" asked Mark. "I mean *everyone!*" answered Barkley. With more than a few misgivings, Mark set out for the Mayflower Hotel to seek the volatile bachelor from Tennessee. When Senator McKellar did not answer the house telephone, Mark enlisted the aid of a hotel official who suggested that they get a maid to knock on the door. Obviously the hotel man knew McKellar well! The Senator opened the door at the maid's request to discover Mark Trice outside. McKellar welcomed him and seemed surprised to learn that he was needed at the Senate. Though Mark carried a subpoena in his pocket, it never became necessary to mention it.

The old Senator came along in a friendly spirit, chatting with Mark as though they were on a normal trip together. Then suddenly, as the car climbed Capitol Hill, the light in the dome made

McKellar put two and two together. He realized that he was about
to help the leadership get a quorum that would foil his fellow
Southerners. He stopped talking to Mark. His face grew redder
and redder. By the time the car reached the Senate entrance,
McKellar shot out and barrelled through the corridors to find the
source of his summons to the Capitol in the middle of the night. He
was so angry with Barkley that he would not speak to him for
months, though as senior Democrat, Senator McKellar sat beside
the Majority Leader in the front row. Then came the day when
Barkley dramatically resigned the leadership in protest against
President Roosevelt's tax bill veto. McKellar's delight with the
Leader surpassed his ebbing anger, and he began speaking once
more. In time he also forgave Mark Trice, who went on to become
Secretary of the Senate in the 83rd Congress.

This was the last time a Senator has been subpoenaed. In the
past quarter-century the tactic of hiding out has been abandoned
by filibustering members. For their part, Leaders are never anxious
to embarrass fellow Senators. It is not the Senate way.

A night session can become a spirited occasion depending on
the brand of the spirits. Hardworking Hubert Stephens of Mississippi was like a faithful puppy, trotting along with the New Deal.
A most gracious and mild-mannered Southern gentleman, he had
been a neighbor on Capitol Hill during his days as a Congressman.
The only time I ever knew him to have too much to drink was one
time too many for his distressed colleagues.

One late session I was astounded to see the temperate Senator
Stephens rear up on the Floor and raise his drawling voice to a
shrill whine reminiscent of his predecessor John Sharp Williams.
To the consternation of his Democratic colleagues, Stephens
launched into a diatribe against the New Deal. Horrified Senators
nearby pulled at his coat in genuine alarm while across the aisle,
Leader McNary and the small band of Republicans kicked up their
heels in delight. Senator Stephens whined on for about fifteen
minutes on the theme of the famous brain trusters who were
brought from the academic world into government posts by FDR.
Throughout it all, Stephens kept wailing time and again, "I cam-

PAIGNED for Franklin D. ROOOOO-she-velt! He ish a GRRR-eat Pre-shi-DENT! But again I shay, shish country has TOOO many college professhors!"

During the filibusters of the 1920's and the 1930's, one of life's compensations was a storytelling session in the cloakroom with Henry Fountain Ashurst of Arizona. The Senator was tall and dashing, often wearing a cutaway to daily sessions. He had all the flourishes of gesture and voice that belong on the stage: a sweeping half-bow, clear enunciation, and dramatic intonation. Like Everett Dirksen, Ashurst took obvious pleasure in charming an audience.

Standing under a small chandelier in the cloakroom, surrounded by colleagues on leather sofas and at writing desks, Senator Ashurst would take us back to his early days in Arizona. There he knew Wyatt Earp and grew to distrust him when Ashurst found that on several occasions the lawman had shot a man in the back and reported falsely, "Shot while resisting an officer."

Senator Ashurst's best story described the great celebration when the railroad first came to Tucson. With his vivid word pictures the Senator could transform the cloakroom into the main street of the Arizona desert community. There was a speaker's stand covered with bunting, a citizens' band playing its loudest and a proud mayor presiding over his most glorious day in office. His Honor began to glow as he read aloud one telegram after another from the Governor and prominent citizens of the territory, congratulating him on the arrival of the railroad in Tucson. Each was addressed to him as the Honorable Robert Nelson Leatherwood; the Mayor was carried away with his own importance.

Seeing their opportunity, some of the boys from the saloon hurried over to the telegraph office where they hastily drafted a message with the look of an official communication. This they rushed to the speaker's stand and thrust into the hands of the irrepressible mayor.

Holding it aloft he cried, "Look! Here is a message from the Pope himself!" And he raised his voice so that everyone could hear each immortal word, "To the Honorable Robert Nelson Leatherwood, Mayor of Tucson. His Holiness wishes to felicitate you on the coming of the railroad to Tucson. It is indeed a great symbol of progress for your fair city. However, His Holiness wishes to make one inquiry, where in Hell *is* Tucson?"

Stories fade, snores rise and fall to be interrupted by quorums and roll-call votes on amendments. The long night drags on until the first rays of the sun over the Supreme Court building give news that the second day of the filibuster is beginning. In the days before the original glass roof was replaced, the dawn would announce itself, turning the Chamber into an eerie conservatory without flowers. Senators under the old roof were subject to the terrible clatter of a rare hailstorm, an occasional leak, cracks of thunder and flashes of lightning that were dazzling enough to stop a speech. The beautifully remodeled Chamber of the past two decades leaves the Senate insulated against both the wrath and beauties of nature.

Senators who have been trying to sleep in the Marble Room walk out onto the balcony over the north terrace. They can stretch under the classical pillars, take deep breaths of outside air and listen to the chorus of birds singing in the Capitol grounds before the morning rush begins on Constitution Avenue. On the Floor the night speaker's voice is dry, thin, and growing steadily weaker. His morning replacement comes bounding in with fresh enthusiasm that jars the nerves of his bleary-eyed colleagues. Only Wayne Morse could speak all night and still greet the morning with energy to spare.

A new crew of correspondents come in, fresh from a good night's sleep, quickly popping questions right and left. I have gone like a somnambulist through the Chamber, trying to find Senators who could not see any better than I could. Meanwhile the photographers come to photograph the remains of "the world's greatest deliberative body." It takes perspective at such an hour to give three cheers for the rights of a Senate minority.

If a marathon speaker has proven himself during the night, he is certain to capture the big headlines as a kind of trophy for his display of strong voice, will power, and sturdy feet. For forty-five years the senior Bob LaFollette held the record for making the longest speech—over eighteen hours in 1908. I watched Huey Long come close when he exceeded sixteen hours in the early 1930's. It took the strength of Wayne Morse to set a new record when he spoke twenty-two hours and twenty-six minutes against the Offshore Oil Bill in 1953. Morse held the title until four years later when Strom Thurmond of South Carolina spoke two hours longer against the 1957 Civil Rights Bill. Senator Thurmond's twenty-four hours and eighteen minutes remains officially the all-time high. The South Carolinian's round-the-clock heroics gained him no love from his Southern colleagues, all of whom had agreed not to filibuster but to accept Leader Lyndon Johnson's compromises. It is no accident that all of these Olympic-style speakers have been lone mavericks, out to advance their goals with calculated headlines. In these terms the filibuster could be called the athletic approach to legislation.

Do filibusters succeed in changing the course of history? For thirty years Southern Senators have been successful, using the filibuster and the threat of one to stop or modify civil rights legislation. Throughout the 1940's the Senate wasted months on anti-poll tax measures. Many Senators who were opposed to the poll tax itself took a legal stand against the bill as unconstitutional, arguing that only the states have a right to set voting standards. Senator Spessard Holland of Florida resolved the question for federal elections when his constitutional amendment barring the poll tax was adopted in 1964, but each new civil rights controversy reopens the fight to preserve states' rights.

The poll tax filibusters were holy wars waged on a high level by dedicated constitutionalists like the respected Josiah W. Bailey of North Carolina. On the other end of the scale was a vehement white supremacist Theodore Bilbo of Mississippi, whose antipathy to Negroes literally consumed him. Senator Bilbo looked like a small groundhog who had just crawled out of his burrow, a plausible throwback to a previous order of man. Once another Senator took Bilbo to task for his racist bitterness by asking what his attitude would be if it were discovered that the Unknown Soldier buried in Arlington were a Negro. His instant retort revealed his callous nonchalance as Bilbo assured the Senator, "Oh, the dead ones don't bother me!"

The ultimate finesse in filibustering was achieved in the Southern fight against the Civil Rights Bill in 1964. Under the generalship of Richard Russell, the Southerners organized into three teams headed by John Stennis, Allen Ellender, and Lister Hill. While the rest of the Senate had to remain on alert twenty-four hours a day, each filibuster team alternated on duty only one day out of three. For a while the Southerners had a field day, saluting each other in jest as "Captain Stennis" and "General Russell." But quorum calls and roll-call votes around the clock wore everyone else down to the point where, for the first time in its history, the Senate voted to shut off debate on a civil rights bill. The overwhelming public sentiment in favor of the bill as a memorial to John Kennedy, Lyndon Johnson's high tide as a new President, and Minority Leader Dirksen's compromises proved too much for the best organized filibuster the Senate may ever see.

Nothing amuses the Southern block more than the phenomenon of a liberal filibuster, when minority rights are claimed by those very Senators most anxious to eliminate the Senate's unlimited debate. Liberals answer that as long as the rules are there, they have a right to use them, too. They enjoyed taunting the leadership as Hubert Humphrey teased Majority Leader William F. Knowland during the marathon Atomic Energy debate of 1954 by saying, "If you had changed the rules as we advocated, I wouldn't be able to tie you up like this!" During the same debate Clinton Anderson of New Mexico grinned sheepishly when newsmen asked him how long he thought the round-the-clock filibuster would last. "What's a filibuster?" he demurred. "I thought it meant breaking a female horse!"

Liberals insist that they are not delaying but educating the public as the old Progressives did. But while the Progressives won their educational campaign against the League of Nations in 1919, modern liberals have not been so successful. Albert Gore of Tennessee and others did succeed in modifying the Atomic Energy Act of 1954, but they failed in their main objective to defeat the Dixon-Yates contract within the Act. The contract, which endangered the public power concept of TVA, was discredited later by a conflict of interest case. In another controversy over public versus private control, liberals lost out in the Communications Satellite Act of 1962. They won the last filibuster I witnessed at the Senate in July, 1965, under the leadership of Paul Douglas joined by William Proxmire, when they defeated Everett Dirksen's determined effort to amend the Constitution and thus enable the states to bypass the Supreme Court's one-man-one-vote ruling.

Nevertheless, filibusters by any name do not always work. Why must the Senate suffer the periodic indignities of finding itself hamstrung by a few members? It is not efficient; it is not even democratic for the few to hold up the many. But in a world where the majority pushes through, right or wrong, it is good to have one place where the minority can say, "Stop and listen to me!"

The majority has a weapon which it rarely uses called cloture. Since Rule XXII was adopted in 1917, it has been possible to close off debate, but the procedure is so involved that it was used successfully only seven times during my years at the Senate. Cloture requires a petition signed by sixteen Senators and then presented to the Chair. The melodious language of Rule XXII describes what happens then:

". . . and one hour after the Senate meets on the following calendar day but one, he shall lay the motion before the Senate and direct that the Secretary call the roll, and upon the ascertainment that a quorum is present, the Presiding Officer shall, without debate, submit to the Senate by a yea-and-nay vote the question:

" 'Is it the sense of the Senate that the debate shall be brought to a close?

"And if that question shall be decided in the affirmative by two-thirds of the Senators present and voting, then said measure . . . shall be the unfinished business to the exclusion of all other business until disposed of.

"Thereafter no Senator shall be entitled to speak in all more than one hour on the measure . . . and it shall be the duty of the Presiding Officer to keep the time of each Senator who speaks . . ."
Senate Manual, Rule XXII.

One of the strangest sights to be seen on the Floor is a United States Senator whose time has expired under limitation of debate. One moment he is clamoring to be heard. The next he must take his seat in helpless silence until the vote is over, when he is free to talk like a Senator once again.

The idea of silencing a member is against the very nature of a Senate tolerantly devoted to free and lengthy exploration of fundamental principles. I have never known cloture to be attempted until weeks of such exploration have taken place. This deliberate pace in which every voice can be heard is the Senate's unique role in government. It remains the one place where the individual idea, Senator, or state can make itself heard above the din of the whole.

And so it is important that the minority must be able to challenge the majority but not tie up action indefinitely by going to the extremes of the past. So strong was the coalition of Southern Democrats and conservative Republicans that no cloture was voted for thirty-five years, from 1927 to 1962. This was the extreme of minority rule. The pattern has been broken in this decade as cloture has been achieved several times. Possibly a moderate rule change to allow three-fifths of those present and voting to shut off debate would be reasonable. But if the numbers should be nibbled away bit by bit until a simple majority could silence the rest, the Senate would cease to be the greatest free forum on earth.

ADJOURNMENT FEVER

Adjournment is the spring unwound, the last frantic push to get home before the opposition back in the states can gain ground. With few exceptions Capitol Hill succumbs to adjournment fever, a virulent disease that overpowers legislators and propels them madly to the end. Carefully studied legislation is jettisoned; hastily-put-together compromises are accepted. It is as though a long voyage had been in the planning stage with months of weighing what would be best to take along. At the last moment when the whistle is blowing, whatever can be readily grabbed is thrown in while the rest is abandoned on the wharf. Staff members and legislators rush around at a feverish pace to arrange the necessary conferences. Out of this chaos comes the realization that many bills must be abandoned.

During the last hours it is sometimes possible to slip in a few items unnoticed by the usual watchdogs. At the close of a session in the 1930's, I approached Appropriations Chairman Carter Glass at his desk to ask a routine question for the press. While he answered, parliamentary maneuvers were whizzing past us right and left to the accompaniment of the words spoken with such finality by the Chair, "Without objection, agreed to." Later that day Senator Ashurst told me, "You spoke to Carter Glass at exactly the proper moment. He had planned to object to my amendment, but while you kept him busy talking, I was able to secure a million dollars for Arizona!" Anything can happen during the closing hours of a session.

At some point on the last day Wayne Morse always rose to protest the madness of it all. "Mr. President," he entoned, "we owe it to the American people to stay here and solve the problems yet unsolved." If it had been left up to the indefatigable Senator Morse, Congress would never have adjourned.

Another last-day ritual was Matthew Neely's annual speech against speaking. The Senator from West Virginia asked a page to bring in the volumes of the *Congressional Record* and committee hearings printed during the session, which he stacked up beside his desk until he had a tower waist high. With this evidence before him, Senator Neely attacked the verbosity of his colleagues as only he could. Vigorous beyond belief, the black-haired Neely survived into his eighties but looked as though he were still in his fifties. He shook his head from side to side as he spoke and waved his arms at the stack of printed matter before him, alternately shouting and whispering. In rebuking those "windy Senators" who had filled so many unnecessary and expensive pages, Neely urged them to deliver their speeches during adjournment. He suggested that they speak in highly secluded places where the only listeners would be hoot owls and turkey buzzards. When the birds became vexed, as Senator Neely was certain they would be, they could take the "wings of the morning, noon or night and fly far, far away."

Neely had developed a fabulous memory by which he retained much of the Bible and Shakespeare, learning a new piece each morning while he shaved. When he did give other speeches on rare occasions, they were laced with the poetry he loved. His work was done in committee where he proved himself to be one of labor's firmest friends, but the Senator from West Virginia could never countenance long speeches on the Floor.

Swan songs from departing Senators can be expected to break out at any time during the last week but especially during the last day. Back when Victorian sentimentality held sway, Senatorial farewells could be tearful affairs. As late as 1957 the Senate heard a plaintive lament from William A. Blakley of Texas when he prepared to leave after the first of two interim appointments. Regretting that he had not been able to stay longer, the oil million-aire made a well-chosen observation:

"I should have liked to try to find out what is a liberal and what is a conservative. Perhaps I should have liked to be sure that a liberal is not one who wants to give away the lives and liberties and fortunes of others, or that a conservative is not one who wants to have placed in the hands of a few the privileges and the property of the many."

Then came the heroics as Senator Blakley must have suddenly been overcome by the thought that no longer would the United States Senate be privileged to have him walk among them.

"But now, kind friends and Mr. President, I bid you fare-well. I shall go back to my boots and saddle, to ride toward the Western sunset . . . May the will of providence be with you forever."

Congressional Record, 85th Congress, 1st Session, 1957, p. 5062.

Had Senator Blakley ridden into the setting sun in my page days, half of the Chamber would have been in tears. As it was, he returned in 1960 for another brief tenure, the second time depart-ing without a word.

When an adjournment resolution is passed on the last day, the session must end by midnight despite last minute tie-ups. Any bill which has passed each house in a different form must go to conference where members of the Senate and House have to give and take until they agree on its final provisions. Tension builds if the conferees become deadlocked and neither House nor Senate is willing to compromise. The members on the Floor anxiously await the return of the conferees, glancing up at the clock as it inches toward midnight. Should it become necessary, a gallery doorkeeper leans over the balcony and turns back the hands of the clock while Senators look the other way until the conference report arrives and the vote is taken. The United States Senate is not to be restrained by anything as ephemeral as time.

Except for those who have already left for home, the actual moment of adjournment finds every Senator in his seat. The walls are lined with staff members waiting for the final pronouncement from the Chair. The suddenness of a session's end is a historic moment at which to be present. All stop to listen as the Leaders announce that the President has been informed that the Senate has completed its business and is ready to adjourn. They report that he has no further communications to send to Capitol Hill. When I was a page the Leaders would notify the President in person at the White House or in the President's Room if he had come to the Capitol to sign bills. Now the formalities take place over the telephone. Leaders Mansfield and Dirksen had to awaken President Kennedy at six o'clock the morning of September 27, 1961. Another year they consulted President Johnson by phone on board his plane.

The final sound of any Congress is the pounding of the gavel by the Vice President. Thomas R. Marshall, whose Latin was evidently none too strong, once made the announcement, "The Senate stands adjourned *sine Deo.*" Inadvertently he had substituted "without God" for the proper words "without a day fixed for the next meeting." Every other Congress has heard the Chair proclaim, "The Senate stands adjourned *sine die.*"

Sessions used to end more leisurely to the strains of sentimental songs. After the final gavels had fallen in both wings of the Capitol, the Speaker of the House would welcome Senators to the House Chamber for an informal gathering where old friends and enemies would join together in an hour of singing. A piano would be rolled into the Chamber and Speaker Nicholas Longworth would entertain with his violin. In the 1920's when Uncle Joe Cannon was no longer Speaker but still a member of Congress, the old gentleman would close the hour by leading in the singing of his favorite hymn, "God Be With You Till We Meet Again." In today's matter-of-fact world, sentimentality is out of style. All it takes is a sharp crack of the gavel to send Congress flying home to prepare for the next election.

THE POLITICAL PERSONALITY

In the beginning is the voter. He creates the politician with his vote, sends his choice to Washington, and settles back to analyze him hypercritically ever after. Somewhere along the way the voter can lose sight of the fact that the politician is created in the voters' own image.

It must be admitted that politics is a specialized profession with novel trade skills. What does a politician do that other citizens do not? Traditionally, he kisses babies, but there have not been enough babies around the Senate for me to verify this habit. J. Ham Lewis of Illinois kissed ladies' hands with a continental flair, but evidently kissing is not a required political skill.

Woe be unto the would-be politician if he does not enjoy, even delight in shaking hands, for the hand is to a politician what the tail is to a dog. It expresses warmth, joy, hope, and a host of other positive virtues. In the Senate the handshake becomes a contagious reflex action that continues unabated throughout the day. As though the hand had become magnetized, when another hand comes near, they automatically come together. For Senators and employees alike, the Senate serves as a handshaking gymnasium to keep the politicians' hands in training for the inevitable campaigns to come. I would be the last to criticize legislators for being friendly. This spirit stems from naturally outgoing natures and is well suited to willing servants of the people. Better the extreme of exurberance than the chill of sour aloofness.

101

The master of the art of handshaking was Estes Kefauver of Tennessee, who achieved such perfection that he left one with a glowing sense that no one he had met that day was more important. Senator Kefauver would amble along with a slow, loping motion and come to a complete halt as he quietly put forth his giant hand. In his leisurely Tennessee drawl he would inquire about the family, calling them all by name. Just as one began to feel honored that he was ready to spend the day, in an elusive instant Kefauver would take his leave and again go loping down the corridor. The tableau of his tall frame, stooped slightly forward, and his large wistful face was a familiar sight. Once it elicited from Joseph Alsop the comment, "There goes Estes Kefauver, looking like a hunted moose."

From the days when I first knew Kefauver as a young Congressman, a graduate of Yale Law School, he remained the same unaffected country boy, although he gained considerable public exposure through his hearings on crime and rackets. During his try for the vice presidency as the running mate of Adlai Stevenson, Kefauver's handshaking technique failed to impress one little dog who nipped him when he tried to greet the dog's voting owner. After a brief stop for a bandage, Kefauver kept right on shaking hands.

A good politician also makes certain that he has shown proper gratitude to every soul in his domain. It is part of his general fence maintenance at home and at the Senate. One Senator even goes so far as to move about responding to everyone he meets with an absent-minded muttering, "Thank you, thank you, my friend!" He evidently wants to make sure that he has recognized any favors bestowed in the past, any in the process of being accorded, or possibly those favors that might be contemplated in the future. "Thank you, my friend. Thank you!" It works; he gets reelected every time.

When a skilled politician meets a constituent, he begins to build his image as a matter of course. In my page days I was intrigued with the special knack of Georgia's Hoke Smith, an old-fashioned gentleman who had blazed the way in aid to vocational education. Once I boarded an old Senate subway car and settled back on its wicker seat to watch Senator Smith escorting a group of constituents. The large Senator made a courtly bow, his pale face flushing a bit, as he handed the ladies aboard. When they were seated, one of them gushed, "Oh, Senatah Smith, wherah do these cute little cars go?" "Why, Madam," he answered without a qualm, "these cars go to *my* office." The ladies were charmed to be with such an important person. No one mentioned the fact that Hoke Smith shared the Senate Office Building with ninety-five other Senators. Building egos is very much a political skill.

For his very survival a politician has to master the complicated art of saying nothing. Not that he remains silent before the voters; far from it! But he must convince as many voters as possible that he holds the key to their dreams. This, like all magicians' strategy, requires artful slight of hand.

The neophyte in politics must learn to brandish the abundant clichés that say absolutely nothing. Since my page days, this kind of speech has echoed frequently on the Senate Floor, contrasting sharply with the brilliant debates that illuminate the path of legislation. As a saturated authority, I would offer the following composite speech as a survival kit for politicians who are trying to ride out a tidal wave of public opinion.

"I state without fear of contradiction and without equivocation that, in my opinion, while I agree in part with the distinguished and eminent Senator, insofar as I have been able to learn from the somewhat limited attention I have been able to give the matter, it is the general consensus that a further study of this question might add further light to the subject which has been under discussion for so long. Therefore, I can state categorically that it has been my observation, after consulting with my constituents, that we should come to a meeting of the minds.

"Come next election, we shall hear unmistakably from the people. I wish to say to the Senate and the country that we have no time to lose! It is later than we think! At the same time, we must not rush into this. We must take it under study and advisement and not act with undue haste until we can come up with something concrete. Indeed, we could succeed in cementing our ideas to an extent never before realized. But on the other hand, it presents serious problems and difficulties that have to be ironed out. Broad solutions must be found.

"In passing, permit me to say that the crux of the problem goes to the very heart of the whole matter. As I go through the stacks of communications from my constituents every day, I find that they are completely fed up with everything. When I go back to sample the grass roots, what shall I say to the man in the street? How can we turn a deaf ear to the cries of our constituents? I cannot let this matter pass without raising my voice in protest. I, for one, am for the common people and shall stand behind them to the bitter end.

"However, I wish to state with all candor that, personally, I cannot honestly say what should be done in this case. In truth, we stand at the crossroads. One might say, 'Never have we stood at the crossroads so long.' But casting all doubt aside, we must move on! We must face the future undaunted!"

This speech should succeed in clouding the issues long enough for any politician to survive a temporary emergency. In the old days a lifetime career could be sustained by variations on a theme of clichés, but not today. Scrutiny by newsmen and exposure on television frequently make it necessary for politicians to say what they mean.

Public appearances are an integral element in a Senator's career. Most of them develop poise and assurance through practice, and some reveal a real talent for the theatrical. The Senate's great tragedian was James A. Reed of Missouri, an able lawyer whose arguments were always permeated with emotion. He spoke with the passion of a Patrick Henry, pleading on a precipice of history in an attitude of "Give me liberty or give me death!" Senator Reed always looked as if he expected to be given death. He spoke with his hand to his heart as though saluting the flag with eyes upraised or as if he were dying by an unseen sword. His voice had a steady tremor and his face a deathly pallor which further added to his air of perpetual tragedy. Jim Reed, with his distinguished crown of white hair, made a striking Senatorial appearance equal to Warren Harding and Guy Gillette. His noble bearing could have been displayed to perfection by a Roman toga and an olive wreath around the head.

Senator Reed shared his pet phobia, fear of British imperialism, with Colonel Robert McCormick, publisher of the *Chicago Tribune*. Once in the early 1920's to illustrate his fears, Jim Reed had a large map of the western hemisphere placed in the well of the Senate on which he located all the British bases surrounding the United States. From the rostrum where I sat with the pages, I could study every tragic gesture as he proceeded to describe a phantom attack by Britain on the United States. His finger jabbed at Bermuda on the map; then his hand quickly clutched his chest. With a melodramatic hint of impending doom, Senator Reed thundered the improbable question, "At whose hearrrrrt are those guns aaaaaimed?" Shaking his fist at little British Honduras, he passionately cried out again, "At whose hearrrrrt are those guns aaaaaimed?" As his arm swept across the map to the West Coast and British Columbia, I concluded that as far as Jim Reed was concerned, the American Revolution and the War of 1812 had not settled one thing.

The Senate parallels the theater in many ways, as I discovered when Otto Preminger was shooting Washington scenes of his movie version of Allen Drury's *Advise and Consent*. Charles Laughton, who played the role of an aged Senator, lamented to me during a long delay, "It's very wearisome when they make the same scene agaaan and agaaan and agaaan." I readily sympathized, "I know how it is, Mr. Laughton, because Senators in debate say the same thing again and again and again!"

The surface noises of a politician can obscure his better qualities. Robert Rice Reynolds of North Carolina would swagger down a corridor, bow to the ladies and grab every hand in sight with a hearty, "How are yah, Cuz?" The tall, sandy-haired Senator was the epitome of the middle-aged dandy. But just as real was his desire to be a devoted Senator and diligent Chairman of the Military Affairs Committee during World War II. I have never known a more gracious man in the Senate, or one who tried harder to be helpful at all times to Senators and staff people. What he lacked in depth, Bob Reynolds made up for in bluster. It was easy to enjoy his natural flamboyance.

When Reynolds returned from one of the countless trips which made him possibly the most traveled Senator of all time, he would give travelogues that created much noise but shed little light. With his mouth open to the maximum, Bob Reynolds reached heights of exaggerated enunciation. Place names fascinated him, like "Saaaaan Pierrrrre" and "Ja-maaaaa-ca, that beeeee-uuuuu-ti-ful iiiiisle!" One did not learn much through his reports but he left no doubt that he had been somewhere.

Robert Rice Reynolds was a human paradox: a wealthy man who campaigned in a worn-out jalopy, a ranter who appreciated the quiet beauties of nature, and an all-embracing romantic who nevertheless wanted to exclude whole nationalities and races from our country. Bob Reynolds was a politician I had to disagree with and yet he was a man I could not help but like.

If the landmarks of the Senate scene had parallels in nature, Senator William Langer of North Dakota would have been the active volcano. Wild Bill Langer won his epithet fair and square on the Floor of the Senate. He did not speak; he detonated. Langer took the Floor with the roaring turbulance of a thunderstorm breaking over the Senate Chamber, even to the lightning crashes of his mighty fists literally cracking the desks in front of him.

Bill Langer created a spectacular afterglow of the old pioneer spirit of stubborn independence. He was the voice of frustration who lashed out continually at a society that he believed had dealt unjustly with him, and he championed the underdog at all times. Actually the Senator from North Dakota was a quick-witted debater who had been considered the most outstanding student in his class at Columbia University.

Whatever direction he took, Langer was never lukewarm.

While he could be a most vehement enemy, he could be a strong and loyal friend. Almost more startling than his public bombast was his warm and gusty cordiality toward his friends. It was like being with a grizzly bear who had suddenly become domesticated. He would grab one by the shoulder and give a mighty shake and a friendly hello. Even women reporters did not escape his hearty slap on the back.

In a political world that operates on unwritten rules of mutual cooperation, Langer went out of his way to be unpredictable. One evening the Republican leadership left him to watch the Floor while everyone left for dinner. With no one to object in the empty Chamber, Langer dumbfounded the entire Senate by unexpectedly obtaining unanimous consent that all pages be sent home. For once the boys were relieved of the tedious ordeal of a night session, but the mechanics of running the Senate were thrown awry. Thereafter the Leaders made certain that someone else was on duty, not only to watch the Floor but to watch Langer as well.

Senator Langer was forever the individualist, even to the tortuous way he mistreated a cigar. His answer to the no-smoking rule in the Chamber was to chew at his cigar nervously, never bothering to remove the cellophane wrapper first. When one end of the cigar was reduced to a splintered ruin, he quickly reversed it and began working on the other end. He drove a car through Washington congestion as a Great Plains wind might tear through his own North Dakota country. With his grey hair flying, his shoulders stooped forward in a fighting stance, and the cigar clenched in his teeth, he was ready at the drop of a gavel to add more fire to the legend of Wild Bill Langer.

Among the spellbinders of the half-century, John Sharp Williams of Mississippi was the only one who delivered his finest orations while heavily under the influence of alcohol. He might have needed to be led out of the Chamber afterwards, but the speech itself would have been a model of logic and wit, spoken in a whining voice that cracked like a whiplash for emphasis. Senator Williams' brilliant mind and stinging humor were reminiscent of Mark Twain, whom he also resembled in appearance.

The old gentleman was practically deaf when I was a page, but that did not diminish his disgust at the roaring broadsides of Tom Heflin from Williams' neighboring state of Alabama. One day I heard them exchange words in the middle aisle when Heflin puffed up to say, "At least I am in full command of my faculties." John Sharp Williams retorted, "And what difference does that make?"

Senator Williams proudly used the desk of Mississippi's best known Senator Jefferson Davis, who had closed it for the last time on January 21, 1861, when he left Washington to become President of the Confederate States of America. The desk is identified by the small patch on the side which covers the place where a Union soldier in a moment of passion thrust his sword into the wood when he was told it had been used by Jefferson Davis.

Using the Davis desk today is John Stennis of Mississippi, who sternly maintains the traditions of the old South and is one of the hardest workers in the Senate. When he made possible the microfilming of Confederate records in the National Archives, Senator Stennis was awarded a citation from the United Daughters of the Confederacy by my mother-in-law Mrs. Robert Bachman, then President General.

Southern Senators have been among the most memorable figures in Congress. They used to be secure in the Senate because of their relatively unchallenged positions at home. Many have stayed long enough to become institutions in the way that Ellison D. "Cotton Ed" Smith of South Carolina became the authority on cotton during his thirty-five years as a Senator. In a voice choked by chewing tobacco, Agriculture Chairman Smith would deliver speeches no one could understand on "fightin' the booooll weevil." The leathery old Senator was a bitter opponent of Franklin Roosevelt. When someone suggested that FDR was really his own worst enemy, Cotton Ed snorted, "No, damn it, not as long as I live he isn't!"

During Smith's last years his colleague was Burnet Maybank, an aristocratic cotton exporter whose Charleston accent trimmed every word to its bare essentials. Maybank would lament, "Mist'

Pres-dent, we-ah *giv'n* away cot'n! We-ah *giv'n* away cot'n!" Gesturing in an upward spiral, Senator Maybank brought one speech
to a climax with the declaration, "I stan'—wheah I've always
stood—right heah!" at which point he sat down.

If a politician forgets his home base and looses touch with the
voters who keep him in Washington, he will inevitably find himself
without a job. His approach to national and world problems may
be outstanding, but before anything else, he must be the Senator
from his home state, responsive to its needs and supporter of its
way of life.

Alabama's two Senators for over twenty years were creative
legislators in fields that were acceptable at home. John Sparkman
in his self-effacing way has starred in housing legislation as Chairman of the Committee on Banking and Currency. Lister Hill
specialized in the field of health. He is the son of a prominent
surgeon who named him for Joseph Lister. As Chairman of the
Labor and Education Committee, Senator Hill used his remarkable
energies to sponsor more health legislation than any other person
in our history. Both John Sparkman and Lister Hill have been able
to help *all* Americans without disavowing the home base that made
their Senate careers possible.

Olin Johnston of South Carolina never forgot his boyhood
struggles as a poorly-paid textile mill worker. His concern for little
people was circumscribed by the prejudices of his native environ-
ment, but it led him to become, together with Frank Carlson of
Kansas and Hiram Fong of Hawaii, the champion of government
workers. In the same way, sharecroppers never had a better friend
than North Carolina's Kerr, pronounced car, Scott, whose earnestness and humility made him a beloved Senator. He, too,
worked within the political limits of his home state, as any successful legislator must do.

To keep in touch with the voters back home, a Senator's staff
devotes a great portion of its time to handling the mail that pours
into Washington. The writers ask for information, intercession with
government agencies, and most important, they express their feelings about legislation, the administration, or the Senator himself.

Morris Sheppard of Texas was one of those steady, quiet men who makes any institution function well. Elected with Woodrow Wilson, he stayed in the Senate for the rest of his life, almost thirty years. One of his secrets was to give personal attention to every letter that came to his office, signing each answer by hand. Back in his day it was a monumental achievement. Today it is almost humanly impossible, though Margaret Chase Smith succeeds in meeting the challenge, and Kenneth Keating of New York was another in recent years who gave full attention to his mail. It is remarkable how many letters still get a Senator's direct scrutiny; and with mass answering equipment, each letter at least has the appearance of the personal touch.

Who is the politician? What kind of life has he led before coming to Washington? Of the 558 Senators in my time, over three-fifths have been lawyers, as one might expect, but the remaining two-fifths have represented an interesting cross section of life. Long before coming to the Senate Ralph Flanders of Vermont was a machinist, Magnus Johnson of Minnesota was a glass blower in his native Sweden, and Harry Darby of Kansas was a boilermaker prior to making railroad cars among other enterprises.

Well-known men from labor have included Patrick McNamara of Michigan, who began in the construction business as a plumber; William Calder of New York, who apprenticed as a carpenter; and James J. Davis of Pennsylvania, who after immigrating from Wales, began in a steel factory as a puddler when he was eleven. "Puddler" Jim, as he was called, rose in the Iron, Steel and Tin Workers of America and became Secretary of Labor under Presidents Harding, Coolidge, and Hoover. George Berry of Tennessee spent his life as a pressman, becoming President of the Pressmen's Union for forty-one years with a brief tenure in the Senate.

Six Senators were once printers including "Honest Vic" Donahey of Ohio and Henry Dworshak of Idaho. Among the nine

Senators who were miners was Samuel Nicholson of Colorado, discoverer of the zinc ore Nicholsoiti. Ralph Cameron of Arizona not only prospected for and mined many kinds of ore but located and built the Bright Angel Trail into the Grand Canyon. Senators have manufactured everything from Stuart Symington's electric products, William Brock's candy, and Glen Taylor's wigs to Homer Capehart's radio-phonographs.

There have been athletes like Birch Bayh, who played semi-professional baseball in Indiana, and Warren Barbour of New Jersey, who held the title of amateur heavyweight boxing champion of the United States and Canada before turning to the manufacture of thread. Walter E. Edge of New Jersey, a champion bicycle racer, walked with a forward tilt to his shoulders as though he were poised over handlebars, ready to race again.

Forty have left the academic world to become Senators, including twelve current members who have taught in institutions of higher education: Eugene McCarthy of Minnesota, George McGovern and Karl Mundt of South Dakota, Gale McGee of Wyoming, Mark Hatfield of Oregon, Jack Miller of Iowa, Jennings Randolph of West Virginia, Frank Yarborough and John Tower of Texas, John Sparkman of Alabama, Mike Mansfield of Montana, and William Fulbright, who also served as President of the University of Arkansas. Other college presidents who came to the Senate were Simeon Fess of Antioch College, Frank Graham of the University of North Carolina, and Joseph Rosier of West Virginia's Fairmont State College. Frank B. Willis of Ohio Northern University was another noted educator turned politician.

The prime example of the college professor in the Senate was Paul Douglas of Illinois, who could not restrain himself from teaching as he expounded his ideas. Deep in thought most of the time, Senator Douglas would come out to see the press willingly, but when a newsman asked a poorly-phrased question, the professor in Douglas would sometimes point out, "Now you *should* have asked me this way . . ."

Perhaps the most learned man to have served in the Senate, Douglas taught at six institutions of higher learning. Speaking in the scholarly tones of his native New England, he managed to make theories applicable to daily life. A big polar bear of a man, Douglas showed in the Senate the kind of courage that led him to join the Marines in 1942 at the age of fifty, advancing through the ranks from private to lieutenant colonel, being twice wounded in action. The Senator has inspired his liberal followers with a brand of thoughtful independence uniquely his own.

Accustomed to a roomful of eager students, Paul Douglas found the Senate Chamber uninspiring in its tomblike moments. As he would walk back and forth, gesturing mildly, the Senator would direct his lecture to an assistant seated in a low chair beside his desk, who would nod animatedly from time to time. Sometimes Phil Weymouth, Assistant to the Sergeant at Arms, or I would slip into the Chamber to stand by the wall and listen. When we were spotted by Senator Douglas, he would begin directing his remarks to us as though we were students late for class. In the same way Olin Johnston and Wayne Morse would single me out as a straight man. Without realizing it, each of these Senators would often walk toward me, pointing a forefinger and saying, "Now you *know* . . ." By the time they began shaking a fist in my direction, I would slip out into the Lobby, grateful that none of them could give me a written examination.

In the 1920's the most professor-like Senator was Hiram Bingham of Connecticut, a statuesque figure with prematurely white hair. Born in Hawaii of missionary parents, Bingham married into the Tiffany family and had seven sons. Before he became Governor of Connecticut and a Senator, he taught at Harvard, Princeton, and Yale and organized and commanded flying schools during World War I in this country and in France. He was best known, however, as the discoverer of Machu Picchu, remote capital of the Inca civilization, which he found during one of five archaeological expeditions that he led in South America. Senator Bingham literally looked down on the world from his towering height of six foot six, greeting everyone with a formal bow, but his natural reserve disguised a warm personality. He was censured on a technicality by the Senate in 1929 because his adviser on the

Robert Taft of Ohio always said what he thought.—photo: USIA, National Archives

Among the great minds of the Senate.

Paul Douglas of Illinois was the scholar in politics.—photo: Harris & Ewing

Floor during the Smoot-Hawley Tariff debate was an expert from
Connecticut manufacturing interests. Though this cast a shadow
over Bingham's political career, it did not diminish the varied
accomplishments of one of the most striking personalities ever to
serve in the Senate.

The most interesting historical figure to serve in my time was
the youngest son of Sam Houston, Andrew Jackson Houston, who
came to the Senate in 1941 when he was eighty-seven to serve the
last two months of his life. His appointment was a gesture of
respect from the State of Texas, which had also made him Superintendent of the San Jacinto Battlefield where his father had become
a hero by defeating the Mexican General Santa Anna. Andrew
Jackson Houston was only seven when Governor Houston, then
sixty-eight, was deposed because he courageously refused to go
along with the Confederacy. Sam Houston was born while George
Washington was President, which meant that his son, the kindly
old Senator, represented in his frail person a remarkable span of
American history.

During the last decade the Senate has gradually become more
representative of the ethnic groups that make up the American
people. Hawaii's admission into the Union brought as one of its
first Senators Harvard graduate Hiram Fong, whose parents had
come as laborers from China to the sugar fields of the Islands.
Daniel Inouye became the first Senator of Japanese ancestry and
Edward Brooke of Massachusetts the first Negro to be elected
Senator by popular vote.

With their varied backgrounds and personalities, there is no
stereotype Senator. Each has a unique approach; most have the
perspective that comes from a highly developed sense of humor. I
often wished that Will Rogers had become a Senator, but the next
best thing was having South Dakota's William Bulow in the Senate.
His common sense and homespun humor made him welcome
everywhere. In his well-mannered drawl, Senator Bulow would tell
how back home when he had been governor, he had vetoed a bill
because it required spending half a million dollars more than had
been appropriated. Then he came to Washington to find that the

federal government dealt in billions of dollars, not millions. Senator Bulow liked doing what he called "whittlin' things down to size." In trying to figure out just what a billion dollars really was, he started with the annual $10,000 salary paid to Senators in his day. At that rate, Bulow reasoned, he would have to be elected for one hundred thousand years to earn a billion dollars. He concluded that it was not worth it. "In all that time, some Republican would surely come along and want the job!"

Even Robert Taft had to take his share of political ribbing from a liberal Democrat like Glen Taylor of Idaho. One evening when Taft had brought the Senate to the verge of a vote, Taylor decided to have some fun with the serious Republican. A humorist and maverick by nature, Taylor always had an up-to-something look which suited his background as a professional entertainer and leader of his family hillbilly band. Senator Taylor alerted me as I went by his back row seat, saying, "Watch Bob Taft! I'm going to play a joke on him and make him think I'm getting ready for a long speech!" He began stacking his desk with piles of documents and every book within reach. Joining in the spirit, I returned from the Lobby with the unabridged dictionary and several bound copies of the *Congressional Record*.

As the mountain of literature on Taylor's desk grew, Senator Taft's cheerful smile began to fade. I walked over to the Republican side to hear him exclaiming to his colleagues in a tone of alarm, "Look at Glen Taylor! He's going to filibuster when we are all ready to vote!" Taft began to pace the aisle in acute distress while Taylor wore the deadpan expression of a boy who had fooled the teacher. Finally the suspense was too much for Bob Taft. He came around the back of the Chamber, obviously seething inside but forcing a sickly smile as with great restraint he asked Taylor what he planned to do. The Senator from Idaho shrugged and with a poker face answered, "I just want to make a few remarks. It's hard to say how long it will take." When he got the Floor, Glen Taylor proceeded to make one of his shortest speeches and abruptly sat down to enjoy Taft's look of surprise and relief as the yeas and nays were ordered and the Senate began to vote.

Generally, the politician reflects mankind in its more outgoing and effervescent moods, but the complete range of mortal frailties can be found in any group of political beings. If Shakespeare were writing his classic interpretations of human nature in our time, he could readily use the United States Senate as the scene of countless personality dramas. While the stage set of the Chamber never really varies, the electorate has chosen the cast so that on the Senate stage at any given time there will appear an amazing variety of types. While some of the more celebrated members of the Senate are depicted in individual portraits throughout the book, here are anonymous vignettes of some of the lesser aspects of human nature I have observed in watching these men play their chosen roles.

All Senators must enter the Chamber through one of the seven pairs of bronze-decorated, swinging glass doors, and there were those whose entrance style was unique. There was the knight-errant who, amid the ruffles and flourishes in his own mind, strode into the Chamber as though he were mounted on a charger. With his lance raised on high and his cold, steely eyes fixed on the target at hand, he was more than ready to do battle with every windmill in Washington.

There was also the Mr. Dick, straight out of *David Copperfield*. He was a true, gentle-hearted fuddy-duddy who meant no harm and somehow managed to do some good.

Another had come to the Senate with refreshing eagerness, his open countenance reflecting a mind receptive to the country's needs. In time, his mouth gradually twisted down as though the years had left a sour taste, and his narrowing eyes could see no farther than his next election.

There was always at least one Senator resigned to a continual state of boredom. He had the condescending disdain of one who had seen it all and done it all until he felt it was hardly worth his while to bother.

Slouched at his desk was one whose youthful career once gave buoyant promise but whose vital energies had dissolved into a sluggish bog. With his brilliant mind perpetually pickled in alcohol, he was highly vulnerable to manipulation and lived a tragedy on which the curtain would soon be lowered.

Not far away sat a granite pharaoh on his throne watching his slaves lift a new pillar into place. He had only to lift a finger for his quaking staff to come running.

We all have our egos. It was part of my shell to march around the Floor at full speed with austere, military-like precision. One day I burst into the Republican cloakroom on the trail of a Senator and stood surveying the scene with stern concentration. Senator Bourke Hickenlooper, a friend of many years, looked up from the sofa where he was relaxing and took me down a peg or two. In his broad Iowa accent he said, "Richard, you look just like a Russian army officer!"

There was always a Senator who paused to look up at the galleries while he adjusted his handkerchief. He seemed to believe that all attention was riveted on him in a silent accolade that said, "You're wonderful! You're wonderful!" His self-satisfied look seemed to reply, "I know it! I know it!"

One quickly recognized the malcontent who prowled his dark way through the Lobby like the bully in *The Hoosier Schoolmaster*. His oaths filled the cloakroom and even when he joked, the sneer never left his bony face. On the Floor he could not speak without bitterness, as he snarled out speeches so crass they made his few partisans shudder.

The full cast of human characters exists today as it has since man began. The Senate is a mirror in which the voter can find an accurate reflection of himself.

One unique personality of recent years was not a Senator. Bobby Baker managed to become an integral part of the Senate scene with a rise to power that was unmatched in its swiftness. I knew Bobby Baker from the day in 1943 that he came as a small page boy fresh from South Carolina until his last day as Secretary of the Majority. He stood in the center aisle to make a ceremonial announcement of a message from the President and then left the Chamber to resign under fire, never to return.

Bobby had been a brattish page whose manner said, "I'm coming through and if anything gets in my way, *it* has to move, not I!" His first promotion went to his head when he became chief telephone page in the Democratic cloakroom and he sought to push staff personnel around. He and I had one strongly-worded confrontation, after which his attitude toward me was always courteous. Bobby matured into a dignified young man, valedictorian of his class at the Capitol Page School and a hardworking law student at the American University. He performed his duties with unusual energy and consideration for those under his supervision. When Bobby became, at the age of twenty-six, the youngest Secretary of the Majority, he had before him the potential of a long life of service to the Senate.

There was always something questionable about Bobby Baker. Perhaps it was the unrestrained ambition that showed through his every move calculated to increase his standing with the Senators. Perhaps it was the way he kept glancing up at the Press Gallery to be sure they were watching his every step. Perhaps it was his habit of speaking out of the corners of his mouth, alternating one side and then the other as he circulated among the Senators and newsmen. His closely-set eyes were focused dead ahead, fixed on goals known only to him.

A prominent columnist always referred to Bobby Baker as the "Junior Genius." His management skills were such that very little business of the Senate was transacted in which Baker's counsel was not sought. Republicans and Democrats alike would call for him constantly. "Let's get Bobby over here. He'll straighten things out! Where is Bobby Baker?" There is an extraordinary element of irony in the almost unanimous denunciation of Baker among Senate Republicans who, in fact, had placed unusual confidence and trust in him.

Bobby seemed to be everywhere at once. His job as Secretary of the Majority centered on aiding the leadership in the expediting, planning, and channeling of legislation. He was an active secretary to the majority conferences and caucuses, kept track of roll-call votes, arranged voting pairs for absent Senators, and maintained close contact between the leadership, the Democratic Policy Committee, and the Senate as a whole. Until the Republicans objected, he would stand at the center door to the Chamber during a vote and say to each Senator who entered, "Our vote is aye or no" as the case might be. Senators voted the way they wanted to, but Bobby left no doubt as to the party stand on each issue. The pressures and tensions of his job may have produced his ulcer, but that is only part of the story of a young man in a hurry.

Bobby Baker's incredible business involvements were one of the best kept secrets since the Manhattan Project. Not even the alert press corps discovered them. Two of the young men who were assigned as my assistants were close friends of Bobby Baker though they later broke with him; but in all the years I knew them, not one inkling of his business life leaked out. I did think it strange that corporation executives would meet with Bobby Baker in the President's Room from time to time. Senators, too, may have wondered at his amazing power, but he was a highly skilled young man on the staff who had made himself all but indispensible to the operation of the Senate. Who would have supposed that he sought anything beyond the normal political goals? The story as it gradually unfolded came as such a stunning shock to the entire Capitol community that even the newsmen were reluctant to write about it for weeks. After all, for years Bobby Baker had cultivated first-name friendships among the press by becoming one of their best news sources on the Hill.

The first news broke in the *Washington Post* in a story of a lawsuit against him which charged that Bobby Baker had used his government position to persuade a large corporation to favor his vending machine company. Baker remained as unshaken as though it were a minor inconvenience and no cause for embarrassment. For a while he came to see the press in his old confidential way, undoubtedly assuring himself that anyone with his great prestige and his friends on both sides of the aisle had nothing to fear. As time went on, one business involvement after another became known until the story broke wide open when the sex angle made headlines across the nation. By then Baker refused to see any members of the press, saying, "Tell them to see my lawyer." He began slipping out the south or west doors to dodge the newsmen.

Where before I had never seen anything on Bobby Baker's face but an overdose of assurance, now he tried hard to mask his anxiety. He could not walk across the Chamber without generating an atmosphere charged with tension and a noticeable wariness on the part of Senators. The hint of corruption was too close to home. There were long conferences with Senators on the Floor during which Bobby would talk very fast and then blanch when the Senator would shake his head slowly from side to side. It began to look as though he were beyond the help of those who had trusted him as an official of the Senate.

One Senator and one newsman were principally responsible for Bobby Baker's resigning his Senate position rather than facing the charges against him. When I saw the huge frame of Clark Mollenhoff of the *Des Moines Register and Tribune* and the *Minneapolis Star and Tribune* coming down the corridor, I automatically went in search of Senator John Williams of Delaware, knowing that the two would have much to talk over in the sanctuary of the President's Room. Williams, who looks like Daniel Webster, is a self-made multimillionaire and beholden to no one; the Senator from Delaware has none of the areas of caution that even some of the best Senators must often reserve for their political longevity. During the tax scandals of 1950 the independent Williams found a kindred spirit in the uncompromising approach of Clark Mollenhoff. Through the years they have unearthed and made public evidence that many people would have preferred to have forgotten.

Clark Mollenhoff pursued the Baker leads with the same investigative thoroughness and responsibility that won him a Pulitzer Prize for his news stories on racketeers in labor unions. It was Mollenhoff who first interested Senator John McClellan and his counsel Bobby Kennedy in the racketeering investigation. At six foot four, Clark is the giant of the press corps, a crusader with the unpretentious manner of his native Iowa. A lawyer by training and an aggressive detective by instinct, Clark is Perry Mason and Superman rolled into one. The similarity between the crusading Clark Kent and Clark Mollenhoff was so real that Mollenhoff's young son insisted his father kept the Superman suit hidden in the office filing cabinet. As Jimmy Hoffa and Bobby Baker have discovered, lawyer-reporter-author Mollenhoff is no fictional character but a very real threat to anyone who has something to hide.

At the opposite poles of the political personality can be found two types of Senators: those who are hungry for power alone and those who seek only the chance to serve the public good. Somewhere in between are the vast majority who recognize that in order to continue serving, they must achieve some degree of power.

The two Senators under whose patronage I spent my page days, Boies Penrose and George Wharton Pepper, illustrate these two poles. Boies Penrose was the embodiment of the machine politician whose Senate seat was secure for life. He had only to issue commands to have politicians and businessmen do his bidding the length and breadth of Pennsylvania. Penrose's successor was appointed from outside of politics and later elected because of his ability as a lawyer, scholar, and public-spirited citizen of Philadelphia. George Wharton Pepper found that because he represented no political organization, his Senate career was limited to five years.

Boies Penrose was not only a heavyweight politically but also physically; he was the largest Senator I have known. His six-foot-four, four-hundred-pound frame cruised like a battleship in and out of the Chamber. Though he inspired fear in staff members and Senators alike, Penrose was never gruff with me but took a certain pride that he had sponsored so young a page. In those days, pages were strictly cautioned never to speak to a Senator until first spoken to, but I could not resist saying each day, "Good morning, Senator Penrose!" He would answer with a solemn "How de do,

young man," which constituted a speech from Penrose. I knew that
he watched when it was my turn to take a bill to the rostrum. Once
when another page tried to elbow ahead of me, Senator Penrose
grabbed the bill and thrust it deliberately toward me. *His* page was
not to be beaten out!

When I was sent on an errand to the Senators' private dining
room, I would find Penrose seated at the table like Henry the
Eighth with a cloth napkin tied around his neck. He consumed
milk by the quart, impressive evidence that it took a lot of fuel to
maintain his huge form.

Senator Penrose had no wish to hide himself in the background, an impossibility for one of his bulk. Instead, he viewed the
world from a fiery red touring car, a Winton Six, with its top down
no matter what the weather. The Senator all but filled the back seat
himself, protected partially by a large hat whose broad brim would
flap in the breeze. Penrose and his Winton Six were a conspicuous
sight on the streets of Washington and throughout Pennsylvania.
Any local politician who could be seen riding with the Senator
gained status on the spot. His closest companion was Senator Jim
Watson of Indiana whose jovial nature complimented the outward
austerity of the Pennsylvanian. Years later, Senator Watson told
me that many of their trips together were spent enjoying the
beauties of nature. Penrose, who was graduated from Harvard
magna cum laude in 1881, was a devoted and knowledgeable
naturalist, a remnant of his early days when he gave promise of a
scholarly career in keeping with his family tradition. Instead, he
became a protégé of the ruthless politician Senator Matthew Stan-
ley Quay, and the rest of his life was spent in spinning his own
political spider web.

Senator Penrose had a serious illness in 1919 which reduced
him by one hundred pounds to a mere three hundred. His illness
also made him extremely irritable. I remember the day he waited
too long for the Senators' private elevator. In those days it was an
open cage that ascended and descended in full sight at a leisurely
pace that was maddening to anyone in a hurry. In a fit of impa-

tience Senator Penrose took hold of the cage bars and rattled them vehemently. As the elevator approached, I hoped for the sake of the operator that he had sufficient skill to stop at the exact level of the floor or else the door would not open. More than one new patronage operator had bounced a restless Senator up and down in trying to find the right place to stop, while those waiting outside would first have a view of the Senator's head and then a sight of his feet. Those manually-controlled lifts took more composure than an ailing man like Penrose could muster.

Another time the Senator found a medium-sized man, a member of the general public, standing in front of him ready to board the elevator. Not hesitating a moment, the giant Penrose picked up the unsuspecting man, set him neatly to one side, and walked alone, unhindered, into the elevator. That incident remains for me a symbol of Penrose and his type of political sovereignty.

The last day of 1921 saw the end of an era when, as the czar of Pennsylvania and the Republican Party, Boies Penrose died. Senator Jim Watson, who would never be classified as a liberal, characterized his friend Penrose as the most reactionary man he had ever known.

When George Wharton Pepper succeeded Penrose, everything about him contrasted sharply with the austere figure of the old political boss. Pepper was animated and articulate in the manner of a well-rounded intellectual. Despite his wealthy, aristocratic background, he approached life with a warm-hearted interest in the welfare of every individual, showing his consideration for others in small but telling ways.

Again an elevator provided the insight. A Senator can let himself feel very important when he pushes the buzzer three times in a signal that means, "Senator waiting! . . . Top priority! . . . Come quickly!" One day I accompanied Senator Pepper when he entered an elevator and found a waiter carrying a large tray of dishes. Senator Pepper had the right to be delivered immediately to his floor, but he said to the operator, "Please take this man first. He has a heavy load." In recent years I saw Senator Quentin

Pennsylvania's czar, Senator Boies Penrose, in his red Winton Six, was the antithesis of his successor, George Wharton Pepper, Philadelphia lawyer, outdoorsman and best friend of Senate pages.—photos: Herbert French Collection, Library of Congress

Burdick of North Dakota perform a similar kindness, but unfortunately there have always been a few Senators who have lived in the self-contained world of a Boies Penrose.

Senator Pepper had universal interests and talents that made him a valuable addition to the Senate. He was the Lyman Beecher lecturer at Yale in 1915. For sixteen years he held the Algernon Sydney Biddle chair of law at the University of Pennsylvania. When he became a Senator, this led in 1925 to his key role in the codification of federal statutes in a single volume. With his brilliant mind and sense of proportion, Senator Pepper would have made a Supreme Court justice of the highest caliber.

Baseball was high on Pepper's list of interests. He was a natural athlete himself, with a robust frame. He sensed the page boys' need for fun and exercise to counteract their long hours indoors breathing stale cigarette smoke. With his own funds, Senator Pepper bought the twenty-one pages complete baseball equipment, including uniforms and an elaborate backstop to protect the nearby Senate Office Building. Sometimes he would join them in their games. To this day, no other Senator has taken as keen an interest in the welfare of Senate pages. Professional baseball benefited from his legal skill. In one of his many cases before the Supreme Court, Senator Pepper successfully defended the American and National Leagues, arguing that they were not subject to antitrust laws, thereby assuring that the world series games could continue. It was never enough for Senator Pepper to believe in a cause; he had to take direct action to carry out his beliefs. In the same spirit he was an enthusiastic supporter of the Washington Cathedral, preaching at times from its pulpit.

It must have come as a shock to the boss politicians of his state when they realized that a man representing them in the Senate could not be controlled. When they awakened to the fact that George Wharton Pepper was a nonpolitical statesman, they made certain that he was defeated in a three-way race in 1926 with William S. Vare, Old Guard, and Gifford Pinchot, Independent Republican. Vare won the election but the Senate refused to seat him, so questionable was his campaign.

Afterwards Pepper showed his rare perspective when he admitted that if he could do it over again, he would not change any of his votes in the Senate but would spend time in building up his own political organization. Obviously, courage and dedication alone do not return a man to the Senate. Had Senator Pepper been allowed to serve longer, he would have continued to gain stature. He had the dignity, fairness, and humility of Walter F. George, the approachability of George Aiken, and the scholarly mind of Henry Cabot Lodge, Sr. George Wharton Pepper was one of those who truly sought to serve the public good.

All manner of character sketches and caricatures can be drawn of the politician, but it must be remembered that he is nothing more than one of us. He literally represents the species *homo sapiens*. Politics itself is a human phenomenon. Wherever there is more than one person, you will find the practice of exchanging favors and support which is the essence of politics, and from it will emerge the many facets of the political personality.

THE SENATE FAMILY

In circulating behind the Senate's public facade I have often searched for and seldom found any evidence of "the world's most exclusive club." That overworked sobriquet for the United States Senate is largely inept. Club implies an austere, impersonal setting where aloof gentlemen seek seclusion from the world. The Senate I know is a warm, friendly, hyperactive community whose members are deeply involved in solving the problems of their country and the world. After a lifetime spent in their midst I could compare the Senators to members of one great varied family who are subjected to all of the rigors that living with relatives entails. Yet their tolerance of each other and their loyalty to the whole membership permeates every aspect of Senate life. Whether they agree or disagree, this overall spirit of pulling together is the key to what makes the Senate a constructive instrument of government.

Among the one hundred Senators a few choose to maintain a strictly official relationship. When they confer together, it is as though one state were talking to another. But it is when the official side and the human side can be combined that Senators are most effective, and the combination is a powerful one. Throughout Floor debates that are reported by the press and in the *Congressional Record,* Senators state their cases formally and hammer

away verbally at each other from what would seem to be irrecon-
cilable stands on issues such as states' rights or foreign aid. After
they have finished, it would not be unusual to encounter the same
two Senators in the cloakroom, shaking hands in the best prizefight
tradition. More often it would go deeper than that. The defiant
adversaries of the Floor would sit down to confer quietly in the
sanctuary of the cloakroom. Here as friends, they could frankly
and objectively discuss the very problems that seemed so insolu-
able on the Floor. In this personal way more momentous questions
are resolved at Senators' desks, offices, and in the cloakrooms than
ever are in public debate, not necessarily by vote trading and other
crude political arts, but by an honest attempt at reason and mutual
understanding.

Friendships among the members of the Senate are such reser-
voirs of strength that they often transcend political parties, those
rigid power structures on which the entire Senate operates. However, a Senator's closest friendships are usually within his own
party. One rarely finds a Democrat in the Republican cloakroom
or a Republican in the Democratic cloakroom. Party members
even eat together at special tables in the private dining rooms, but
there are exceptions. Democratic Leader Mansfield and Republican dean George Aiken begin each day by having breakfast together. Their mutual world outlook and warm personal friendship
overshadow their differences in background and party affiliation.
When Hubert Humphrey was Majority Whip, his seat adjoined
that of Harry F. Byrd, Sr. Their respect for each other bridged vast
chasms between their divergent political philosophies. If all the
conservatives were on one side of the aisle and all the liberals on
the other, there would exist a wide and difficult gulf between them.
Since each party reflects the full spectrum of political beliefs from
ultraliberal to extreme conservative, like-thinking members of opposite parties are naturally drawn together across party lines,
creating a closely-knit Senate family.

Not always does the Senate family work together smoothly
and resolve issues neatly. For one thing, every clan has its stubborn
members—or heroes, depending on one's point of view—who

insist that theirs is the only way. In defense of his cause one single Senator can freeze legislative operations for hours or even days by resorting to a variety of parliamentary tricks. By objecting, a Senator can prevent unanimous consent agreements, such as limiting debate or rescinding quorum calls which would result in requiring the continual presence of a quorum.

If he wants to be genuinely obstreperous, a Senator can begin the day by objecting to dispensing with the reading of the *Journal*. Rather than a verbatim report of debates like the *Congressional Record,* the large red *Journal* includes legislative action and official communications, recorded in longhand by Journal Clerk Bernard Somers, who sits on the rostrum beside the Parliamentarian. Somers' job is provided for in the Constitution which states, "Each House shall keep a Journal of its proceedings . . ." To read aloud the *Journal* of the previous legislative day usually requires an hour's delay and sometimes longer. During a 1942 poll tax filibuster, the Senate stalled for a hectic two days on a point of order raised when Richard Russell and Kenneth McKellar insisted that the *Journal* be read.

Surely in the world of deliberative bodies, few are so liberal in guaranteeing individual freedom as the United States Senate. For that reason the fraternal spirit of the Senate family is an all-important and much needed cohesive force.

Like any large group of strong-willed persons, the Senate has to admit to quarrels that have varied from temporary spats in the heat of an angry debate to outright feuds. It can be more than inconvenient when colleagues from one state break openly with one another, as did Matthew Neely of West Virginia and his handpicked protégé Rush Holt. Neely's vigorous support plus the backing of the United Mine Workers won Holt his Senate seat in 1934. Holt had to wait six months before he became thirty and old enough to take the oath of office, not long after which the young Senator made it clear that he was his own man and would vote his own way. This kind of disloyalty was more than a man like Neely, long schooled in practical politics, could countenance. Matthew Neely became as powerful an enemy as he had once been a friend.

The two did not speak to each other during most of Holt's single term in the Senate, delegating to their office staffs the job of coordinating legislation for West Virginia. In the 1950's a similar enmity grew up between the two Senators from Oregon, when Richard Neuberger steered a separate course from his senior colleague and one-time law professor Wayne Morse.

The most bitter Senatorial feud resulted in an icy silence for years between Kenneth McKellar of Tennessee and Royal S. Copeland of New York. There seemed to be a natural antipathy between the quick-tempered Tennessean and the mild-mannered doctor from New York, who always wore a red carnation. They clashed verbally many times on the Floor, but on one occasion the argument became so heated that a physical clash seemed eminent. McKellar lunged toward Copeland muttering under his breath, but that was all. A sensation-seeking columnist asked me repeatedly, "McKellar had a knife, didn't he? You saw him go after Copeland, didn't you?" Senator McKellar did wear a pocket knife on his watch chain, but though I stood only a few feet away, I did not see him touch it during the disagreement. Despite my repeated denial, this rumor has never died.

In half a century I have met only one Senatorial temper of greater dimension than that of Kenneth McKellar. No one has ever equaled the perpetual fury of Senator Stephen Young of Ohio who daily seethes from some mysterious volcano of hatred burning deep within him. While Senator McKellar took out his frustrations on his peers, Stephen Young has directed his ire primarily toward the Senate staff.

The wonder is there have been comparatively few open hostilities among men who are constantly in opposition. Most Senators fight over issues rather than personalities. Though several have become bitterly angry in debate, in my time no Senators have ever come to blows. However, sporadically a quarrel does take place in which one Senator is accused by another of impuning his motives and is therefore required to take his seat under Rule XIX. This portion of the Senate Rules is similar to a parental code under which the children are not allowed to call each other names.

Thomas Jefferson's Manual, compiled when he was Vice President
from 1797 to 1801, established part of Rule XIX.

> "No Senator in debate shall, directly or indirectly, by any
> form of words impute to another Senator or to other Senators
> any conduct or motive unworthy or unbecoming a Senator."

The remainder of Rule XIX has been added in subsequent years:

> "No Senator in debate shall refer offensively to any State of
> the Union.

> "If any Senator, in speaking or otherwise, in the opinion of
> the Presiding Officer transgresses the rules of the Senate, the
> Presiding Officer shall, either on his own motion or at the
> request of any other Senator, call him to order; and when a
> Senator shall be called to order he shall take his seat, and may
> not proceed without leave of the Senate . . ."

Whenever I heard a harsh tone of voice or the angry invective
turned against a Senator, I stopped in my tracks to listen. There
would be a rustle over the Chamber and a mumbling in the
galleries when it became obvious that a family quarrel was taking
place. Everything ground to a halt to see what would happen as the
Senator who had been speaking was ordered to take his seat.

There was the unforgettable day of March 13, 1925, when
Richard P. Ernst of Kentucky became so upset as to produce the
following scene:

> "Mr. Ernst: I wish to know if there be any way under the rules
> of the Senate whereby I can, without breaking those rules and
> without offending the Senators about me, call a fellow mem-
> ber a willful, malicious, wicked liar? Is there any way of doing
> that?
> "Mr. Robinson: Mr. President—
> "Mr. Glass: Let me ask the Senator—
> "Mr. Robinson: Mr. President, I rise to a point of order.
> "Mr. Moses: So do I.
> "Mr. Robinson: The Senator from Kentucky is not in order.
> "Mr. Moses: I wish to make the same point.
> "Mr. Robinson: I insist that the Senator from Kentucky be in
> order.

"Mr. Glass: I want the Senator to be specific.

"Mr. Ernst: Mr. President—

"Mr. Robinson: Just a minute, Mr. President—"

Congressional Record, 69th Congress, Special Session, 1925, p. 226.

Senator Ernst was immediately ordered to take his seat under Rule XIX and never did explain which Senator was the target of his wrath. Thomas Jefferson in his Manual had made no provisions whatever for calling a fellow member a liar.

Senators are usually tolerant of each other when it comes to overlooking faults and extreme views, to the extent of an indulgence that far exceeds public toleration. When one Senator incurs public wrath and condemnation, it is rare for him to find that among his colleagues, he has become yesterday's friend. There is an atmosphere of general regard in which all Senators maintain at least an official respect for one another, if only to sustain the elevated office which they mutually hold. To diminish the power and influence of one member might affect them all. For whatever reasons the Senators work together, the net result of the family's personal approach is a pooling of ideas which makes it possible to fit the needs of the country together like the pieces of a puzzle into one usually workable whole.

LEADERS

My work as Press Liaison brought me into constant contact with the Floor Leaders more than with any other members of the Senate family. As the Leaders were generally the greatest news sources, yet could spare the least time to leave the Floor, I had to question them continually for the press. I hiked many a mile along the Barkley, Taft, Johnson, Mansfield, and Dirksen trails.

Leadership of the Senate is a traditional post, not provided for in the Constitution. The Leader is elected by his party to the overall task of directing the course of legislation. Whether he heads the majority party or the minority, the Leader's role is akin to that of a military commander who must decide priority moves in various sectors of a war and at the same time present a unified front. In expediting the most vital legislation, intuitive timing is often the key factor. The Leader must ride the high tide to take advantage of public sentiment or slow down the progress of legislation until votes can be won over to his side. As he builds up support for a bill, he maneuvers like a general to strike at his opponents' weakest points, rushing to overwhelm the opposition when the victory is certain.

No matter how creative a Leader is expected to be, his daily work is drudgery. He bears the brunt of the organization of the Senate's business, involving the day-to-day, hour-by-hour toil of overseeing the parliamentary action on the Floor. Even the most

obscure Leaders have gone at it doggedly, faithful to their staggering tasks and responsibilities.

A Leader has many loyalties: to the *state* that sent him to
Congress, to his *party* as its spokesman in the Senate, to the *Senate*
whose integrity as a part of government he must guard with his
decisions, to the *President* for whom he is the main trunk line of
communication, and above all, to the *nation* whose interests should
be his first consideration. After reconciling his own conflicting
loyalties, a Leader must know how to focus and transform the
thinking of others into concerted action. This requires political
genius. Of the nine Democrats and ten Republicans who have led
the Senate in the last half century, the quality and type of leadership has been as varied as the men themselves.

Wartime Republican leadership in 1918 was in the hands of
sprightly Henry Cabot Lodge, Sr., of Massachusetts who commanded a healthy and growing minority that would soon win a
Senate majority in the November election. Democrats were led by
an aging Confederate veteran Thomas S. Martin of Virigina, the
Harry F. Byrd of his day, who seemed to belong to another age
and another war. I vainly tried to picture this white-haired gentleman as a sharp, young cadet in 1865, marching with his VMI class
to defend New Market, Virginia.

When Leader Martin died in 1919, it was the first time that I
had seen the Senate in mourning; and a somber experience it was.
His desk on the front row became a spectre, enshrouded in folds of
black crepe. The sight was sobering enough during the day, but
after an evening session as the pages were going home, the only
light came from the cloakrooms in dim streaks reaching out across
the darkened Chamber. Then the funereal desk inspired us to taunt
one another in hollow tones, "There —is —the —ghost —of
—Senator —Martin!" Fortunately this melancholy custom disappeared along with black arm bands and widow's weeds.

When a Leader dies, the resulting power vacuum can precipitate a close fight, as it did when the Democratic caucus split evenly between Oscar Underwood of Alabama and Gilbert Hitchcock of Nebraska. Publisher Hitchcock of the *Omaha World-Herald* settled for the honor of serving a difficult two months during the League of Nations fight. Afterwards Oscar Underwood became Democratic Leader, a post he had once held in the House of Representatives, which made him the only man ever to lead his party in both houses of Congress. The Alabamian had insured his fame as a Congressman in the early Wilson years by authoring the liberal Underwood Tariff. With his cherubic countenance neatly bordered by a rounded collar, Senator Underwood specialized in a low-keyed serenity and moderation every bit as mild as Mike Mansfield's approach, proving that a successful Leader need not be vehement or spectacular.

Oscar Underwood came of that impeccable breed of contemplative statesmen like Walter F. George of Georgia, who was a freshman Senator during Underwood's leadership. I have watched both cross the Chamber with a weighty, measured step that reflected their steady determination. Thoughtful but not cautious, Underwood fought a losing battle to make the 1924 Democratic Convention go on record against the Ku Klux Klan, even though it was a rising political force in his home state. His stand against the Klan not only failed, but reduced his own presidential hopes to a pitiful echo during the protracted balloting of that convention. His state delegation loyally insisted one hundred three times, "Alabama casts twenty-four votes for Oscar W. Underwood!" A prototype of the honorable man in defeat, he quietly retired when his Senate term expired.

In those early days before bipartisan foreign policy was known, the political law of fang and claw was the unquestioned rule. Oscar Underwood came close to a nonpolitical ideal when he accepted an appointment from President Harding to the 1921 Washington Disarmament Conference, but Underwood incurred the wrath of his Democratic colleagues at the time by his audacious disregard of party lines.

The Senator who best represented the party-oriented politics of the day was Henry Cabot Lodge. Both a wiry fighter and a courtly figure, his curly white hair, mustache, and goatee created a perfectly matched tonsorial ensemble. Forcefully articulate, he used elegant, short phrases in the highest tradition of Massachusetts culture.

Lodge's very being embodied that heritage, from his mother who was a Cabot to his father who had sent clipper ships around the world to trade with China. Holding three degrees from Harvard, Henry Cabot Lodge had begun his career as an editor of the *North American Review* and as a historian who lectured at Harvard. Throughout his life he remained a prolific writer, publishing at least twenty-two scholarly works. His interest in history soon led him into the more activist field of politics, where Lodge became a great admirer and valued adviser to Teddy Roosevelt. He was elected to the House of Representatives in 1887, serving until he came to the Senate in 1893 where he represented Massachusetts for the rest of his life, a total of thirty-seven years in Congress.

As Leader Henry Cabot Lodge, Sr., commanded from the second row surrounded by his own colleagues, rather than from the front row by the center aisle where the Leaders sit today. He inherited the desk of Daniel Webster, another famous Senator from Massachusetts. It was one of the desks that had been moved from the old Senate Chamber in 1859 when the new Senate and House wings were completed. From this historic piece of furniture, Lodge waged his successful campaign against the League of Nations.

My Senate days had just gotten under way when World War I ended in November, 1918, and the final battle of that "war to end wars" raged on the Senate Floor throughout 1919 over the ratification of the Versailles Treaty. In adamant rigidity from the White House, Woodrow Wilson insisted on all or nothing in a one-package treatment of the Treaty with the League of Nations hitched to it like a rider on an appropriation bill. Pitted against Wilson was the rocky determination of the senior Lodge and his fellow Irreconcilables that the League would not involve us in the internal affairs of Europe. They were also convinced that the Versailles

Treaty had within it the seeds of future war rather than a hope for world peace.

As a young page and new recruit, I considered myself already a loyal Senate trooper, ready to follow the lead of Henry Cabot Lodge in his double command post as Majority Leader and Chairman of the Foreign Relations Committee that brought the Treaty to the Senate Floor. If the picturesque Lodge with his elfin face and satisfied twinkle in his eyes was an uncompromising partisan lining up his forces against President Wilson, then I could only conclude that that was the way it should be. A Leader of the opposition opposed; how else could it happen? To be the Leader was to be right.

I felt as though I were going to save the colors in the midst of the firing line when I would take a new reservation to the Versailles Treaty from Lodge's hands and rush it to the rostrum to be read aloud by the clerk. In my most memorable charge down the center aisle I stumbled on the steps and fell flat on my face, setting up a resounding boom from the hollow floor beneath. Amid a chorus of laughter from the surrounding Senators, I scrambled up and without taking time to brush my blue knickers, continued the sprint up to the waiting clerk. In subsequent years I never had to look at the steps. Each one of the five levels, unevenly spaced and several feet apart, is etched on my mind.

Throughout the vivid battle over the League, I also watched and listened from the rostrum. In this verbal war, humor was employed to the point of ridicule. In the thick of the fray I can remember the giant form of Boies Penrose rising in debate and in his deep bass voice asserting, "Mr. President, I fail to see any sign of divine annointment on the head of Woodrow Wilson." The choice proverb of the battle came from sharp-witted Lawrence Sherman of Illinois who exclaimed, "Blessed are the peace makers for they shall see Paris!"

The defeat of the League and the Versailles Treaty is a classic example of the lack of understanding that results when the President and the Senate do not communicate. Looking back over the sweep of history, one can believe that a President Eisenhower with

The subway connecting the Capitol
with the Senate Office Buildings has
been the only free ride in Washington in this century. Majority Leader
James E. Watson of Indiana (with
glasses) surrounded by visitors. Arizona's Henry F. Ashurst looks over
his shoulder.—photo: Herbert French
Collection, Library of Congress

Senators relax in the Marble Room.
Powerful Republicans in the 1920s
were (left to right) George H. Moses
of New Hampshire, Charles Curtis of
Kansas, Charles McNary of Oregon,
and James E. Watson of Indiana.—
photo: Herbert French Collection, Library of Congress

a Majority Leader Johnson, or a President Johnson with a Henry Cabot Lodge, *Junior,* could have worked out a constructive solution without bitterness and intransigence.

When the senior Lodge died in 1924, the greatest legacy that he left his country was the grandson whom he had trained in the ways of statecraft. Henry Cabot Lodge, Jr., was to serve his government well in a later day of stress when newer and more flexible approaches would be demanded.

In 1924 the whole tone and tempo of leadership shifted abruptly from the patrician, scholarly Lodge to the roughhewn man from the prairies of Kansas Charles Curtis, who could proudly boast of considerable Indian ancestry. That Curtis retained his seat in the back row is symbolic of his custodial type of leadership. Though he was destined to rise to the vice presidency in the Hoover administration, Curtis lacked the qualities that inspire men. He was not an orator or even a smooth politician. His sparse code of employee relations and possibly all human relations was succinctly put in his comment, "I always take the word of the employer, never the word of the employee." Curtis made his surefooted way along the bed rock of the doctrinaire party man, overshadowed by his remarkable Whip, James E. Watson of Indiana. When Curtis became the first of three Leaders whom I would see take the Vice President's chair, he made way for Watson to become Majority Leader in name as he had been in fact.

Jim Watson was a professional politician of the highest order, comparable in skill, diligence and even hair style to Everett Dirksen. He looked like the Hollywood stereotype of a florid Senator with his wavy hair, round face, and rotund figure. Watson was one of the most attractive speakers in the old-fashioned Hoosier style that required a powerful voice, moderate desk pounding, and above-average humor. The Republican Party was the basis of all political action for Jim Watson. It was inevitable that he would tangle frequently with James Couzens of Michigan, whose independent philosophy Watson could never understand. He could appreciate equally-dedicated Democrats like Pat Harrison of Mississippi, but the Progressives of his own party were nothing but insurgents. They did not play according to the rules.

Jim Watson's organizational skill was proven long before he became Majority Leader. I remember the day in June, 1919, when, as Chairman of the Woman Suffrage Committee, he succeeded in getting the Senate to pass at last the Nineteenth Amendment giving women the right to vote. It was over forty years since the "Susan B. Anthony" Amendment had first been introduced, but few politicians took it seriously until the National Woman's Party led by Alice Paul began their vociferous campaign during Wilson's first term. They paraded and went to jail to dramatize their cause, eventually winning the support of President Wilson and a sufficient number of Congressmen and Senators. Andrieus Jones of New Mexico made several attempts to get the amendment through the Senate in 1918–19 while the Democrats were in control. Early in the next Congress Jim Watson put it through winning the credit for the Republicans.

The fight for suffrage took an unusual turn one day when I was a new page. The galleries were full, particularly the one east of center which was filled with ladies intent upon the debate. I did not realize what they were doing until I saw the ladies quickly lower a golden sateen banner over the railing. Startled Senators looked up to read the words, "WHAT WILL YOU DO FOR WOMAN SUFFRAGE?"

No one said a word to them, but quiet consternation swept the Chamber. Doorkeepers tried to reach the ladies only to find the aisle blocked by fellow suffragettes. In a few minutes a page was sent to climb upon someone's shoulders, reach up and yank the banner from the ladies' hands. Mabel Vernon who had smuggled the banner in beneath her coat had to watch in disappointment as it disappeared from the Chamber. She and the others continued to listen to the debate for a while before they filed out of the gallery without incident, trusting that their quiet demonstration had added to the suffragettes' cause. Since that day no one has been permitted to lean upon or even touch the gallery railing. Their colorful banners, the persistent lobbying by the ladies, and their nights spent in jail finally won for the women the vote that should have been theirs all along.

Senator Watson with his discerning eye as a practical politician was not fooled by the crowds who came out to greet him and President Hoover in the campaign of 1932. "They are only here to see a President of the United States," Watson told an incredulous Hoover. "We are all going out on the ash heap together." Jim Watson accurately forecast his own political funeral as well as Hoover's with the victory of Franklin Roosevelt in November.

In the early years of the century the post of Floor Leader, then sometimes called manager, was considered to be such a thankless and demanding post that no one remained Leader for any length of time. It was rare for a man to serve longer than one session, though he might come back after a respite of a year or two and have another go at it. The *Congressional Directory* did not even list the Leaders until the 1940's. But Henry Cabot Lodge, Jim Watson, and Joseph T. Robinson of Arkansas realized the full potential of the post and established the precedent of retaining the job as long as the Leader remains in the Senate.

Senator Robinson set a record by leading the Democrats for fourteen years from 1923–37. He led partisan guerilla warfare as Minority Leader for ten years before the Roosevelt landslide suddenly gave him overwhelming command in 1933 of sixty Democrats out of a total of ninety-six Senators. In a rising tide of victory the New Deal swept across the middle aisle to inundate the Republicans even more completely in 1935 when the Democratic majority swelled to a record-breaking seventy-seven.

The few GOP members floated in an ocean of space on their side, while the majority determined to squeeze every one of their members onto their half of the Floor. The solid mass of desks left no room to move. Other large victories have created similar seating problems. After the Harding landslide in 1920 the overflow of Republicans sat on the Democratic side in what was called the "Cherokee Strip." New Democrats in 1965 chose to form a "rumble seat" row in the back of the Chamber. Any Leader would welcome the problem of seating a huge majority.

Leader Robinson directed the Senate through the New Deal
avalanche of legislation, the sheer quantity of which had never
before been seen. The period is aptly described by Will Rogers'
quip at the time, "Congress doesn't pass legislation any more; they
just wave at the bills as they go by!" To witness this phenomenon
in the Senate was to watch a great river at flood stage sweeping the
debris of tradition before it.

Robinson was well suited to control the Democratic jugger-
naut as Franklin Roosevelt's field marshal in the Senate, taking
orders seemingly without question from his chief. The Arkansan
was a mighty Leader in a dictatorial, ruthless way. His reptilian
complexion gave him the look of a great horned toad, yet his
keen-edged mind and sharp reactions were anything but sluggish.
When he would go into one of his rages, it took little imagination
to see fire and smoke rolling out of his mouth like some fierce
dragon. Even when he kidded me, he spoke in loud gasps while
puffing at his cigar. Robinson could make Senators and everyone
in his presence quake by the burning fire in his eyes, the baring of
his teeth as he ground out his words, and the clenching of his
mighty fists as he beat on the desk before him. His voice had
tremendous volume like the crackling roar of a forest fire. His was
a combination of mental agility and physical power that made
him a devastating adversary and the iron master of the Senate.

The irascible Robinson, who had neither the personality nor
the need to be conciliatory, was the antithesis of his counterpart
across the aisle. Charles McNary of Oregon, quiet and personable,
guided his small band of Republicans skillfully through New Deal
waters. McNary was the only Progressive Republican to become
Leader and, in fact, the most liberal member of either party ever to
rise to leadership. He not only supported Roosevelt's National
Recovery Administration and the Tennessee Valley Authority, but
he wanted to go farther than the President in the field of social
security. Farm legislation had always been McNary's special
concern. In the conservative 1920's he had coauthored the most
liberal measure to pass Congress during that era, the McNary-
Haugen Farm Bill, twice vetoed by President Coolidge.

Although he led the smallest minority in Senate history, Charles McNary's outstanding effectiveness came from his persuasive personality as well as his sympathy with many New Deal measures. A roaring, all-day debate could not accomplish what McNary could in minutes of quiet, personal conversation urging compromise. Throughout his convincing talks, he would jerk his arms in an unending struggle to achieve a properly balanced length between coat sleeves and shirt cuffs. McNary was so skilled a parliamentarian and so likeable a person that he was often called across the aisle to straighten out a Democratic hassle. At a distance the sandy-haired Oregonian looked like a person in his early forties; only close up did the wrinkles suggest that he was actually in his sixties. A slightly-built man who walked with a cheery bounce, McNary did not look, act, or sound like a politician. Throughout the crucial fight over the Supreme Court packing proposal, however, McNary proved himself a graduate politician by keeping hands off and letting the Democrats battle out the critical issue among themselves.

By 1937 several controversial measures such as the National Industrial Recovery Act, the Agricultural Adjustment Act and minimum wage laws had been ruled unconstitutional by a conservative Supreme Court, much to the consternation of Franklin Roosevelt and his followers. The President countered with a judiciary reform bill which, among other provisions, would have made it possible for him to appoint six new justices to the Supreme Court. It was a quick move to liberalize the Court, the arrogance of which alienated many liberals who were in sympathy with the New Deal programs at stake. The issues were obscured by the extreme loyalty of many to the popular President, regardless of what he advocated; but there were Senators, notably the Progressives, who cut through the maze of short-term goals to uncover the real dangers of the plan.

The proposed packing of the Supreme Court was the greatest frontal attack by one branch of government toward another with the aim of changing the constitutional balance of power since the House passed a resolution of impeachment against President An-

drew Johnson in 1868. It shook the very foundations of the
country and the Senate itself, forcing Senators to go beyond mere
platitudes and dire predictions of the destruction of our form of
government.

The showdown, led by Burton K. Wheeler, Democrat of
Montana, was unlike anything I have seen, save a declaration of
war, for solemnity, sheer grimness, and an unsmiling determination
to duel to the death. Despite appeals from the President, Gerald
Nye, joined by Wheeler, Borah, and Hiram Johnson, began a radio
campaign to win public support for the defeat of the proposal.
Henry F. Ashurst, Chairman of the Judiciary Committee, used his
powerful influence against the bill.

If the majority of a committee opposes a bill, it usually dies
without reaching the Floor. However the court-packing plan involved such basic issues that the bill was reported out unfavorably
so that the entire Senate could consider it. Joseph C. O'Mahoney
of Wyoming fought for liberal measures throughout his twenty-six
years in the Senate, but he was most proud of authoring the
committee report which rejected the President's bill.

After fourteen years as Leader, the court fight became Joseph
Robinson's greatest challenge. He loomed as the key figure in the
Senate, the only one who could effect a victory for his supreme
commander in the White House. Tensions mounted as the issue
came closer to a vote, while a loyal Robinson, seething as usual,
tapped every reservoir of friendship and political indebtedness at
his command. The Majority Leader seemed to be a boiling caldron
of conflicting loyalties where country and party and Senate and
President and self battled for supremacy.

Suddenly, as in a well-staged melodrama, Senator Robinson
fell dead in his apartment in the Methodist Building on Capitol
Hill. With him died the entire court-packing scheme. The moment
the judiciary bill was scrapped, soon after Robinson's funeral, I
saw Hiram Johnson spring to his feet on the Floor, throw his
hands over his head and shout a hearty, "Thank God!" The
Republic had weathered a serious crisis.

To insure another loyal Leader to replace the fallen Robinson, Roosevelt seemingly hand picked Alben Barkley of Kentucky,
a proven party regular who had been Whip under Robinson. By
sending him a letter which became famous for its salutation of
"Dear Alben," Roosevelt seemed to turn the trick for Barkley.
Actually Roosevelt's interference in internal Senate affairs may
have made it more difficult for Barkley who won in the Democratic
caucus by only one vote over conservative Pat Harrison of Mississippi. By this narrow margin, another leadership devoted to serving
the chief in the White House was launched.

Rather than the heavy-handed iron rule of a Robinson, Barkley's method was one of easygoing rapport with a warm undercur-
rent of laughter. He would sit down by a colleague, ease him into a
benevolent mood with a bit of droll humor, and while they were
chuckling together, Barkley would solidly close in with his reasoning on the issue at hand. He relied equally on his considerable
ability to deliver vehement speeches. Schooled in the old courthouse square oratory of Kentucky, Barkley would roar in a powerful rather than an eloquent manner, his face reddening as though
on the verge of a massive cerebral hemorrhage. At the close of a
long paragraph he would come up for a gulp of air.

Far from being a Kentucky colonel type, Alben Barkley
resembled another plain son of Paducah, humorist Irvin S. Cobb.
Each had the earthy look of a healthy potato, and both were
experts in the high folk art of storytelling. One of Barkley's best
stories in the tradition concerns a politician who specialized in
spellbinding speeches on the courthouse steps. He found himself
running for office in the pre-prohibition days when the issues were
sharply drawn between the Wets and the Drys. The politician in
question would meet the issue of prohibition head on with unparalleled skill, "Now, some of my friends are Wet, and some of my
friends are Dry; and I want to tell you here and now that *I* am for
my friends!"

This tale was possibly more than a story to Alben Barkley. As
a young Congressman he was influential in drafting the Volstead

Act implementing the Eighteenth Amendment that prohibited the sale of alcoholic beverages. Nevertheless, within eleven years he was seeking to run with Al Smith on a ticket to repeal prohibition. Throughout his long career, Senator Barkley was for his friends.

With all of his shouting Barkley was an effective and moving speaker who could tap the resources of history from a lifetime of study. Like Everett Dirkson, Barkley maintained an unusual historical insight with deep emotional and romantic undertones. Congress was a great drama to him. He loved politics as an actor loves the stage, and he cherished the nation with the fervor of an early patriot. But Barkley tempered his genuinely emotional nature with a firm sense of the dignity and decorum necessary for his image as Senate Leader.

Alben Barkley and Charles McNary were more than concurrent Leaders of the Senate; they were excellent friends. Not until they became Leaders together did they discover that their forebears had farmed adjoining land in North Carolina in the early days before the Barkleys moved to Kentucky and the McNarys to Oregon. They were the first Leaders to take the front seats on the center aisle, an arm's length and a convenient conferring distance away.

In Alben Barkley's mind, a Majority Leader could not function unless he saw eye to eye with his President, a harmonious state which he was able to maintain consistently for over six years. Finally the day came in 1944 when he could not countenance a tax bill veto message sent by Roosevelt in which the President said, "It is not a tax bill but a tax-relief bill providing relief not for the needy but for the greedy." Consequently, Barkley gravely took his stand on the Senate Floor to offer his resignation as Leader in the most solemn tones he had ever used. The word of his intentions had brought every Senator to the Floor. There was no sound other than his stirring words:

"That statement, Mr. President, is a calculated and deliberate assault upon the legislative integrity of every Member of Congress. Other Members of Congress may do as they please, but as for me, I do not propose to take this unjustifiable assault lying down . . . If the Congress of the United States has any self-respect yet left, it will override the veto of the President and enact this tax bill into law, his objections to the contrary notwithstanding."

Congressional Record, 78th Congress, 2nd Session, 1944, p. 1966.

In one of the most dramatic moments in the Chamber's history, I saw the Senate rise as a body to give Alben Barkley a thunderous ovation that lasted several minutes. Republicans and Democrats alike acclaimed him at that moment the Senate's Leader. Many of the old independents were still there to cheer a Senator's Senator: Hiram Johnson, Burt Wheeler, and Gerald Nye along with Harry Byrd, Richard Russell, and relative newcomers like Robert Taft and George Aiken. When Barkley resigned as Leader the next morning at the Democratic caucus, he was immediately reelected and proceeded to lead the Senate in passing the tax bill over the President's veto.

This act of honest courage ultimately cost Barkley the presidency itself. Though "Dear Alben" sought to make amends, Roosevelt never forgot that day of insubordination, naming another Senator instead to be his running mate in 1944. Within the year, FDR was dead and Vice President Harry Truman succeeded to the presidency. Always one to recognize service and faithfulness, Truman rewarded Barkley in 1948 by choosing him as the vice presidential candidate, salvaging for his old friend and Leader the post Barkley had sought since the Al Smith race in 1928. As the "Veep," Barkley welcomed the social status of his ceremonial position with his customary good nature and made his vice presidential shelf a cheerful one.

It took courage for him to make his comeback to the Senate two years after his term as Vice President had ended. His eyesight was failing, but with the old dignity and spirit, Barkley made a heroic effort to rally his oratorical abilities. Like all Senators whose terms of office are not consecutive, Barkley returned with the status of a new Senator without seniority, as though his thirty-five years in Congress had counted for naught. He made an almost

pitiful figure sitting in the back of the Chamber with the new
Senators, while his colleagues of old were either gone or sitting at
the senior desks up front.

Day after day it depressed me to see the lonely figure of
Barkley. Formerly the valued Leader's peers had beaten a path to
his desk; now his colleagues continued to pass by but they no
longer stopped. The old gentleman's friends seemed to have faded
away along with his power and influence. In our last talks together
it was pleasant to arouse a little chuckle from him or even a
vehement statement on current legislation. Before long, word came
that Alben Barkley had dropped dead while delivering what became his valedictory, an address to the students of Washington and
Lee University.

The leadership of Robert Alphonso Taft was not through the
personal magnetism of a Barkley or a McNary but through his
intellectual powers. That an independent thinker could amass so
many willing followers was a unique tribute to Bob Taft. In
retrospect, his leadership of his party seems to have spanned most
of the decade and a half that he was Senator from Ohio. Actually
he became Floor Leader only during the last few months of his life
in 1953. Taft chose instead to pilot the Senate in the 80th Congress as Chairman of the Republican Steering Committee, where
he could make policy decisions without being tied down by Floor
duties.

The focus of power does not necessarily center in the Floor
Leader if he is overshadowed by a personality of the magnitude of
Taft. His influence predominated over that of the three hardworking but much lesser figures who served as Republican Leaders in
the narrow party sense from 1944–52, Wallace White of Maine,
Kenneth Wherry of Nebraska, and Styles Bridges of New Hampshire. While Taft kept too busy with legislation to bother with
routine political touches, Styles Bridges specialized in them. He
was a prototype of the back-room politician who spoke out of the

corner of his mouth, but he was a well-informed Senator and one of the very few who had known in advance about the Manhattan Project that produced the atomic bomb.

When Bridges stepped up to the ceremonial office of President Pro Tem, it left the position of Leader open to Taft in January, 1953, as the new Eisenhower administration got under way. Knowing that there would never be a Robert Taft administration since his party had rejected him with finality as the presidential nominee in 1952, Taft was gallant in defeat. He accepted the Leader's job, not realizing how little time he had left to give to his party, his new Republican President and his country.

As moral and practical head of his party, Taft earned the title Mr. Republican. Yet he could lead on a level above party where issues are weighed on merit and by the standard of constitutional law rather than by political label alone. When he sensed a need for revision of the labor codes, he supplied it in the Taft-Hartley Law. When he saw the striking railroad workers about to be drafted into the armed forces by President Truman, he opposed the move as a slave-labor measure, and he blocked it in one of the most incongruous alliances of all time with ultra-liberal Senator Claude Pepper of Florida.

Bob Taft was far more open to change than his conservative reputation would indicate. For years he sat beside liberal George Aiken, who undoubtedly influenced Taft to support such measures as public housing, farm cooperatives, and federal aid to libraries. During the McCarthy era when anyone in disagreement with the reactionaries was labeled a red, Aiken's standard greeting for his seatmate was a teasing, "You're looking a little pink this morning, Bob!"

Robert Taft was nothing less than a portable university. The campus was plain but the faculty first-rate. His exceptionally brilliant mind had the computer-like qualities of speed, accuracy, and utter thoroughness. He was always alert, brisk in step, and quick in speech with the broad, crisp accents of Ohio.

Taft would display a noticeable impatience with those who failed to measure up to his expectations. Yet, he was most considerate of those of us in whom he had confidence but who could not be expected to match his brilliance. Taft might become riled at the attitude of a Senator or the "foolish question" of a newsman, but he would always listen and hear me out. He confided in me his opinions of various newsmen, whether they dealt fairly with him or whether Taft thought they got their facts mixed. In knowing his feelings, I could be more explicit in relaying Taft's information to those newsmen who had perhaps inadvertently distorted previous statements he had made. It worked to their mutual benefit.

Despite a few misunderstandings, Bob Taft was a newspaper-man's Senator, available whenever possible and always a veritable library of information. Because he could outthink almost everyone, Taft was not an easy Senator to question. Phil Dodd of the *Chicago Tribune* found it disconcerting when Senator Taft would read a newspaper throughout their interview, until he realized that the Ohioan could dispense sharper answers while reading than could others who were giving him their undivided attention.

Besides the informal press conferences at his Leader's desk on the Floor minutes before the Senate convened, Taft submitted to frequent interviews with a score of newsmen in the President's Room. Sitting cross-legged on the Lincoln Table under the chande-lier, he sometimes gave a rueful smile or scowl at a poor question, but he never hedged. Taft stated facts so clearly and succinctly that it was never necessary to ask him to repeat what he said. He spoke what he thought without counting the consequences, a rare attrib-ute that was deeply appreciated by the press.

Taft had all the dynamic quality of a glamorous person without being either colorful or remotely handsome. On the Floor he stood with a slight slouch, usually putting his hands in his trouser pockets and making no attempt to hide his moderate bay window. His bland but intelligent countenance was completely open with a kind of little boy guilelessness that affirmed his total honesty. When he spoke, always with crystal clarity, people lis-tened to him as attentively as they would have to a great orator. Yet while he had all of the substance, Taft had none of the oratory. He was simply one of the plainest but most convincing speakers ever to rise on the Senate Floor.

There were certain limits to Taft's endurance. I have seen him in moments of exasperation when he grabbed the arm rests of his chair and scrunched deeper and deeper into its cushioned seat as though to match the stubbornness around him with a grim determination to outlast his adversaries if it meant staying all night.

A facet of Taft's greatness was his modesty, though at times he carried it to the extreme of bashfulness. Without a hint of ostentation he worked unstintingly, usually preferring to go it alone. One night after a late session I was leaving the Capitol heading for my car in its parking space on the grounds when Taft leaned out of his car, characteristically one of modest price, and offered, "Dick, may I give you a lift?" He would be very tired and probably preferred to rest alone in his thoughts after a tedious day at the Senate, but he could be selfless to the point of putting another first.

From an authoritative source I learned weeks before his death that Taft was hopelessly ill with cancer. As he made his way on crutches to the Majority Leader's desk, he had the wan look of a man undergoing an ordeal but with such a brave front that there were only a few ghastly glimpses to reveal the extent of his inward struggle. When I mentioned to some of his closest friends among the Republican Senators that I understood his illness would prove fatal, their unbelieving answer was, "Oh, no! Impossible! Bob Taft is going to get along all right." His death came as a severe shock to his colleagues since comparatively few were aware of the severity of his condition. The deep mourning for Taft was akin to the gloom that settled upon the Senate following the deaths of William E. Borah and Franklin Roosevelt and, in a later year, the grim news of the assassination of John F. Kennedy. The medical verdict was cancer but there were those at the Senate who believed that Bob Taft died of a tumor psychosomatically induced through disappointment at not being given the presidential nomination.

Taft had absorbed his family's tradition of public service as the son of a President and Chief Justice of the United States. Combined with his natural endowments of brilliance and drive were his own considerable legal and legislative experience. Taft felt that he was ably prepared to be Chief Executive, but it was not to be. In history he joins the senior Bob LaFollette, Borah, Wheeler, and Hiram Johnson as among the giants who never became President. The Kennedy Committee placed his portrait in the Senate Reception Room, naming Robert Taft one of the Five Greats of the Senate along with LaFollette, Henry Clay, Daniel Webster, and John C. Calhoun.

The poignancy of Taft's death at a point of incompleted mission in life brought to his devotees extreme anguish and frustration. His congressional colleagues set out to pay him rare homage by according him the honor of lying in state on the Lincoln catafalque in the Rotunda under the Capitol dome. If their candidate could not be President, he would be paid a tribute reserved only for Presidents, commanders of the armed forces and the three Unknown Soldiers. Within an amazingly short time a marble carillon was built in clear sight of the Senate. It is placed alone in the Capitol grounds where no other memorial honors a Senator, Congressman, or President. It is a unique tribute to the solitary and monumental spirit of Robert A. Taft.

In rapid succession two Democratic Leaders after Barkley became political casualties, a fate attributed to their devoting more time in Washington to the duties of leadership than to campaigning back home. Leader of the Senate in the 81st Congress in 1949–50, Scott Lucas of Illinois forfeited his seat to Everett Dirksen; while two years later Arizona's Ernest McFarland lost to Barry Goldwater, after leading the Senate in 1951–52 during the 82nd Congress. Upon these isolated events determined by a few thousand voters in Arizona and Illinois turned the future of the Senate and the country. Through the defeat of the two Leaders, Dirksen, Goldwater, and new Democratic Leader Lyndon Johnson rose to fame.

The Leaders of today compare favorably with the highest tradition of Senate leadership and rise far above its lesser periods. Majority Leader Mike Mansfield, who has led the Democrats since 1961, combines the intellectual perspective of the college professor with a realistic, fresh-air virility typical of his home state of Montana. Knowledgeable and deceptively mild, Mansfield is consistently fair as he exerts a constant effort to protect his fellow Senators' Floor rights. He is selfless, possessing little vanity and great stoicism. When the occasion is sufficiently stirring, Senator Mansfield's Irish spunk raises his voice in righteous indignation, but he quickly returns to the poker-faced demeanor that is his natural style.

Though his wiry appearance hints at Mansfield's sturdiness, it comes as a surprise to learn that this pallid intellectual has had a hearty career. For a landlocked Western lad whose parents had brought him to Montana from New York City at the age of three, young Mansfield showed an amazing determination to serve his country and see the world. He enlisted as a seaman in World War I by managing to look older than his fourteen years and performed ten months' overseas duty with the Navy before his age was discovered. Immediately he tried the Army where he spent a year of underaged service. Mansfield finally came of age during two years in the Marine Corps which included a tour of duty in the Far East, a part of the world which was later to become his particular concern. In this unorthodox fashion he became the youngest World War I veteran and the only Senator to have served in the Army, Navy, and Marine Corps. Returning to Montana, young Mansfield devoted eight years to the gritty profession of mining, first as a mucker in the Anaconda copper mines and then as a mining engineer. Ultimately he chose the academic world, becoming professor of Far Eastern and Latin American history at Montana State University [in Missoula] for almost a decade before coming to Congress. Understandably Mansfield has been one of the men to consult on Asian affairs since his freshman days as a Congressman.

When President Roosevelt sent him to the Far East on a fact-finding mission in 1944, Mansfield proved himself a good politician by taking with him the location of every Montana serviceman in the area. In Burma he borrowed a jeep and bounced ten miles down a jungle trail to visit John Kamps, a constituent who was on duty elsewhere when the Congressman arrived. The note

Everett Dirksen, as Congressman from Illinois, was dusted with DDT before an inspection tour of war torn Germany in 1945.—photo: U.S. Army

TODAY'S LEADERS YESTERDAY.

Montana's Representative Mike Mansfield, in Burma during World War II, borrowed a jeep to visit servicemen on the Ledo Road.— photo: U.S. Army

Mike Mansfield left for him began a friendship which still continues when John, now with the Associated Press, interviews the Majority Leader in the President's Room.

Relaxation for a Leader is almost unknown, but when Mansfield can leave the Floor, he heads toward the Lobby in a mood of deep contemplation, reaching in his pocket for his pipe as he goes. Standing by the clicking news tickers in the Lobby, he cradles his pipe in hand while reading the latest news, some of which he has helped to make. When word comes that he is needed back on the Floor, he can empty the ashes from his pipe in an instant, and with quick strides be back at his desk to take the reins.

Even though Mansfield's leadership began when he was Lyndon Johnson's choice for Whip, he did not always follow the President's policies. Like his mentor Johnson, Mansfield has ability to reconcile differences between Senators. Displaying a patience that has become famous at the Senate, he goes a little farther than most Leaders in making certain that all Senators are treated equally.

One colleague with whom Mike Mansfield works closely at all times is Minority Leader Dirksen, whose term as Republican Leader began in 1959. The two Leaders strive together in true harmony reminiscent of the amity between Barkley and McNary and more recently between Dirksen and Lyndon Johnson. The analogy of a Senate Leader to a commanding general is no longer valid when discussing the relationship between Leaders Mansfield and Dirksen. No two opposing generals would sit down together at frequent intervals as the Majority and Minority Leaders do daily. They are more often than not in disagreement on the issues before the Senate but they always agree on the *procedure* they will follow in disagreeing. "I have consulted with the Minority Leader and he agrees that the Senate should limit debate on the bill to three hours, with half an hour on each amendment," is an often-heard result of the indispensible planning between the two men. Gentlemen's agreements between them are trusted guarantees that neither will take unfair advantage of the other by trying to slip through

legislation without the other's knowledge. This atmosphere of cooperation between the opposing Leaders is conclusive evidence of
their mutual loyalty to the Senate.

When I first knew Everett McKinley Dirksen as an affable
young Congressman known only as Chairman Dirksen of the
House District of Columbia Committee, there was little hint that
he would become one of the best known and most revered Senators
of the twentieth century. The climate for growth in the stimulating
atmosphere of the Senate has nurtured the Senator from Illinois to
a degree parallelling that of one of the tallest trees in the forest.
Starting with a provincially partisan approach, he has through the
years acquired the statesmanlike qualities that have made him a
responsible leader of the national community without losing his
loyalty to small-town America.

Everett Dirksen is a living, walking, historical encyclopedia
who lends force and dimension to sentiment by basing it in historical fact and thus avoiding sentimentality. In any commentary on
government he continually draws comparisons, making vivid and
pertinent to contemporary life what would otherwise be a drab
discussion of legislation. To point up the change in the value of the
dollar, Dirksen recalls his mother's giving him a penny and saying
gravely, "Now Everett, don't spend it all in one place."

When Dirksen takes the Floor it is as though the greatest
contemporary actor in the Senate has come on stage. The Senators
settle back in their chairs, eyes sparkling in anticipation of a
moment of high entertainment as they prepare to listen attentively
to his opinions. With a style all his own Dirksen has studiously
played the role of the nineteenth century orator so long that the
man and the role have become one.

Savoring each syllable, he speaks with the undulating rhythm
of an old square-rigger, majestically riding great smooth swells of
the sea. Dirksen creates the deeply emotional effect produced when
a virtuoso, seated at the console of a great organ, achieves a
fervent rising crescendo and the next moment charms his audience
with the most mellow and soothing of melodic tones. The Senator
has a complete repertoire from quiet tone poems to thundering

Wagnerian passages. On the few occasions when his arguments are more airy than erudite, he can make them sound more convincing with his unique delivery than the most factual presentation of a less-talented opponent. One thing is certain: what Senator Dirksen says will be different. Others quote from the Bible, or refer to the Scriptures, or read from Holy Writ. But Dirksen comes up to one's expectation by intoning, "We read in the Sacred Parchments . . ."

Such a distinctive Senatorial type as Everett McKinley Dirksen can scarcely be envisioned in his early nonpolitical days as a balloon observer and intelligence officer in Europe during World War I and the owner of a bakery after the war. It is in politics that Dirksen shines in an element well suited to his talents. The Senator has described his love of public life in his own way:

"When I got my first taste of Congress in 1933, and I was called Honorable, and invited to dinners without having to pay for them and people came saluting me in my office, I thought, 'This is for me. I do not wish ever to give up this office.' And I fought to keep it until a malady made me resign; and later, by the grace of the voters of Illinois, I was sent to the Senate in 1950, and I thought, 'The Senate is for me . . .'"
Congressional Record, 89th Congress, 1st Session, 1965, p. 19349.

Senator Dirksen enjoys the most strategic position of any Minority Leader I have known. Controversial legislation such as civil rights must meet his approval before it has a good chance of passing the Senate. Everett Dirksen has become the balance of power in the Senate and the best known member. He is *the* Senator, as William E. Borah was in his day.

Many of the Leaders of the Senate over the past half-century have excelled in distinctive skills: McNary and Barkley in personal persuasion, Robinson in sheer command of power, Taft in intellect, Dirksen in eloquence, and Mansfield in fair management. None, however, developed as remarkable a synthesis of gifts and skills vital to leadership as Lyndon Johnson. He combined an energetic tenaciousness with a mastery of dynamic persuasion and a thorough understanding of the use of power. Lyndon Johnson was without doubt the greatest Senate Leader of this century.

Only his inexhaustible drive was obvious at first. Despite an apprenticeship of twelve years in the House of Representatives, Lyndon Johnson appeared on the Senate scene in 1949 like a fiery young stallion not yet broken in, charging about with an overdose of self-confidence. When he was a new Senator, I avoided him as much as possible. No one goes into the teeth of a whirlwind without a good reason. Later his election as Whip in 1951, Minority Leader in 1953, and Majority Leader two years later required that I approach him many times a day for national as well as Texas correspondents. This very necessity to confront him daily gradually revealed the real Lyndon Johnson. I found that what seemed on the surface to be brazenness was actually a burning desire to meet social needs wherever he saw them and a powerful determination to overcome all obstacles in the path. By the time Lyndon Johnson became Majority Leader, I looked forward with enthusiasm to his morning press conferences which never failed to be a fascinating experience. The Texas whirlwind had substance, a penetrating mind, and keen perception.

There was also a temper, subject to incendiary flare-ups, that was a distinct liability. Ironically, it was destined to be checked by a severe antidote in the form of his near-fatal heart attack in 1955. At all times immediacy was the key word with Lyndon Johnson and with it came part of his capability. Aides had to be on tap at all hours, ready to jump instantly. When things failed to happen the moment words came out of his mouth, Johnson would curl his lips and bawl everyone out in all directions. "Where's George Reedy and Harry McPherson? Get them here right away!" he would bellow from the cloakroom while biting into a sandwich. But even in the days when his temper flared the highest, he was never vicious nor one to hound people in perpetual moodiness. Fifteen minutes after cussing someone out, he would be talking to him as though nothing had happened.

After the heart attack Lyndon Johnson's sense of immediacy remained the same, but the bursts of fury were replaced by a stern, determined request. He still gunned his own motor and that of everyone around him, but there was far less chance of a blowup. The new Lyndon Johnson came back to the next session of Congress from Bethesda Naval Hospital a stronger man in all ways. The humbling brush with death was worth more to him than a bevy of ministers and an office full of psychiatrists. A man who has learned to control himself becomes infinitely more effective in dealing with others. He began to approach everything and everyone more thoughtfully. I never saw a Leader or anyone else grow as much in stature over a short period of time. To watch the metamorphosis of Lyndon Johnson was to see a future President of the United States evolve.

Johnson's dynamic genius can be traced beyond his phenomenal energy to the all but hypnotic sway he exercised over his fellow Senators. Like any good teacher, he knew to convince others by starting at the level of their understanding, as he must have learned when teaching in Texas schools. His was not a Socratic questioning, but rather a fervent leading to the water by prod of reason. He went the old adage about the horse one better; he not only led it to water but he made it want to drink.

Not since Charles McNary had the Senate been captivated by a more magnetic personality. McNary was shrewdly convincing and charmed with an almost ministerial gentleness, albeit flavored with a little cussing. Lyndon Johnson overwhelmed with a style of forceful persuasion unique to him. Dashing from one to another, the tall Texan would sit down beside a Senator, shift to the edge of the chair, lean forward and twist his neck around in order to look up into the face of his now-captive audience. What could be more fascinating to a Senator than a convincing argument coming from beneath his own chin? A Senator was compelled to listen to Lyndon Johnson's earnest pleas which inevitably carried their own weight. Completely absorbed in his own insistent reasoning, Johnson would lock onto the coat lapels of his victim with both hands; and eye to eye, he would hypnotize the Senator into a state ranging from enthusiastic cooperation to suspended animation, or possibly, to complete paralysis.

Appearing in formal speeches on television as President of the United States, Lyndon Johnson could never seem to work the same magic with the millions that he did with individuals. Perhaps if he could have leaned out of the video tube into the nation's living room and grabbed the man of the house by the coat lapels, he could have communicated his compelling intensity in his own element of face-to-face understanding. After all, personal persuaders like McNary and Johnson generally were not orators. Lyndon Johnson was a do-er instead of a say-er, to be appreciated by those who valued the results of action and destined to be underestimated by those who wanted to be captured by philosophical speeches.

The Majority Leader did not always limit his persuading to Senators. At one press conference he told about a crisis which had occurred early that morning in the Johnson family. Just as he was ready to drive his young daughters to the National Cathedral School before coming to the Senate, it was discovered that their new puppy was wetting under a bed. With all the responsibilities awaiting him as Leader, Senator Johnson had to stop, get down on all fours and try to convince the puppy to come out. Not as cooperative as most Senators, the obstinate puppy caused Lyndon Johnson to crawl under the bed and retrieve it by hand. After this delay the future President drove his daughters to school and then on to the Capitol to face the other tasks before him that day.

Lyndon Johnson steered his course of leadership by a firm belief that "reasonable decisions can be arrived at by reasonable men," even though he sometimes had difficulty in finding reasonable men. His majority in the early years was a borderline one, but it swelled to a two-thirds margin by 1959, largely owing to his constructive program. The period in the Eisenhower years of even balance between the two parties was ready-made for Lyndon Johnson's skillful brand of conciliation and compromise.

That his eight years of leadership took place entirely during the Eisenhower administration gave Johnson a measure of freedom he could never have enjoyed had he been Leader for a President of his own party. The kind of opposition he would lead was up to him alone. He elected to cooperate with President Eisenhower and in so doing chose the course of highest loyalty to the nation, putting first a Leader's obligation to his country to keep the legislative machinery operating in good order. Had he adopted a strictly partisan course urged by some in his party, Johnson would have been following past Leaders of opposition parties like Robinson during the Coolidge and Hoover administrations or Wherry and Bridges during the Truman years. But Lyndon Johnson chose instead a new approach based on a constructive relationship between the Legislative and Executive branches; actually he led the administration. By tempering his use of power with reasonable compromise, he achieved remarkable results such as the first civil rights bill to be passed in the twentieth century. His program of action that he defined as "pro-American and not just anti-Republican" fulfilled the goal of Johnson's life, to make government work. Whether agreeing with him or not, his countrymen could take comfort that Lyndon Johnson was no vain obstructionist.

His Republican counterpart, Leader William F. Knowland of California, differed from Johnson in personality, effectiveness, and techniques of leadership. Built like a football tackle, Bill Knowland had a solemn countenance and broad shoulders that, when planted firmly at his Leader's desk, bespoke his unyielding determination to hold the line. In contrast, when faced with balky opposition, Lyndon Johnson would seek reasonable alternatives, preferring half a loaf to none and often walking away with the full loaf. But Knowland stood doggedly by his goals and sought to move forward like a massive Sherman tank through some of the longest and most difficult sessions the Senate has ever known.

During the one Congress [1953–54] when Knowland was Majority Leader, the progress of legislation became a tedious inching through all-night meetings, including the Senate's all-time marathon session in July, 1954. To break the filibuster against the Atomic Energy Bill, Leader Knowland insisted that the Senate continue without adjournment around the clock for almost eighty-six hours. That week Gregor Macpherson, an official reporter of

debates, was carried out of the Chamber on a stretcher. Staff
people and Senators had long since passed the bounds of extreme
exhaustion when Majority Leader Knowland finally agreed to end
the ordeal.

Despite his dominant stubbornness, Bill Knowland was a
courteous gentleman with impeccable decorum. While he lacked
natural spontaneity, he went to the trouble of forcing a smile or a
chuckle in a sincere desire to be gracious to other people. The son
of, and now himself, the publisher of the *Oakland Tribune,* Knowland was born in Washington while his father was serving in
Congress. Though nourishing an almost religious devotion to our
institutions of government, he could not be a rubber stamp Leader
for any President. Differing with Eisenhower on foreign policy,
Senator Knowland stood firm as the conservative Leader in this
field, while Democrat Lyndon Johnson spoke more accurately for
the Republican President's international policies. Nevertheless, Bill
Knowland and Lyndon Johnson worked well together, both having
a strong sense of the Senate's responsibility to the nation.

Lyndon Johnson began his study of government in a basic
way on the staff of the House of Representatives. When Leader he
recounted in one of his press conferences, "I used to do work over
in the House similar to what Richard does here at the Senate for
the press." As secretary to Congressman Richard M. Kleberg of
Texas, an affable southwesterner and son-in-law of the owner of
the gigantic King Ranch, Lyndon Johnson's experience in Congress dated back to 1932. Years later, instead of letting his position as Senator to go to his head, Johnson drew on his experiences
on the Capitol staff to give him insight into the problems of staff
people. While he had a reputation as a slave driver, he drove
himself at a faster pace, much like a hard-riding, Civil War general
whose staff had to race frantically to follow him into battle.

Lyndon Johnson considered all newsmen important, yet as
Leader his time was too limited to permit him to see everyone. He
discussed with me the current attitudes of the press, giving me
briefings as to what to say to them. I had blanket instructions to
weed out and relay routine queries. Beyond that he was always

willing to rush out to give what time he could to those who were writing special articles or gathering background information for their news stories. Among those covering the Leader for Texas papers was husband-and-wife team Les and Liz Carpenter. When the Johnsons moved into the White House, Liz left the Gallery to become Mrs. Johnson's press secretary.

In those on-the-Floor press conferences just before convening, Lyndon Johnson was quite relaxed. He slumped down in his Leader's chair, surrounded by a knot of listening newsmen, and discoursed with disarming perspective about the legislative hurdles before him. When he got in a story-telling mood, Johnson could be like Will Rogers—droll wit, country voice, wry facial expressions, and all. Like another Texan Senator Tom Connally, he specialized in good-natured mimicking of his colleagues. "You take ol' Joe over there," he began and launched into a hilarious imitation of voice and gestures.

But nine seconds out of ten Johnson was the intense Leader with his penetrating eye peering into every corner of the Senate's activities. A moment's wait for a parliamentary ruling from the Chair stirred Johnson into action even while sitting at his desk. If the presiding officer paused before acting on a parliamentary procedure, such as directing the clerk to call the roll when the yeas and nays had been ordered, Lyndon Johnson gave an anxious look at the Chair, leaned to one side toward the center aisle and impatiently signaled with his right hand spinning round and round as though he were cranking up an old Model T Ford. Not a moment should be lost when the legislative battle was almost won.

In keeping his majority together Johnson was everywhere at once rallying his troops. Often he would play the referee between adversaries, getting them together or pulling them apart. I have seen him do everything but throw a bucket of water over their heads to bring recalcitrant Senators around.

The Johnson methods worked to create two new states from territories that had long awaited admission to the Union. Alaska's Delegate Bob Bartlett and Governor Ernest Gruening and Hawaii's Delegates Joseph and Betty Farrington labored without success until 1958. That year in the last session of the 85th Congress, Leader Lyndon Johnson and Speaker Sam Rayburn said, "Let there be Alaska first and then Hawaii," and it was so!

In all the many private conversations that I witnessed between Lyndon Johnson and his colleagues, I never heard him talk one way in the cloakroom and another way on the Floor. When reason and persuasion failed and he was forced to wield political power, he was simply more frank and obvious about it than the usual politician.

The other consistent theme underlying his strategy was his genuine concern for human need. I remember the day he came back to the Senate after a trip in which he had seen the plight of bitterly impoverished people. In conveying his concern to surrounding Senators, I heard him say, "We've got to help these people! We can't let them live under those conditions."

With Lyndon Johnson's inborn sense of urgency he never stopped at mere expression of regret. The words "might" or "should be" and "sometime" were rarely in his vocabulary. Any issue he felt was right became an imperative for him. He could not rest until his ideal was at least approached if not attained. It would be impossible for any Leader to have given more of himself than did Lyndon Johnson.

Of all people to accept the ceremonial job of Vice President, Johnson was one of the last I would have expected to find in that serene presiding Chair. Like a supreme commander who had died, he could look down from his celestial perch and watch his old colleagues fighting the good fight, but he could no longer lead them out of their difficulties. Vice President Johnson had many active outlets in the useful assignments given him by President Kennedy, but these activities were outside the Senate and often abroad. What we at the Senate saw in his immobile state on the rostrum was an incongruous figure full of pent-up energy, energy that had previously been the vital fuel propelling the Senate.

When he climbed up to the vice presidency, again there were longer sessions and the Senate again knew what it was like to bog down without his unparalleled leadership. If he were inwardly chafing, Lyndon Johnson showed no signs. He would call down cheerfully across the rostrum, "Richard! How ya doin'?" For one who understood the workings of power better than anyone else in Washington, it could not have been easy for him to be no longer a main source of power himself.

Lyndon Johnson was the only Senate Leader to become President. His skill in legislative procedure, conciliation, and concentration on issues made possible his phenomenal record of domestic legislation, both as Leader and as President. Lyndon Johnson and leadership will always be synonymous at the Senate.

President Lyndon Johnson escorts Senators Margaret Chase Smith of Maine and Maurine Neuberger of Oregon.—photo: Arthur E. Scott

John Kennedy talks with Senators Glenn Beall of Maryland, John Carroll of Colorado and Clair Engle of California as the author waits to accompany the President to the President's Room.—photo: Frank Muto

PRESIDENTS

"Ladies and Gentlemen, the President of the United States!" The closest contacts most people have with our Chief Executive are telecasts and the printed word. This is not so at the Capitol where I have had the singular experience of knowing twelve Presidents in relationships ranging from a speaking acquaintance to close friendship.

To a boy growing up on Capitol Hill, the President and former Presidents were real, flesh-and-blood people who might be seen at any time. One day when my father was introducing me to the stuffed wonders of the Smithsonian's Museum of Natural History, we rounded a corner to find a very much alive Theodore Roosevelt. In his inimitably vigorous style the former President was regaling a small group with tales of his big-game hunts in Africa, pointing out the various specimens he had contributed to the museum. "There's where I shot him!" he pointed to the neck of a giraffe who still towers over a jungle diorama. While talking with my admiring father, Roosevelt patted me on the head and in his rapid-fire way said, "God bless you, little man!" To be spoken to at the age of six by Teddy Roosevelt was to feel blessed indeed.

The rotund silhouette of another former President was an imposing and familiar sight to those of us who lived on Capitol Hill. With his umbrella in hand William Howard Taft, at that time Chief Justice Taft, came paddling up the Hill each morning en

route to the Supreme Court. He walked from his home on Wyoming Avenue over three miles away. It was entertaining to watch
his measured progress across the street to the accompaniment of
automobile horns whose owners had no idea that they were sounding off at the Chief Justice of the United States. As the Supreme
Court was housed in the Capitol building in the original Senate
Chamber, I often encountered Mr. Taft when I was a page. Like
his son Robert who was to become Senator after his father's death,
President Taft was exceedingly plain. But the elder Taft was
gregarious; and when he laughed, it was a total experience. His
entire rotundity shook, even to his handlebar mustache. A visit
with him in Capitol corridors was a bright spot in any page's day.

To meet a President is one thing; to know him first as a
personal friend is quite another. If anyone had asked me when I
was a new page whom I would name as my favorite Senators, I
most certainly would have included Warren G. Harding. I knew
him as a friendly Ohioan who took time to encourage a page boy,
walking the length of the Lobby with his arm around my shoulders.
His huge head with its classically chiseled features gave him a
Senatorial appearance which he backed up with diligence and a
sincere regard for other people.

When he progressed from minor candidate for the Republican
nomination to the party's nominee in 1920 and then went on to
become the nation's President-elect, I could hardly contain my
amazement. An everyday friend had actually been selected as
President of the United States! I watched wide-eyed the day President-elect Harding came to the Chamber to stand at his desk and
tender his resignation as Senator from Ohio. As I stood a few feet
from him on his inaugural platform in front of the Capitol the
following March of 1921, his inauguration was no less impressive.

During his presidential visits to the Senate I observed Harding
closely to note what effect the presidency would have upon this
gracious man. He did not bear his responsibilities easily with the
bounce of a Harry Truman. Once I remember seeing the cold
sweat on his brow as with hands shaking, he paused before enter-
ing the Senate Chamber to make a speech explaining his reasons

for reluctantly vetoing legislation passed by his former colleagues.

President Harding's administration remains under a cloud. Two cabinet members were discredited, Harding's good friend Harry M. Daughtery and Albert B. Fall, one of the first Senators from New Mexico. The latter was jailed for accepting a bribe in the Teapot Dome scandals. In the same Harding cabinet, however, were conscientious men like Charles Evans Hughes, Andrew W. Mellon, Dr. Hubert Work, and Henry C. Wallace father of the Vice President. As for Warren Harding, I remember the man himself, his warm personality and his trusting nature.

After Harding's sudden death, another friend Calvin Coolidge left the Capitol to live in the White House. For over two years this quiet, undemonstrative New Englander performed the ceremonial duties of Vice President with dignity. His was hardly a bubbling personality, but it was certainly free from affectation. There was not one ounce of pretense in this imperturbable man who was born on an isolated Vermont farm, was graduated from Amherst, won fame as Governor of Massachusetts by settling the Boston police strike, and while Vice President went back to Vermont during vacations to plow his fields again.

Though frugal with speech, Coolidge himself was not as taciturn as is generally believed. As Vice President he would sit in the Lobby smoking cigars while talking and laughing with the Senators around him. He could make long, dry speeches that said comparatively little in a great many words; but he was noted for his quaint quips and droll New England humor. One of his wittiest cracks came out when he was presiding over the Massachusetts legislature as Lieutenant Governor. In a heated moment one member told another to go to Hell. Coolidge replied from the Chair, "I looked up the law and you don't have to go."

In his quiet simplicity Coolidge was at home with unsophisticated people and ill at ease in the artificialities of society. Within a month after Coolidge had become President, I phoned to make a special appointment with him through George Christian, President Harding's secretary who had remained during the customary transition period. Two elderly gentlemen from Marion, Ohio, who had known Warren Harding all of his life, wanted to go to the White House and "see where their friend Warren had lived." Coolidge greeted us in his executive office with unhurried cordiality. He felt at ease with these fellow small-towners and sympathized with them at the loss of their personal friend the late President.

The only statesman of recent times with whom I could compare Coolidge would be Harry F. Byrd, Sr. Both were conservative and economy-minded. Their sharp, penetrating eyes missed little about them, but their natures demanded that change come slowly if at all. Coolidge was a symbol of his times of "normalcy" after the upheaval caused by World War I. In his role of quiet helmsman, he was popular by most standards of the day. He studiously performed the duties of caretaker of a federal government that he, like Senator Byrd, believed should be kept at its minimum level. In contrast to the more vivid men who have followed him as President, Calvin Coolidge seems to be a black and white sketch. Actually his very colorlessness was unique.

Looking back over the last half-century, four Presidents in that time have not come from the Senate: Wilson, Hoover, Franklin Roosevelt, and Eisenhower. Understandably my recollections of them are limited to casual meetings at the Capitol or at White House receptions.

On the few occasions when the Chief Executive comes to Congress to deliver a message in person, no amount of legislative opposition can dim the fascination of the event. This was particularly true when Woodrow Wilson returned from Paris in 1919 and addressed the Senate in support of his much criticized League of Nations. I sat with the other pages within a few feet of him, studying this stern, intensely serious intellectual who was at one time president of Princeton University. At a White House reception before he went to Paris, I had met another Woodrow Wilson who was cheerful, cordial, and in good health, in sharp contrast to the frustrated President who came to address the Senate. As he stood on the Senate rostrum, what impressed me was his bony forefinger. He kept it in motion throughout the speech, shaking it at the Senators as an irritated schoolmaster might have at a group of recalcitrant students. The set of Woodrow Wilson's sharp jaw and the zeal reflected by the glare in his eyes made an unforgettable picture.

That other dynamic, legendary world figure among our Presidents, Franklin Delano Roosevelt, presented quite a different face to Congress during the crises of another world war. Because so many Senators had come into office on his coattails, Roosevelt held a superiority that made his the master's voice. His relationship to Congress was all but that of a king, both feared and loved.

Often wearing a majestic cloak, Roosevelt arrived at the Capitol near the ramp built especially for him that still remains in use. With an understandable lack of dignity the Secret Service men literally had to drag his crippled form out of the car feet first, place him in a waiting wheelchair, and roll him quickly to an elevator. In no time at all with the aid of his braces and the strong arm of his son James, President Roosevelt entered the House Chamber amid tumultuous cheers. Mounting the rostrum and locking his braces in place, he performed courageously before the assembly as though he were in perfect physical condition, as though inconvenience and pain were nonexistent in his life. Few Americans living outside Washington realized how severely incapacitated the President was. The photographs and newsreels by which they knew him showed a seated or standing figure, glowing with vitality.

Unlike Wilson, Roosevelt led not by moral lectures but through his enormous charm. He exuded a hypnotic confidence that reassured with a bouyant toss of the head and the knowing smile of the suave diplomat. His sweeping phrase, "You and I know . . ." brought Congress into an assumed agreement as magically as "My Friends . . ." united his radio audiences.

When meeting him personally, the famous Roosevelt charm was just as evident at close range as in his speeches. Seated in the East Room of the White House during the annual press receptions, the President received his guests with a greeting that made each individual feel that the party was a success because that person had come. Though these were receptions requiring formal attire, the press parties had an informal warmth. One could dance in the East Room to the music of the Marine Band, explore at leisure other historic rooms of the mansion, and while enjoying the sumptuous buffet, chat with Mrs. Roosevelt or sit on the south portico overlooking the illuminated Washington Monument. In the warm evening scented with magnolia, it had the mellow flavor of an old Southern plantation, seemingly remote from the pressures of Washington. It took some self-prodding to remember that the genial host was himself the powerful symbol of Big Government.

Franklin Roosevelt made his last visit to Capitol Hill on March 1, 1945, a month before his death, to report on the Yalta Conference. It was his first visit to the Capitol in over two years, and it left us with a shocking memory. As he sat in the Well of the House, instead of standing on the rostrum, I was startled by his saffron complexion and his cheeks that seemed to have fallen away. Only Roosevelt could have managed to begin in his best fireside-chat manner, apologizing in an informal aside for having to remain seated while he spoke. He brushed away the problem by explaining that his braces had been giving him trouble lately, hurting his ankles when he stood. He made a heroic effort to launch into a typical Roosevelt speech, even to flashing a broad grin. At about the halfway point his head dropped perceptibly, his tongue thickened and he made a few incoherent sounds. I thought he had had a stroke on the spot. But in the spirit with which he had overcome polio, FDR gave another toss of his head and completed his last speech before Congress, a truly indomitable man.

The office of the presidency holds glamour regardless of the individual who occupies it. Whoever he may be, from the moment the President walks into a joint session of Congress the atmosphere becomes supercharged. No one proved this more conclusively than the blandly nonaggressive Herbert Hoover whose entrance into the

House Chamber, reminiscent of Coolidge, was as totally undramatic as that of the most obscure citizen. Facing the gathering of hopeful Republicans and dour Democrats, Hoover would address them in the flatly factual monotone of a businessman reporting to his board of directors. Hoover's dedication was apparent in unobtrusive acts such as his unprecedented gesture of returning his presidential salary to the Treasury.

While Hoover had the misfortune to preside over the depression and personify its tense, bleak days in the public's memory, the next Republican President, twenty years later, never lost the popular appeal of the victorious general. Dwight Eisenhower spoke to joint sessions of Congress with equal formality and nonpolitical adornments but with considerable more punch than Hoover. The legislators always listened to him with the respect they had given him as the conquering hero. It was as though General, rather than President, Eisenhower continued to report to Congress as he had when he returned the victor from the European front.

In contrast, the President who immediately preceded Eisenhower was one of the Senate's own and another personal friend. Harry Truman was one of the liveliest, most vital Senators in my time. Almost from the day he became Senator, Truman felt at home. I doubt if anyone ever enjoyed public office or took it in stride more than Truman, from his Senate days right through the presidency. An easygoing joviality emanated from him in a constant stream of lighthearted banter with the Senators around him. Many times I found him trading yarns with his seatmate Nate Bachman of Tennessee, another cordial kidder and a first-rate storyteller. Years after Senator Bachman's death I discovered upon first meeting my wife Angela that her father Robert Bachman of Johnson City, Tennessee, was a cousin of the Senator who had been one of Truman's best friends.

Harry Truman was one of those who wrote his own speeches. This did not change when he became Chairman of the Special

Committee to Investigate the National Defense Program, better known as the War Investigating Committee or the Truman Committee. He pulled no punches in his disclosures, regardless of the politics of those who had made dishonest war profits. For this reason the Senator from Missouri became a national news-maker during the war years, in greater demand by the press than any other Senator.

Harry Truman had the same bubbling interest in everything and everyone that Hubert Humphrey evinces. Working quickly at all times, Truman took his duties as Senator extremely seriously for an ebullient man. And like most quick people, Truman's anger had a flash-fire quality, as his publicized flare-ups when President demonstrated. When he got down to business, the twinkle in his eyes would be replaced by a look of concentration. At such times, at close range the thick lenses of his glasses gave his eyes a fearsome, eerie stare so stern that it gave the weird illusion that one was confronting an entirely different person. The impact of these more serious moments made me grateful that Senator Truman was a good friend. The country would find out what a devastating adversary he could be. He was certainly not one to underestimate in ability.

As an advocate of brisk walking, Truman seemed fascinated by the pace I set as I pursued Senators. One day in a typical kidding mood he started in behind me and walked lockstep through the Lobby to the amusement of all who saw him. In his offhand way I doubt that Vice President Truman worried too much about the failing health of Roosevelt. While we were walking briskly about the Capitol together one afternoon, I reminded him that the weight of the world would fall on his shoulders should he become President. Truman replied with a jaunty, "Oh, nothin's goin' to happen to him!"

As Vice President he had been presiding over the Senate on that quiet afternoon of April 12, 1945, when Roosevelt died an hour after adjournment. The next day Truman returned to Capitol Hill as the President of the United States to start the mundane chore of moving his office. As his presidential press secretary,

Truman appointed Charlie Ross, the soft-spoken correspondent of the *St. Louis Post-Dispatch*, who had interviewed him daily in the President's Room.

Harry Truman was not only popular with newsmen and his fellow Senators but he remained a pal of staff members, and became the all-time favorite of the White House News Photographers. It was no chore to photograph a cheerful, understanding subject like Truman. After making an appointment with the President through Charlie Ross, I made a movie of Truman in the White House Rose Garden. He remarked, "I'll have to be careful what I say if this is sound film." Assured that the movie was silent, the President said, "Good, then I can cuss all I want to!"

Truman never left the Senate family in the larger sense; he made more informal visits to Capitol Hill than any other Chief Executive. On one of these occasions President Truman went in on the Floor and sat at the desk where he had spent ten of the happiest years of his life. For the moment the Senate assumed a festive air of welcome led by Senator Vandenberg, then President Pro Tem, who gave a broad grin when he drawled, "The Chair recognizes the former Senator from Missouri." The Senate listened gleefully to his impromptu remarks as it did at a later date when Truman became the only former President to address the Senate in my time. In recent years the rules have been amended to provide that former Presidents may speak before the Senate, which constitutes a standing invitation. Whether he was the personable pal of the cloakroom, the serious statesman, or a private citizen, Harry Truman was always himself.

The Senate at any given time contains an array of talented men, a number of whom could lead the country well as President. In 1960 there sat in the Senate a man of rare genius, another of proven leadership, many with uncommon capabilities, several with exceptional courage, and some with vast wealth, yet none of these were able to reach the Presidency at that time. What *does* it take to be elected to our highest office? The prize was captured that year by one who had marked ability, confidence, and fortunately for him, youth, a handsome appearance, and wealth as well, at a strategic moment when all of these qualities held a magic appeal to the voters.

Only seven years before, John Fitzgerald Kennedy first appeared on the Senate scene by defeating Henry Cabot Lodge, Jr. Often a noted Senator is replaced by an unknown quantity, and this was no exception. What would young Kennedy be like, I wondered, as he walked down the center aisle to the rostrum with the senior Senator from Massachusetts Leverett Saltonstall to take the oath of office. It soon became apparent that John Kennedy had a keen mind and was going to become an able Senator.

For me, Kennedy's capability was established on the Floor of the Senate during extemporaneous debate, which I have usually found to be an accurate gauge of a Senator's ability to construct an argument from his stockpile of information. Some Senators have the spontaneity to debate on a myriad of subjects that flare up like a flash fire on the Senate Floor when least expected. Others are taken off balance, reeling back and needing time to prepare for a verbal battle. Few of the younger Senators have impressed me as significantly as did John Kennedy in skillful debate. He left his desk in the back row, taking on one Senator after another. Moving down the aisle, he became so engrossed in debate that he progressed from desk to desk without thought as to where he was, shuffling papers and moving pens and pencils on the desks of other Senators as well as his own. Not only his well-marshaled facts and sophisticated wit but his entire bearing inspired confidence in a manner suggesting the assurance of Franklin Roosevelt.

The Kennedy gestures were distinctive and natural to him, growing out of his intense personality. Never flamboyant but always patrician in manner, his graceful and rhythmic arm movements were synchronized with a ceaseless progression of thought patterns. The chopping motion indicated the agile mind behind the hand, the restlessness to get things done, the hammering away at the problems before him. The sweeping gestures together with a measured nod of the head suited Kennedy perfectly but when copied by anyone else became awkwardly artificial. His gestures began an epidemic of imitations that started among his Senate colleagues and swept the country after Kennedy became President. So many caught them that it was nothing to see an entire roomful of people chopping away with the fervor of adolescents copying their latest hero.

Like Hollywood stars or European royalty, the entire Kennedy family is enveloped in a cloud of legendary lore and superficial glamor that obscures a deeper evaluation of them. Established by their father in wealth and social position, the three Kennedy brothers might have followed paths of ease and frivolity rather than choosing as they did to dedicate themselves to the hard work of public service, a choice that has cost two of them their very lives. With a compelling force of nervous energy and idealism characteristic of all the brothers, John Kennedy came to the Senate as an urbane young man with a distant goal. He devoted himself to being a good Senator first of all, much as his brother Teddy is doing today.

When I would contact John Kennedy for newsmen, it was a study to observe him at close range while standing in front of his desk. Under the fair, almost orange eyebrows, there was a remote, pensive look as though he were looking far into the future. Sometimes before he would answer a question, Kennedy would pick up a pencil half a dozen times, lay it down, and tap on the desk, completely absorbed in thought with the scholar's unawareness of the human scene around him.

While calling from a cloakroom telephone booth, Senator Kennedy propped his feet against the wall in an unpretentious pose. It was natural that when he became President, he did not always go through the formality of asking a member of the White House staff to place his calls. Pat Hynes, assistant to the Secretary of the Majority, would answer a cloakroom phone to hear a familiar voice saying, "This is John Kennedy. May I speak to Senator Mansfield, please!"

There was a natural aloofness about Senator Kennedy that let him relax only with his closest friends, particularly Senator George Smathers of Florida and columnist Charlie Bartlett who then represented the *Chattanooga Times*. However, foremost among his intimates was his brother Bobby, then on the Senate staff as counsel to the Government Operations Committee and never very far away. Bobby was his indispensible mentor so when John Kennedy momentarily could not locate his brother, he would sometimes ask me anxiously, "Have you seen Bobby?" One could sense a spiritual and mental unity between the two that transcended any dissimilarity in appearance. Yet within Bobby there was an unusual composure that enabled him to become a leading political force on his own.

Behind Bobby's wistful and ingratiating smile was a man of iron. Beneath the tousled hair was a professional who sternly approached politics with a determination to be unthwarted regardless. He had the maneuverability of the political opportunist who could accommodate himself to all situations, and it was this very flexibility that some found disconcerting. On the other side of the coin, Bobby had a remarkable sense of personal rapport with a faculty for understanding and blending in with people of varied backgrounds. The person to whom he was talking came away with the feeling that his problems were of the utmost importance to Bobby Kennedy. Throughout his years in government, whether as a crusading committee counsel, as Attorney General and troubleshooter at the storm center of the Kennedy administration, or as Senator from New York, he never varied his responsive personality or his goal to create a better world.

The Kennedys each had an air of complete self-assurance, at times undiluted by humility. This was apparent when President Kennedy in his inaugural address stated without hesitation, "We are able." Senator Teddy combines with this a gentleness that is distinctly his own. Beginning with the advantages of his legendary family, Teddy is also the near twin of an admired and martyred President. It is all but eerie to find him looking and sounding so much like John Kennedy, even to shuffling papers on the desks around him as he speaks. He has a similar patrician reserve which stems from intense concentration. As the youngest and only surviving brother with the future before him, Teddy is following the paths upon which progressive growth is found: hard work, study, devotion to being a good Senator from Massachusetts, and tending strictly to the Senate's business. In recognition of this, his colleagues elected him Majority Whip.

Bobby and Teddy were close companions in the Senate. With heads together they talked earnestly as Bobby occasionally ruffled his shock of hair. When they took the Floor in friendly colloquy, it brought to mind their uniqueness as the only brothers of this century who served in the Senate together.

The stiff, erect walk which Teddy bears today as a reminder of the broken back he suffered in his narrow escape from a private plane crash in 1964 makes him all the more like his older brother. John Kennedy had not been a Senator long when he was stricken by a flare-up from his wartime back injury. After almost losing his life, he came back to the Senate on crutches with his back in a brace. Like other Senators with back problems, John Kennedy had special leather cushions fastened to the back and seat of his chair.

During these months of pain he came out willingly to see the newsmen though I asked him questions whenever possible to save him the trip. At times I helped him move his chair while he managed the crutches, but always very independent, Kennedy insisted on pushing doors open with his shoulder. Among the hundreds of newsmen he would see, one was a wartime friend Pat Munroe, who was then correspondent for several western newspapers. As commanders of PT boats in the Pacific, Pat and John Kennedy had once tossed a coin to see who would take that fateful mission on which Kennedy's boat was torpedoed.

Senator Kennedy's individualism was noticeable even in his manner of having lunch. Many Senators when pressed for time, had the pages bring their lunches from the Senate Restaurant and ate from a tray on a cloakroom desk, while others grabbed a sandwich and munched on the run. John Kennedy was the only Senator to eat from a large picnic basket containing a special diet lunch sent from home. If a photographer had been admitted to the

sanctuary of the cloakroom, he would have readily snapped a
picture of Kennedy sitting on a cloakroom sofa, eating alone with
the basket open beside him.

The one movie that I most regret not taking could have been
made of Senator and Mrs. John Kennedy as they sat on the Senate
steps watching President Eisenhower's second inaugural parade in
1957. My wife and I were sitting on the same step about ten feet
away. Afraid that I would run out of film for the parade, I decided
that the Kennedys' picture could be taken at a later time. Had I
captured on film a portrait of this young couple dreaming of
inaugurations, it would have been historic indeed. Four years later
they had exchanged the cold marble steps of the Capitol for the
heated reviewing stand in front of the White House as the stars of
Kennedy's own inaugural parade.

During his last years in the Senate John Kennedy applied his
talents by assuming greater responsibilities on committees. Before
his successful presidential campaign he floor-managed a labor
anticorruption bill, taking on all comers in debate, as chairman of
a subcommittee of the Committee on Labor and Public Welfare.
Like all Senators, Kennedy had aides to help him with research on
legislation, and he knew how to utilize his staff. The modest
Theodore Sorensen remained in the background as his most valued
speechwriter whose eloquence and clarity of expression could be
termed Sorensenian prose. In addition to such outstanding assistance, Kennedy acquitted himself admirably on his own and was
genuinely admired within the Senate. He found, as Bobby did later,
that being a presidential candidate requires much time away from
Washington. But when he would appear on the Floor, colleagues
gravitated to the likely winner, drawn by his quiet magnetism and
the pull of a potential power base.

As the stage was set for the 1960 campaign, many of us at the
Senate were in a singular position to know the major candidates
John Kennedy and Richard Nixon and the supporting cast of
Lyndon Johnson and Henry Cabot Lodge. They had all learned
and practiced their skills on the Floor of the Senate and then
stepped up to the national scene. August of 1960 saw a spectacular

production which ran for a limited engagement of three weeks only, never before and perhaps never again to be seen on the historic stage of the Senate. Three of the newly-designated candidates came bounding back after the political conventions to complete the second session of the 86th Congress. It was the first time in history that both candidates were in the Senate Chamber at the same time: Nixon as Vice President, President of the Senate, and Republican nominee for President of the United States, and Kennedy as Senator from Massachusetts and Democratic nominee for President. No less conspicuous was Lyndon Johnson, Senator from Texas, Majority Leader, and the Democratic nominee for Vice President. Daily I wondered if I were talking to the next President at Kennedy's desk, or if I had left him on the rostrum in the Vice President's chair. One of them would head the Executive Branch within a very few months.

Waiting to get in the galleries were the longest lines of people in Capitol history, lines that stretched through the halls of the Senate wing, down the main corridor and across the Rotunda. Even with only a limited stay permitted in the galleries, many were turned away as the day's session ended. When Vice President Nixon discovered that so many could not get in to see the Senate, he made it a point to go down the line, taking time for personal chats with entire families. The last week before adjournment, Senator Kennedy copied this by quickly shaking hands down the hall. Squeals of excitement greeted them everywhere they went among these waiting crowds.

Visitors in the galleries are not permitted to display emotions of any sort, but their hushed excitement was a study in suspended animation. No opera stars on the stage of the Metropolitan received more audience appreciation than did Nixon and Kennedy. Had the rules not prevented it, gallery applause for the candidates would have brought down the house! As the hour of climax neared when John Kennedy would be elected thirty-fifth President of the United States, no one could foresee the great tragedy that lay only three years ahead which would rock to the core the Chamber then so humming with excitement. Little did one know that within such a short span of time the assassination of John Kennedy would thrust Lyndon Johnson from the supporting cast into the role of leading man.

The last time I talked with President Kennedy was the day he visited the new Senate conference room in the extension of the East Front of the Capitol. It is a beautiful walnut paneled room with gleaming chandeliers adorned with hurricane globes. A party officially opened this important unit in the East Front extension and President Kennedy came to honor the occasion.

I was standing with a group of Senators who were waiting to speak to him. When my turn came, after a smile and a handshake, I said, "Mr. President, do you realize that you are the only President who has not visited the President's Room since Abraham Lincoln first signed bills there?" His answer indicated how preoccupied he had become by the presidency for he looked rather puzzled for a moment before he asked, "Where's that?" I replied, "Why, you know, it's just off the Lobby, the room where the news correspondents meet the Senators, where you used to be interviewed by the press when you were a Senator, and where Mrs. Kennedy came to see you when she was a reporter."

He looked exceptionally thoughtful for a moment. There was a quizzical look as he promised to try and go with me when the party was over. When he indicated to me his readiness, President Kennedy and I walked around the corridors and through the Senate Lobby, side by side. He paused to open a door to the Chamber where he glimpsed Senator Wayne Morse speaking. "Everything's normal," he quipped.

Arriving at the President's Room, only the President and I went in while the Secret Service men waited outside. As we discussed the long history of the room and Brumidi's colorful frescoes, his appreciation was that of a young historian. Realizing that he was the eighteenth President since Lincoln to visit the room, Kennedy seemed quite pleased at what Robert Albright of the *Washington Post* called a "rendezvous with history."

His manner throughout was the most relaxed since his early days in the Senate. He had tremendous responsibility but he was taking it in stride. John Kennedy had arrived; he was the President of the United States. The long race was won. The far goal that he had set was reached. The years ahead seemed full of promise.

One quiet afternoon a few months later during a rare absence of newsmen from the President's Room, I was able to read accounts in the morning papers of the Kennedys' "successful" visit to Texas. The smiling pictures of the President and Mrs. Kennedy reflected their pleasure at the cordial reception accorded them during the first part of their visit. Meanwhile in an almost empty Chamber, not over eight Senators were listening to Senator Prouty of Vermont soberly discuss a library bill.

Suddenly my assistant Tom Pellikaan came rushing out of the Lobby to report that Phyllis Rock, research assistant to Senator Morse, had just read on the AP news ticker that President Kennedy had been shot. I dashed to the ticker to read for myself that first sickening but brief dispatch, "President Kennedy was shot as he rode in a motorcade in Dallas. Two shots rang out. Blood was seen streaming from his head."

Usually when I entered the Senate Chamber, I walked rather rapidly but in as dignified a manner as possible. I did not realize it at the time but Spessard Holland later told me that, looking quite pale, I literally ran into the Chamber bearing the dreadful news. Senator Holland's desk near the door was my first stop. After telling him that the President had been shot, I went on to inform the other Senators present, including Minority Leader Dirksen. The Majority Leader was not in the Chamber at the time.

When I turned toward the rostrum and saw Senator Teddy Kennedy seated in the Vice President's chair, calmly giving his attention to the portfolio full of correspondence before him, I realized that he was utterly oblivious of the great tragedy that had taken place. The event that was already shocking the world had brought to a close the most notable chapter in the history of the Kennedy family.

Knowing that Senator Kennedy could not leave the Chair, I dashed up on the rostrum and leaned over the Vice President's desk to say, "Senator Kennedy, your brother the President has been shot!" The young Senator looked as though he had been dealt a stunning blow. He instantly, though calmly, asked me the source of my information and if it had been verified. I replied that I had just read the dispatch from Dallas on the AP ticker.

Senator Holland, having observed the conversation, anticipated the situation by coming up to take the Chair himself. Teddy Kennedy hurriedly gathered up his papers and walked off the rostrum and out into the Lobby. I walked with him, my hand on his shoulder, offering words of sympathy. When he indicated that he would call the White House, I left him as he placed his call on a Lobby phone. Later I learned that about this time J. Edgar Hoover was notifying by telephone the President's other brother Attorney General Robert Kennedy, at his home Hickory Hill in McLean, Virginia. Senator Bobby's assassination in Los Angeles almost five years later would reopen the raw wounds with a sickening sense of national and personal loss.

Back in the Chamber the solemn news had reached Senator Prouty who relinquished the Floor so that the Senate could recess subject to the call of the Chair. Upon reconvening shortly afterward, Majority Leader Mansfield made a formal announcement of the tragedy that had occurred. A meaningful prayer for the life of the President by Senate Chaplain Dr. Frederick Brown Harris brought the day's session to a close.

Over the years I had seen Senators in other times of sorrow, as when the sad news came of Robert Taft's death. But this was the first time I had seen the Senate actually in session when word came of the death of a President. Never had the Senators appeared so shaken, so enveloped in a pall of gloom. Aside from the Chaplain's prayer and the quiet, pained tones of Leaders Mansfield and Dirksen on the Floor, stunned silence was the reaction. Everywhere one looked it was as though a funeral service were already in progress. Some of the most powerful men in the country were going about aimlessly. I am certain that they felt as helpless as they looked in the face of the tragedy. Senator Mansfield was exceptionally pale. Senators gathered anxiously and solemnly around small radios in the cloakrooms and watched the UPI and AP news tickers in the Lobby until the final word came that President Kennedy was dead. Reality was an agonizing fact; for the first time in sixty-two years a President of the United States had been assassinated.

Though the shock and sorrow was keen, no one who had known Lyndon Johnson doubted for a moment that he was more than adequate to the task awaiting him. Five days after the assassination Johnson came to make his first address as Chief Executive in what was the most unique of the presidential appearances before Congress that I have witnessed. Never had a President mounted the rostrum of the House of Representatives who had been in that Chamber before in so many different capacities—an integral part of the Capitol scene for thirty years: as an employee of the House, a Congressman, a Senator, Majority Leader of the Senate, and Vice President of the United States and President of the Senate. At that solemn moment Lyndon Johnson was able to rally Congress as no one else could have done. From his practiced leadership came one of the most dramatic stimulus to Congress, resulting in an avalanche of legislation unequaled since the era of Franklin Roosevelt. President Johnson expanded his former Senate pace until his working day included most of the twenty-four hours, as though he combined the energies of several Presidents.

When Lyndon Johnson returned to Capitol Hill on many occasions, he was welcomed with a spontaneity surpassing that enjoyed by Harry Truman. Both men remained so natural and unchanged by the presidency that their visits were more like the return of Senator Truman or Senator Johnson. After each speech to Congress President Johnson went to the Speaker's Office where he vigorously renewed friendships with Congressmen, Senators, employees, and the top echelon of government. An Old Home Week atmosphere prevailed amid the ring of first-name calling as the President himself rounded up old friends for picture taking. "Come on over here, Carl, and get in this picture," he said while nabbing Senator Hayden of Arizona. Even in all the familiar surroundings of his past, no one forgot that Lyndon Johnson was a figure set apart whose decisions could literally make or break civilization. When we who had known him for so long addressed him as "Mr. President," we fully realized that we were speaking with the most powerful man in the world.

In the past fifty years the Senate has emerged as a training center for future Presidents. All major candidates in the three elections of the 1960's had served in the Senate. President Richard Nixon, who is described in the following chapter, is the sixth Chief Executive of this century to have "graduated" from the legislative experiences of the upper house where every area of government is studied and decision-making is a way of life. With its curriculum of state, national, and international affairs, the Senate may well continue to be a virtual presidential academy.

VICE PRESIDENTS

The Vice President is a hybrid creature of the Constitution, a sort of noble mongrel who belongs partly to the Legislative and partly to the Executive branch of government. Until a few years ago his only roost was on Capitol Hill among the legislators. Now he migrates between his offices at the Senate and his quarters in the White House.

Though he is given the elevated title of President of the Senate, he has less actual power than the newest Senator. Unlike the Speaker of the House or the Prime Minister of Great Britain who are voting members of their houses of government, the solitary Vice President cannot address the Senate or even cast a vote except to break a tie.

Since John Adams it has been the special quandary of the Vice President to hit a useful stride beyond the ceremonial duties of a figurehead. The Constitution guarantees him official entree, but each Vice President must make his own way on Capitol Hill, determining his place in the order of things by virtue of his personality, the breadth of his political skills, and the assignments given him by the President.

Vice Presidents have always fascinated me because at any given moment they could become the Chief Executive. In half a century I have seen three men do just that: Calvin Coolidge, Harry Truman, and Lyndon Johnson.

When my first Vice President Thomas R. Marshall (1913–21) presided from the rostrum where we pages sat, I would try to picture the old-fashioned Hoosier in the White House, but it was difficult to do. The jovial, one-time Governor of Indiana was a complete opposite to high-strung, erudite Woodrow Wilson. Marshall specialized in cigar-flavored social diversions such as cloakroom stories and his special brand of quick wit. One day when walking by the gleaming white-marbled first Senate Office Building, Marshall pointed to the then-unfinished facing on one side and remarked, "It has a Queen Anne front and a Mary Ann rear." His most enduring retort continues to be the enigmatic saying, "What this country needs is a good five-cent cigar!" Vice President Marshall was never given the chance to try any solutions, profound or otherwise, to our nation's problems, since Woodrow Wilson would not relinquish the presidency despite his severe physical collapse. I doubt that the relaxed Marshall really wanted to take on the burdens of the White House in any case.

Thomas R. Marshall established a custom at the Senate which gave the Vice President at least one yearly duty, that of giving a Christmas dinner for the pages. Held in the Senators' private dining room, they were traditional feasts of turkey and trimmings, followed by humorous speeches by the pages who often gave parodies on Senate figures. Each boy received a book from Senator James D. Phelan of California and another from Senator John B. Kendrick of Wyoming. Vice President Marshall dropped in to say Merry Christmas, but Calvin Coolidge actually ate with us. The Vermonter had paid for that meal and he was bound to enjoy every mouthful. Coolidge's Vice President, wealthy Charles Dawes, could afford to enlarge the dinner so that the entire Floor staff of the Senate was included as his guests, while Charles Curtis, under Hoover, had to return to treating the pages alone. By John Nance Garner's time in 1933, the pages' dinner faded into history when the Lame Duck Amendment delayed the convening of Congress until after the Christmas season. Besides giving the Vice President favorable publicity, the dinner was the social event of the year for pages, elevating them to a place of honor and appreciation. Senator Davis Elkins of West Virginia reserved his annual entertainment for the pages until spring when he treated them to front-row seats at the circus.

The vice presidency has never been a disagreeable job. It was a pleasant if innocuous promotion for a popular governor, as Calvin Coolidge discovered. The daily routine suited his sober temperament. Each morning he arrived in his chauffeur-driven limousine without Secret Service men, since no one thought of protecting the Vice President until Alben Barkley's time. Coolidge went quietly to the resplendent Vice President's Room at the east end of the Lobby where he could greet visitors if they came. Just before twelve o'clock he came out to meet Chaplain J. J. Muir in the Lobby and the two entered the Chamber together upon the stroke of noon. Coolidge carefully banged the ivory gavel and called the Senate to order.

For a stoical man like Coolidge it caused him no anxiety to settle back in the Chair and preside the length of the afternoon, taking an hour out for lunch. No one kept track of the Vice President in those days. No newsman asked me to contact him for comments. No party caucus needed his opinion. Protocol placed the Vice President near the head of the formal dinner table, but for any real purposes, Coolidge had an all-or-nothing job. President Harding's death changed it abruptly from nothing to all.

Into this restraining atmosphere stepped Coolidge's remarkable Vice President Charles Gates Dawes, a banker of many talents with a wary glint in his eyes that warned the Senate to beware. The versatile Dawes had been the first director of the Bureau of the Budget, was an amateur violinist and composer of a piece called "Dawes' Melody," and remained head of a Chicago bank throughout his vice presidency. General "Hell and Maria" Dawes of World War I fame was accustomed to action rather than talk, and he could never become reconciled to the deliberateness of Senate procedure. Though his father and brother had both been members of Congress, Dawes regarded politicians as curiosities to be tolerated and hopefully to be reformed. With determination he set out in a vain attempt to do so.

Instead of leaning back and contenting himself with the ceremonial amenities, Dawes undertook a major crusade to do for the Senate's efficiency what he had done for the Army and the Executive branch. To limit debate, he decided, would cut out the useless chatter and get the Senate down to the business of passing bills. I would see Dawes brandishing his underslung pipe as he set about lobbying among the Senators to change Rule XXII and permit cloture by a simple majority vote. Their response was cool and Dawes' activist role was unpopular. Like Senators Paul Douglas and Joseph Clark in recent years, he came up against the unbending nature of a Senate convinced of its unique place in our republic. Coolidge called the Senate "the citadel of liberty" in describing it as the last forum of free debate.

Though his cloture fight was unsuccessful, Vice President Dawes exerted considerable influence by the sheer force of his personality. Sympathetic with agrarian causes, he was able to convince conservative Senator Jim Watson that the McNary-Haugen Farm Bill merited support even though it departed from tradition. When Dawes believed in a bill, he did not sit by and watch it flounder, but called together the key people to hammer out a compromise. Had the opportunity come, Charles G. Dawes would have been a creditable President.

Herbert Hoover in 1928 chose his Vice President directly from the Senate, elevating Majority Leader Charles Curtis of Kansas into the Chair. Curtis was no guest to be welcomed with formal politeness but a member of the family, whose rough-and-tumble ways were familiar to all. Roy Roberts, publisher of the *Kansas City Star,* described to me the Curtis he first knew when Roberts was a newsboy selling papers on the streets of Kansas City and Curtis was a swarthy young man who drove a horse-drawn hack for hire.

Charles Curtis' distinction as Vice President rested on two counts. No one wielded the gavel as often or with more ferocity than the gentleman from Kansas. With no warning at all he would swing it from high in the air with the marksmanship of a prairie pioneer chopping wood. The sharp crack was deafening to the clerks beneath him. I saw genteel Charles Watkins, the Parliamentarian, visibly jump at the report of Curtis' gavel. Because of his Indian ancestry, I called it Curtis' tom-tom.

His other distinction was an awe-inspiring, thick black mustache. It gave him a fearsome quality if only because it hid so much of his face that I could never tell exactly what his expression meant. One day word came that Curtis wanted to see me at once. Puzzled, I hurried to the Vice President's Room, wondering what I had done that might have displeased him. Curtis was sitting behind his desk, his expressionless eyes boring into the gangly young man called on the carpet before him. "I have been worried about you," the Vice President began in his flat voice. "This mustache you have been trying to grow during the past year has had quite a struggle. I've been wondering if there's some kind of fertilizer we could use on it." It was then that I noticed the gleam in the eyes above his own healthy black plumage. We joined in a hearty laugh together. Not long after that I took a good look at my anemic pink growth and concluded that the cause of my mustache would have to be abandoned.

Charles Curtis was every inch the politician of the back-room species and his vice presidency was as unimaginative as his leadership of the Senate had been. It took his successor John Nance Garner of Texas to demonstrate what a master politician could do with the remote office so devoid of influence. Fresh from two years as the Speaker of the House of Representatives, rugged "Cactus Jack" never doubted his ability to make the Vice President a veritable "Speaker of the Senate."

Because of the desperate economic conditions of the times and the popularity of Roosevelt, Garner was able to perform politically during the first hundred days of the administration as no Vice President has before or since. He was a faithful if fitful spokesman for his overpowering President. More than an adviser, Garner was a good strategist. When I would hear him shouting in the Lobby and shaking his fist at a circle of Senators, he would be cussing out some portions of Roosevelt's legislation with which he did not agree, but his loyalty and effective lobbying was such that the net result would be to cuss it into law.

As the Roosevelt administration opened the door for government to enter more and more areas of life, Senator Frederick Van Nuys of Indiana muttered to Garner one day, "They used to talk about looking after people from the cradle to the grave; now it looks like the New Deal is going to take care of them from the conception to the resurrection!"

As the years progressed, Garner became more and more disillusioned with what he considered FDR's extremes, finally breaking with the President completely on the principle of the third term. Garner proved that he was a congressional type to the roots of his bushy white eyebrows when he told a group of us, "I don't want this country to have a dictatorship; but if there ever has to be one, it ought to be Congress, not the President."

Red-faced Cactus Jack was a chain drinker. He never stopped except while in the Senate Chamber. After he had stayed in the Chair awhile, he would motion to one or two Senators to come out with him to the Vice President's Room where he would pour them drinks. "Let's strike a blow for liberty" was the toast. The effect on Senators often belied his words, but somehow strong intoxicants had less adverse effect on Garner than any one person had a right to expect. That he survived in spite of it to the age of ninety-nine is a remarkable testimonial to his native stamina.

When he left Washington in 1941 to return to Texas, Garner vowed he would never cross the Potomac River again; he kept his vow, remaining the rest of his life only a few miles from the Rio Grande. I saw him once more in 1947 when I was driving back from the Pacific coast through West Texas. Garner welcomed me in shirt sleeves, coming across the dry, grassless yard from feeding his turkeys. I wondered if the sharp-eyed gobblers reminded him of any cloakroom friends in Washington. Garner still lived in Uvalde, Texas, when President Kennedy telephoned from Dallas to wish him a happy ninety-fifth birthday, one of the President's last acts on the morning of November 22, 1963.

When Garner opposed the third term for Roosevelt, FDR could not have chosen a running mate of greater contrast to the gritty Texan than Henry A. Wallace of Iowa. The least congressional of all the Vice Presidents, Wallace was an aloof idealist who had been most at home as Roosevelt's Secretary of Agriculture, the post his father Henry C. Wallace had held under both Harding and Coolidge. With his background as an experimental farmer of note and editor of *Wallace's Farmer* of Des Moines, Vice President Wallace had never held an elective office before. He had none of the political talents that enable public figures to mingle with and influence each other. Instead he was the mystic thinker with his mind seemingly in the future at all times. Basically rather solemn, he spoke in short, serious sentences. Though not warm, he had a friendly, quick smile that disappeared as quickly as it had come. When not presiding over the Senate, Wallace stayed in his office, studied Spanish with one of his assistants, and gave little evidence of enjoying his four years as Vice President.

Only once did I see him feel at home among the Senators and that was not at the Capitol but at the old Griffith Stadium where Lowell Thomas staged a baseball contest between congressional players and the "nine old men," a group which included the famous Washington pitcher Walter Johnson. Vice President Wallace's simple Spartan habits gave him an athletic advantage over more sedentary Senators. The antithesis of Garner, Wallace neither smoked nor drank. The home run he made that afternoon furnished him with more outright pleasure than any political contest.

Henry Wallace was a fighter as his deep, burning look confirmed. An earnest reformer, he later realized he was mistaken in his association with communists when he ran on a third party ticket in 1948. He was an intellectual dreamer whose dreams went unrealized. Eighty-two days after Wallace left office, Roosevelt died, and Vice President Harry Truman moved into the White House.

It may not be necessary to enjoy the vice presidency but both Truman and Alben Barkley proved that it could be done with relish. While Truman had less than three months to sample the

atmosphere, Barkley wore his office like a medal of honor given to
the deserving party man.

The vice presidency came to Richard Nixon at the age of
forty, not in the afternoon of a long Congressional career as it had
to his predecessor Alben Barkley. The Californian's three years in
the House were made spectacular by his part in the Alger Hiss
case, but his new Senate career had been underway only two years
when Eisenhower chose him as a running mate. Nixon did not
have time to cement the friendships among members of both
parties as Truman and Barkley had done during their years at the
heart of the Senate family. Because of President Eisenhower's
nonpolitical nature, Nixon undertook partisan chores with a ve-
hemence that made him an anathema to Democrats. The result was
that he was never received at the Senate with the universal benevo-
lence accorded to Alben Barkley.

Despite these disadvantages, Richard Nixon carried a full
share of the load as a regular trooper of the Eisenhower administration. Leaving the Vice President's Chair, he circulated among
the Senators with his eyes searchingly intent as he engaged individuals in serious conversation. Majority Leader Lyndon Johnson
and the Vice President had much to say to each other on occasion,
all of it in deadly earnest.

The two political leaders had an unfortunate failing in common. Neither Johnson nor Nixon appeared on television as I knew
them in real life. The cameras seemed to freeze their true personalities into a masked stage appearance. Lyndon Johnson's hard-
hitting verve was transformed into a benign, pastoral smile. Richard
Nixon's clean-cut, direct look that is so strikingly effective face to
face, used to be distorted on television into an unfavorable stealthi-
ness. Recent years have brought such a remarkable improvement,
however, that the real Nixon now comes through.

Richard Nixon, the politician, does have a straitlaced, thor-
oughgoing sternness and a total poise that gives him the air of an

unbending man of steel. But Dick Nixon, the friend, can discard this in a moment. In nonpolitical conversations he has an outgoing warmth that quietly envelops the person he meets with a glow of genuine cordiality. Oddly enough, his political opposite Hubert Humphrey shares with Nixon this rare ability to put a person completely at ease. Nixon's friendliness enfolds; Humphrey's effervesces. When I talked with them, there was no sense of the "Great" Nixon or the "Mighty" Humphrey. It was as though each were saying, "I am the one who is privileged to see you!"

The consideration for others that is part of this quality made Richard Nixon one of the fairest and most efficient presiding officers in Senate history. To aid the clerks at the rostrum, the Vice President presented to the Senate a handsome five-minute glass timer for use during the call of the calendar under Rule VIII which allows each Senator only five minutes to discuss a bill. In the Senate where traditions are cherished, the Nixon timer has already become a venerated momento.

Vice President Nixon often showed his sympathy for the tourist who might be seeing Washington for the only time. One morning the Senate had agreed to a *pro forma* session in which it is predetermined that no business will be conducted, not even the Chaplain's opening prayer. At such times it has become a parliamentary sport to see how quickly the presiding officer can rap the gavel and pronounce, "The Senate stands adjourned according to previous agreement until Monday noon." That day the clerks used a stop watch to prove that Nixon had set a new record of six seconds. To the bewilderment of the tourists packed in the galleries, they had just witnessed all the business to be conducted by the Senate. Quick to understand their unspoken disappointment, the Vice President gave an unprecedented impromptu talk from the rostrum. He explained that since the Constitution requires that neither the Senate or the House can adjourn longer than three days without the consent of the other, *pro forma* sessions make brief recesses possible without going through the complications of a formal adjournment. After Nixon had expressed regret that they could not see a full session and wished them a pleasant stay in

President Richard Nixon, as a busy Vice President, pauses to chat with author Riedel.

Majority Leader Mike Mansfield, Vice President Hubert Humphrey, and Minority Leader Everett Dirksen congratulate Richard Riedel on his retirement.—photo: Frank Muto

Washington, I could sense that the tourists felt their visit to the Senate had been worthwhile. The human touch distinguishes Nixon, as it does Humphrey. Unspoiled by success, neither man has lost touch with the modest level of society from which he came.

The immediacy of the presidency hovered about Dick Nixon as it has about no Vice President since Thomas R. Marshall. The uneasy Marshall was apprehensive lest Woodrow Wilson die; but during President Eisenhower's two illnesses, Nixon successfully walked a delicate tightrope in which he had to be ready to take command but careful not to appear anxious to do so. When he lost the 1960 presidential election to John Kennedy, Richard Nixon had come within a hair's breadth of the presidency three times in eight years. I have marveled that he could live with suspense and defeat in at least outward equanimity and go on to achieve the most remarkable political comeback in American history by being elected the thirty-seventh President of the United States.

By Nixon's time there were no more long, quiet afternoons for the Vice President to spend at the Senate. World events have become too critical to leave the "Second Man" sitting immobile at the Capitol as Marshall and Coolidge did. Vice Presidents of an earlier age had been mildly occupied with various historic commemorations and the perennial problem of extending the Capitol building. But not until John Nance Garner became a member of the National Emergency Council did our ranking official have an acknowledged part in the Executive branch. Henry Wallace's administrative talents were put to work as Chairman of the Board of Economic Welfare. Finally by 1949 Alben Barkley had status as understudy for the President. It was Harry Truman's conviction that a Vice President must know what is going on in order to be equipped to take over in an emergency. With Nixon's youth and diplomatic talents, he was able to broaden the scope still further when Eisenhower sent him on several missions abroad, establishing a precedent which Johnson and Humphrey were able to pursue. In addition, chairmanship of the National Aeronautics and Space Council was Vice President Johnson's key domestic assignment which he passed along to Hubert Humphrey.

In this way during the past two decades, the atmosphere around the Vice President has become one of activity and expectation. Between trips around the country and the world, he comes to open the Senate when he is in town. He remains at the Capitol usually no more than an hour, sometimes returning in the late afternoon or evening. The routine morning arrivals and quiet evening departures of Coolidge and Curtis have been replaced by the Vice President's informal dash to his waiting limousine, flanked by two Secret Service men, as he hurries on to his various assignments. No matter how busy he might become, the Vice President must always play the game of follow-the-President, which does not come naturally to men like Nixon, Johnson, and Humphrey.

The Capitol's master politician, Vice President Johnson could have jumped feetfirst into cloakroom conferences in the style of John Nance Garner. But Johnson's regard for the Senate and its new Leader Mike Mansfield was such that he carefully restrained his Floor activities to scant circulation, relishing instead the visits with Senators who came up to the Chair to talk with him. During the period of his vice presidency, Lyndon Johnson reminded me of a hound dog in sight of but out of reach of his bone.

For more than two decades the Senate has become the laboratory for developing homegrown Vice Presidents who are no strangers to the scene. When Majority Whip Hubert Humphrey stepped up to take the Chair in 1965, he was the fifth Vice President in succession to come from the Senate. His beaming face from the rostrum radiated more refreshing enthusiasm over the job than anyone since Alben Barkley; but then, Humphrey was the most naturally joyous politician I have known on Capitol Hill.

It would seem that superlatives best describe the gentleman from Minnesota. Nothing less than a genius, Hubert Humphrey was possibly the foremost, original idea man to come to the Senate. He had a fountain of answers to all our social ills—more answers, as someone said, than there were problems. The Peace Corps and the Job Corps were originally his ideas, along with the Great White Fleet and Food for Peace. For Humphrey to be either speechless or idealess would be as unlikely as for an artesian well to run dry.

During his sixteen years as Senator, Humphrey took the Floor more often than anyone except Wayne Morse, often making several speeches a day on a profusion of subjects. If there had been a printed program, it would have read, "Senator Humphrey, followed by Senator Humphrey, with a sequel by Senator Humphrey," and so on, intermittantly throughout the day. Presiding from the Chair, Vice President Humphrey found himself unable to speak except for parliamentary rulings, a fact of life that made him the target of good-natured razzing from his old colleagues. A Senator would gently remind him of his vociferous past and conclude facetiously that if only the Vice President could speak, the Senator knew he would certainly support the Senator's point of view. Unable to answer back, Humphrey would grin in helpless amusement.

A sunny nature was the norm for Humphrey from his earliest days in Washington, but it does not follow that he was always a model of legislative moderation. His early excesses made the Senate shudder. The fledgling Senator Humphrey, who soared down from Minnesota in 1949 after making news as the young reform mayor of Minneapolis and as one of the founders of Americans for Democratic Action, had a cocky disregard of tradition second only to Huey Long.

From the back row Senator Humphrey would bolt up in fervor. Like an ancient Viking at the prow of his ship, he would strike a heroic pose, index finger uplifted and chin jutting out in adamant defiance. I have rarely seen a more enthusiastic speaker. Once when Majority Leader Knowland tried to interrupt, he was waved aside by the Senator from Minnesota who said, "I am in the midst of a wonderful thought!" His voice was light, but it always came through with the ring of sincerity.

Hubert Humphrey was obliging to the press when he came to see them, but it was no small trick to try to catch him between speeches; and newsmen frequently had to wait. Humphrey did not always put correspondents first, but it was typical of him to drop everything to help someone of little political importance. Once he put off a newsman of strategic value to him, saying to me, "I regret it but he'll just have to wait. There's a farmer in my office who is in deep trouble and I must see him first." After a twenty-minute wait the fuming newsman walked off to file his story, in no mood to credit Humphrey with anything that day.

The Senator from Minnesota reached his height of vividness as Hubert the Giant Slayer in those early days when he and his fellow liberals were out in the vanguard alone. Using graphic sarcasm, he would tear into anyone who tried to block his programs. As a result he made the breakthrough in federal aid to education during his first session. The young Humphrey was nothing less than a first-degree maverick in those days. I never expected to see him become part of the Establishment.

But the Senate, like a patient teacher, has moderated many legislators, and Hubert Humphrey was to be one of those who would accept its tempering influence. Crying in the wilderness has rarely been an effective means to change. Ever so gradually Humphrey seemed to realize that the Senate way of working together in compromise had untold advantages for a prolific thinker who wanted to see his ideas become reality. Humphrey had sufficient realism mixed with his innate optimism to accept Lyndon Johnson's tutelage. By 1961 the conversion of the maverick was complete when he became Democratic Whip.

With an average-size body dominated by a massive forehead and prominant eyes, Hubert Humphrey looked like a man of the future—all brain. To see him in operation was to believe it. I have watched him in the center of half a dozen of his staff people, conversing simultaneously with all of them at the back of the Chamber. Had his administrative assistant Herb Waters contacted that cabinet member? Would his legislative assistant Jack Flynn draft an amendment to the current education bill? Had Dave Gartner called Senator Douglas? What was the result of Bill Connell's work on the need for further federal aid to schools in impacted areas? Did Wynn Griffith have the press release ready on his last major speech? Humphrey assessed the answers and gave more directives in quick, sharp order. Instantly he took the Floor to make an extemporaneous speech or joined in a lively debate that he had been following throughout. Then, as though it were his sole delight in life, he found a moment to go out to the Reception Room to greet a Minnesota family, call their children by name, and take a genuine interest in their visit to Washington.

Not a man to nurse defeats, Hubert Humphrey learned from his disasters and moved on. The 1960 presidential primary races against John Kennedy were disheartening to him, but his description of the ordeal was hilarious. He joked about the antiquated bus that was the best he could afford for his campaign transportation. While Humphrey and his entourage were bumping over the roads of Wisconsin and West Virginia in the poorly heated rattletrap, they heard the zoom of Kennedy's private plane overhead as JFK rushed on to get votes by the million. Humphrey's good-natured banter about it reminded one of Lincoln's jests at having to wait on a siding in a freight car while Stephen A. Douglas' special flag-draped private car barreled by in the night.

When Lyndon Johnson first selected him for the vice presidency, it seemed to Humphrey too good to be true. With boyish glee he was enthralled at the prospect, but it all had a storybook quality to him, as though at any moment the golden coach might turn into a pumpkin. With Lyndon Johnson's support, Humphrey went to the threshold of the White House itself, only to lose the 1968 election by a narrow margin. I have seen Hubert Humphrey show sportsmanship in hours of defeat and react with humility in times of triumph, certainly two marks of greatness.

If the vice presidency were the same back shelf that it used to be, Hubert Humphrey and his infinite energies might never have been able to survive the office. Each man who has become Vice President has found a way to cope with the occupational hazards of the office. Marshall had his sense of humor, Coolidge his unrockable serenity. Dawes' fruitless campaign for limitation of debate at least preserved his equilibrium, while Curtis worked off his frustrations by pounding the gavel all day. Ignoring the back shelf altogether, Garner went right on being Jack Garner, but Henry Wallace moved within his dream world to survive. Truman and Barkley simply enjoyed it. Nixon, Johnson, and Humphrey have been fortunate to work with Presidents who have prescribed occupational therapy in the form of important assignments that have added zestful purpose to the vice presidency.

COMMITTEE CHAIRMEN

Within the Senate family circle, committees are the family automobiles, the vehicles by which the legislative work is done. It is the chairmen who drive, each in his own way, directing where and how far his committee will go. It is not the Senate way to push the accelerator to the floor and rush headlong down an unknown road. Neither do chairmen issue orders from the driver's seat with the heavy hand of a Joseph McCarthy. A chairman may sit in the front seat with the adamant dignity of a Harry Byrd, Sr., satisfied to be a moral symbol of his philosophy of government while eventually allowing his committee to determine its course by majority rule. A chairman is apt to be meticulously fair about consulting the other Senators on his committee in the thorough manner of Carl Hayden. At the very least he will be subtle, that is to say, Senatorial.

As unchanging as the Senate seems to be, in half a century I have watched its structure change from an unwieldy dinosaur of seventy-four committees to a more sensible framework of thirty-three, until today the Senate is almost streamlined with sixteen standing committees. However, the bones of the dinosaur are still underneath if the one hundred subcommittees and the standing and select and joint committees are included, but it makes a better story not to count them.

I came just in time to know the ancient and tottering structure of seventy-four committees, each with its own chairman, members, and letterhead. How many Senators could be made happy with a chairmanship in my early days! There were so many plums to go around that they ran out of majority members and had to share the pie by letting twenty-one members of the minority head lesser committees. Today the Democratic majority controls everything except two subcommittees. Republican dean George Aiken chairs the Canadian Affairs Subcommittee of Foreign Relations. Minority Leader Dirksen heads the Judiciary Committee's Subcommittee on Federal Charters, Holidays, and Celebrations, which, he has said, can meet in a telephone booth when Dirksen calls John McClellan, the Subcommittee's only other member.

The early committee names, such as Public Health and National Quarantine, caught the imagination. There was a choice one called Disposition of Useless Papers in the Executive Departments, which on first glance would seem to be janitorial rather than legislative. It seemed that every committee created since George Washington's time had survived to my page days. There was still one on Revolutionary Claims, another to Investigate Trespassers upon Indian Lands and a spine-chiller called Indian Depredations.

My favorite was the Committee on the Five Civilized Tribes of Indians, whose elderly chairman Knute Nelson was as picturesque as his committee's name. The little Senator from Minnesota had a snow-white Santa Claus beard, forever sprinkled with chewing-tobacco stains. Norwegian-born Nelson spoke with a decided accent and was proud to be a Union veteran, once wounded and taken prisoner in Louisiana while serving with the Fourth Wisconsin Regiment. When the Republicans assumed control of the Senate in 1919, Knute Nelson became Chairman of the important Judiciary Committee.

As though there had been no tragic Civil War, the powerful senior Senators of my page days included veterans of both sides of that catastrophe. Besides Majority Leader Martin, a Confederate veteran, there was the imposing elder John Bankhead of Alabama, Chairman of the patronage-rich Post Offices and Post Roads Committee, who had served four years in the Confederate Army. In the 1930's his two sons would be in Congress simultaneously, John H.

Bankhead, Jr., as Senator from Alabama and William Bankhead as
Speaker of the House.

The ranking Republican member in line to become Chairman
of the all-powerful Appropriations Committee was Francis E.
Warren of Wyoming, awarded the Congressional Medal of Honor
for gallant service with the Forty-ninth Massachusetts Infantry of
the Union Army. After being mustered out, Warren moved to
Cheyenne where he prospered in business and became a bulwark
of the territorial government. When Wyoming became a state, he
came in 1890 as one of its first Senators after serving briefly as its
first governor, probably the only man in United States history to
inaugurate both offices. Senator Warren was a kindly millionaire
with a tall, heavy frame, set off by a head of white hair and a full
handlebar mustache. His daughter married General John J. Pershing, and the Senator brought his grandson Warren Pershing for an
unusual visit on the Floor. As Chairman of Appropriations, Warren was an advocate of strict economy who kept a tight hold on the
purse strings in the 1920's. Above all, he was a living monument to
the history of Wyoming and the Old West.

Committee chairmen are the inner circle of the Senate family.
Newer Senators often have that longing, hungry, anxious look of
those who would like to become fully accepted, but committee
chairmen have an aura of assurance and authority that is unmis-
takable. Whether they wear it with the modern, efficient but easy
air of Henry M. "Scoop" Jackson who heads the Interior Committee, the kindly mildness of John Sparkman of Banking and Currency, or the deadly seriousness of Clinton Anderson of the Space
Committee, the chairman lives with the self-assurance of an excellent power base.

A chairman inherits his job by seniority, the one indisputable
way to transfer power without the scars of infighting. Equally
important, seniority guarantees that the chairman has served his
apprenticeship on the committee. The average Senate service of a
chairman in 1968 was greater than twenty-two years, certainly
ample time to have learned his field. A committee chairman has
worked a long time with government problems. In some circles he

may even be considered a problem himself. But he has been around long enough to develop working alliances on both sides of the aisle and to learn many of the lessons of effective, practical action.

However, the seniority system has many disadvantages, the greatest being that the chairmanship may not come to a Senator until he is past his prime. He may have worked strenuously in the committee throughout his career, only to find himself physically unable to carry the load when he becomes chairman in his latter days. The result is that the actual work sometimes falls to younger members, as when George Aiken assumed the burden of the Agriculture Committee for Arthur Capper in the 80th Congress. In the early 1940's Kenneth McKellar steered the Appropriations Committee for Carter Glass whose fatal illness lasted two years. Not long afterwards Richard Russell and Carl Hayden relieved the aging McKellar when he became chairman. Counterbalancing this is the amazing vigor of many Senators who, like Matthew Neely and Rhode Island's Theodore Francis Green, have been more energetic past eighty than most young men. Age is as individualistic as ability.

Seniority has been set aside in rare instances. The Joint Economic Committee, which merely advises Congress in its complex field, has elevated two economists to the chairmanship who were not senior members, Paul Douglas and now William Proxmire of Wisconsin. Like his mentor Douglas, Senator Proxmire does his own thinking, using the statistical wizardry of the economist, without regard to which party will benefit most from his economic diagnosis.

The chairman is to a committee what a Floor Leader is to the entire Senate. By determining the program and priorities of his domain, he can control the life and death of legislation. The ways of killing a bill are so numerous that no chairman has to flat-footedly declare to the world that he is against it. I have listened to chairmen artfully dodge my questions about bills referred to their committees. "That one has yet to be assigned to a subcommittee," the chairman would say in utter innocence, not mentioning that he was the only one who could refer it. "We haven't had a chance to have hearings on that bill . . . The hearings have to be printed . . . We need more information . . . It needs further study . . ." and so on. Burial by delay is an art practiced by design and not without some benefit to the advocates of the philosophy that the best government is the least government. The unyielding head of the Judiciary Committee Senator James Eastland of Mississippi, has been a virtual funeral director over civil rights legislation for over a decade, making it necessary for the leadership to outflank him to pass the civil rights bills.

Other chairmen can be quantitatively-minded like Warren Magnuson of the State of Washington, who has pushed more bills through his Commerce Committee than all his predecessors. When a chairman does wish to breathe life into a bill, he can schedule hearings with dispatch and promote a favorable report from his fellow members, a majority of whom must agree to the final mark-up of a bill before it can be voted out of committee and onto the Floor. There the chairman's prestige can push for a vote and win decisive support from the Senate and possibly the House. The chairman has sole power to call committee meetings if regular ones are not scheduled, which is of key importance near the end of a Congress when all unapproved legislation awaits an instant death sentence. Throughout the long legislative road, the interest and aid of a chairman is vital to the final success of any bill.

Next in importance to the Senators themselves is the staff of a committee, whose appointment has always been in the chairman's hands. Before Congress was reorganized in 1946, a Senator's personal secretaries often did the work that the specialized staff now does: research, preparation for hearings, drafting bills, and writing staff memos and committee reports. Now the groundwork is done in obscure offices by professional committee personnel who know the legislative process thoroughly. In many ways, they are the backbone of Congress. The details of committee work are so complex that only the staff, who devote full time to them, may be familiar with all the technicalities of a bill. Senators often vote on the basis of information given them by the staff, together with the

opinions of their constituents back home. They cannot possibly do
all their own work. It is understandable that a new chairman tends
to keep valuable staff members while adding more.

A record was set by Everard Smith who spanned fifty-three
years with the Senate Appropriations Committee, twenty-seven as
Chief Clerk. When I would see him coming sedately into the
Chamber, I would explain to a new employee, "There goes Mr.
Appropriations!"

Committee clerks are seen but never heard on the Floor, but
Eddie Jarrett, Chief Clerk and mainstay of the Commerce Committee for twenty-five years, usually went only as far as the Lobby.
I was surprised one day to see him going about the Chamber
holding a small box out to each member of his committee who
put something in the slot at the top. What strange new custom
was this? Actually the committee members were casting secret
ballots on a bill to prohibit liquor advertising on radio and television. Such legislation has been introduced in almost every Congress for thirty years, but none has ever passed. The very fact that
it is introduced has been sufficient warning to the broadcasting
industry that if it does not control itself, Congress will. Why the
secret ballots? The committee members were caught between the
temperance groups on the one hand and the powerful liquor lobby
on the other. Unthinkable as it may seem, Senators have been
known to be tattletales, leaking committee votes that would prove
embarrassing to other Senators. A secret ballot guaranteed that
no one would know a Senator's conscience but himself. That year
the Commerce Committee refused to report out the bill by the
narrow vote of seven to six.

A committee leads its own life with meetings and hearings in
distant committee rooms until one of its bills comes up for consideration by the Senate. Then the staff moves onto the Floor with
stacks of documents which are piled on and around the desk of the
chairman, or whoever is to floor-manage the bill, until there is
scarcely room for the Senator's feet. The chairman takes the Floor
to defend the committee's bill against an onslaught of amendments. The chief clerk sits beside him in a small chair, armed with

pertinent information, while other staff members wait at the back of the Chamber. No matter how much support he has, however, it is the chairman who must carry the ball in the debate.

The chairmen of Appropriations have been remarkable men, capable of maneuvering a bill through the Senate. From Francis E. Warren to Carl Hayden and Richard Russell, they have headed the key committee of the Senate, for those who keep the purse have the final word. Both Houses of Congress may agree to authorize a project but until the funds are provided, it cannot get off the ground. When a Senator achieves mere membership on the Appropriations Committee, he has reached the legislative promised land. His state can benefit from the projects he secures; and, if his constituents have enough gratitude and perception to return him to the Senate, he can work for more projects, and so it goes. Since no one ever willingly leaves Appropriations, it boasts the greatest concentration of senior Senators.

The chairman is naturally the senior of seniors who frequently is also President Pro Tempore of the Senate. Awarded to the dean of the majority party, this honorary post ranks him after the Vice President and the Speaker of the House in the line of succession to the presidency of the United States. The President Pro Tem is second only to the Vice President as presiding officer of the Senate, which lets him preside in the Vice President's absence and gives him a chauffeured limousine to certify his VIP status. Carter Glass, Kenneth McKellar, Styles Bridges, Carl Hayden, and Richard Russell have each been President Pro Tem and Chairman of Appropriations simultaneously.

Among the keenest financial minds to hold both positions was Carter Glass of Virginia. Already famous when he came to the Senate in 1920 as father of the Federal Reserve System and President Wilson's Secretary of the Treasury, the little Senator from Virginia more than made up for his size by his fighting nature. Many have compared him with the bantam cocks he liked to watch in combat. Carter Glass would orate from the center aisle, his voice had a rasping tremor, and his sharp face always twisted around to let the words come out of one corner of his mouth. Woodrow Wilson, marveling at Glass's accomplishments once remarked, "Think of what Carter could do if he talked out of both sides of his mouth!" I have watched him work himself into such a frenzy that no one could understand what he was saying. At those times Senator Glass looked and sounded for all the world like a baby robin screaming for a worm.

While he could turn an abrasive side to fellow Senators, even pounding his knuckles bloody in a fit of displeasure, Carter Glass was considerate to me. Evidently his early career as an energetic editor and publisher in Lynchburg, Virginia, made him feel benevolent toward anyone aiding the press.

Senator Glass, a conservative by nature, declared that he had no intention of ever getting into an airplane. After Charles A. Lindbergh's transatlantic flight, however, the Senator conceded that Lindbergh was the *only* pilot with whom he would fly. Glass had his chance in March, 1928, when Lindbergh spent a week in Washington promoting aviation during which he took over three hundred people on flights over the city, where he had lived while his father was a Member of Congress. As the famous aviator was taking up one plane, a second was being loaded with passengers from the Capitol, each strapped into a parachute, gamely waiting to take off. It was for most, as for me, the first plane flight. Carter Glass and Simeon Fess had a look of grim determination that said, "I'm flying with Lindbergh if it's the last thing I do, and it may very well be!" The flight was so smooth that Senator Glass could joke about it when we landed, saying that the plane's motor made such a noise that not even a Senator could hear himself talk.

Carter Glass reluctantly secured appropriations for President Roosevelt's New Deal projects, though as a Jeffersonian Democrat he was devoted to fiscal responsibility. But he never could accept the innovation of the dial phone. I happened to be going through the Democratic cloakroom the day Carter Glass first discovered the new telephones. He had gone into a booth to place a call and came charging out like a snake had bitten him. "What the hell has happened to the phones?" he stormed. The pages tried to explain the dial system to him, but it was obvious that the traditional Senator Glass wanted the telephone left just as Alexander Graham Bell had invented it. An old model was quickly reinstalled and carefully maintained as long as he lived. I hesitate to contemplate what the peppery Virginian would do if he were here today and came face to face with a computer.

A Tennessean with an equally celebrated temper followed Senator Glass as Chairman of Appropriations. Kenneth McKellar was capable of fiery dramatics and chivalrous bows, fierce tantrums and steadfast friendship. He could be narrow and crafty in his ill-fated plan to turn TVA into a patronage plum. But he could prove his worth to the country by pointing among other things to the federal highway system which he pioneered from his earliest days in the House. Whatever Senator McKellar did, there was nothing sinister about him. He was open, some would say blatant, in his political maneuvering. If he wanted patronage, and he frequently did, he said so. If he had it in for someone, McKellar went verbally gunning for him down the main aisle, as he shamelessly attacked TVA Director David Lilienthal year after year.

The Kenneth McKellar of my page days was a real Beau Brummell, jaunty and carefree with wavy brown hair and pink cheeks. He must have been the most eligible young bachelor in Washington in those days, but he was never to marry. By 1953 when Albert Gore defeated him, McKellar was the last Senator to depart who had been in the Senate when I came in 1918. Withered and flabby, he was a lonely, sick old man with an aggravated temper. He had served Tennessee in Congress for forty years and should have retired gracefully. But then, McKellar was never overly graceful, even though he could be, and was to me, a generous friend.

The Senator had a peculiar bent for patronage that became an obsession with him. It seemed that above all, he wanted those around him to be indebted to him, as though to satisfy some deep need. But my experience proves that he could and did perform kindnesses that had no motive other than warmheartedness. Unlike Civil Service workers in the Executive branch, legislative employees on the Hill have not enjoyed automatic raises with length of service. Until recently, salary increases have come to those who went out and got them, and Chairman McKellar of Appropriations was the man to see. Since I had been without a raise for many years, I felt my cause was just. Senator McKellar agreed until I helpfully added, "Les Biffle (then Secretary of the Senate) is for it, too." At that McKellar flew into one of his red-faced fits, the only time he ever lost his temper with me. He became so angry that he could only splutter out sounds that resembled words, "Now-see-here! This is *my* idea! Do you want this raise or don't you? Well then, it's *me* doing this for you, not Biffle. *Me* and nobody else!" After assuring him that I knew it was indeed his initiative that would make it possible, I did get the raise. The important thing to note is that in all the years I knew him, Senator McKellar never cashed in on his aid by asking any special favor of me. I meant nothing to him politically. It was enough for him that he had helped, and that I knew it.

Carl Hayden as Chairman of the Senate Appropriations Committee was nothing short of a phenomenon on Capitol Hill. The Senator from Arizona held an awesome concentration of power, but his fair and unobtrusive manner of exercising it placed him in the best tradition of the Senate elder statesman. In addition to Appropriations, he headed the Joint Committee on Printing, was dean of the Senate and President Pro Tem, and for an amazing thirty-five years, was Chairman of the Democratic Patronage Committee. The majority of his roles Hayden played backstage, but his soundness was such that he could not be classed as a back-room politician. It was simply his nature to work quietly in his office.

In 1962 Senator Hayden made history as the first person to serve in Congress a total of fifty years. When he retired with the 90th Congress, his service of almost fifty-seven years became the all-time record. He was the first man to represent the new State of Arizona in 1912. Carl Hayden, former Sheriff of Maricopa County, was elected to the House of Representatives directly by the people. Immediately he hopped aboard a train and arrived in Washington five days later. Arizona's first two Senators Henry

Fountain Ashurst and Marcus A. Smith had to be chosen by the state legislature and arrived a month later.

The nation has benefited from Hayden's sponsorship of such measures as the establishment of the Grand Canyon National Park and the Hayden-Cartwright Act which expanded the federal highway concept to include area as well as population. When the phrase "student of government" was applied to Senator Hayden, it meant something. During the early New Deal days he made a study of the new federal programs and published guidelines for establishing federal field offices which have been useful for thirty years.

It was part of Hayden's nature to shun publicity. Not until the 1960's did the Senator include on his staff a public relations specialist, Richard Greenwood. Even he had to maneuver around Hayden's natural desire to simply let a job well done speak for itself. All of this contradicted an age in which so many other legislators were vying to make page one. When Senator Hayden came on the Floor, usually to vote, he gave direct, knowing answers without embellishments to my questions for the press. He shied away from photographers with the comment, "I look just like Mahatma Gandhi." But after his fiftieth anniversary, even he had to accept the fact that Hayden of Arizona was a national legend. The Press found him a little more willing to see them and give his shy smile. It is entirely possible that eventually his career will begin to impress the Senator himself.

Better than any one member, Carl Hayden illustrates that the main work of the Senate is done without headlines by tedious study, parliamentary planning, quiet discussion among friends, and the family's respect for an elder statesman's opinion. His career makes a good case for selecting a capable man and returning him again and again to the Senate where each year his experience and influence will increase in direct proportion to his seniority.

The Constitution gives the Senate a voice in our international policies which is expressed with the greatest influence through the

Foreign Relations Committee. Throughout almost half of the past fifty years, the Committee has voiced dissent from the President's policies through Chairmen Henry Cabot Lodge, Sr., William E. Borah, and now J. William Fulbright of Arkansas. Senator Fulbright's current revolt against our participation in the war in Viet Nam, in opposition to President Johnson's equally firm and sincere stand, proves that when the chairman speaks, his voice is interpreted as that of the entire committee.

Senator Fulbright has spoken out against mainstream policies often enough to all but qualify as a maverick along with Wayne Morse. Coming to the Senate with the academic credentials of a Rhodes scholar and former president of the University of Arkansas, Fulbright has blazed a trail of freethinking independence in everything but civil rights. There he maintains an embarrassed acquiescence to the status quo which his liberal colleagues delicately overlook.

When Senator Fulbright comes into the Chamber, he generally looks bored with the whole routine, as though he wishes he were somewhere else—anywhere else. He slumps down at his desk and counters the boredom with satirical comments, laughing with his colleagues. A lively debate on foreign policy serves as a tonic that can kindle him into a persuasive speech with his voice rising to full pitch. But lacking this kind of stimulation, Fulbright reads a prepared statement with all the enthusiasm of a scholar talking to a classroom full of idiots. His every motion says that it is not worth the effort but he will say it and get off the Floor, even if he has to slur a few syllables in his rush to finish. His arguments are discerning and often provocative, but his bored delivery makes one conclude that Fulbright should be read rather than heard.

If Senator Fulbright condescends on the Floor, in the cloakroom or Lobby he is still nonchalant but friendly. There is far more of the down-to-earth flavor of Arkansas about him than the Rhodes scholar. When he relaxes, he slouches on a sofa with the loose-jointed cordiality typical of so many Southern Senators. If I asked him for a comment on the statement of the prime minister of "Outer Utopia" accusing the United States of not having done

enough for them lately, Fulbright would answer with a good-natured growl, "Whyyyy, IIIII don't know. I haven't had time to
study the thing. Besides, I haven't had lunch yet!"

Among Senator Fulbright's favorite newsmen is the erudite
James P. "Scotty" Reston, editor of the *New York Times;* they
talk the same language. The Senator may leave the Chamber like a
pensive commuter but his face will break into a broad smile at the
sight of Scotty waiting by the President's Room. Casually they
adopt a measured pace down the private staircase, deep in conversation on their way to lunch together in the Senators' dining room.
As they brush past the intricate bronze stair railing, cast over a
hundred years ago, their concern is not yesterday but tomorrow.

The greatest living monument to William Fulbright, or possibly to any legislator, continues to be the scholarship program that
bears his name. President Kennedy said that the Senator's plan to
use war surplus property credits abroad for the exchange of students had created more good will than any other act of Congress.
While the Senator had almost full support for the Fulbright Scholarships in 1946, he gives the credit for the bill's final passage to
Walter Reynolds, at that time his legislative assistant and later
chief clerk of the Government Operations Committee.

Mr. Reynolds' story illustrates as well as any the intertwining
pattern of life on Capitol Hill in which no one knows what strands
will connect at some distant date. The Reynolds' story begins in
the 1930's when he was secretary to Hamilton Fish, noted Representative from New York City. As clerk of the House Special
Committee to Investigate Communist Activities in the United
States, known as the Fish Committee, Reynolds went about the
country with the members gathering floods of testimony from
American communists. In those days they were eager for a chance
to spread their ideology openly. Back in Washington Walter Reynolds was surprised to find that a freshman Congressman from
Michigan had as his valued secretary and speech writer a self-ad-
mitted communist who had represented Mexico in Moscow at the
Communist International. Reynolds lost no time in mailing photo-
stats of conclusive testimony to Michigan papers with the result that

the Congressman was defeated by a man Reynolds had never heard of whose name was Clare Hoffman. Representative Hoffman's first move on arriving in Washington was to hunt up Reynolds and proclaim his gratitude. "If there's ever anything I can do for you . . ." were Hoffman's parting words.

Eleven years later in 1946 it happened that Clare Hoffman was the most vocal Member of the House opposing the Fulbright scholarships. Convinced that it would allow communists to represent our country abroad, the ultraconservative Congressman all but created a one-man blockade to prevent the House committee from reporting out the bill. Congress was about to adjourn. The scholarship bill was about to be lost. Senator Fulbright was desperate. "What can we do about Hoffman?" he said to his legislative assistant. "I know exactly what to do about Hoffman," answered Reynolds on his way to the Congressman's office.

Walter Reynolds has an intensive way of presenting facts that would make anyone listen. Congressman Hoffman, aware of his debt to Reynolds, took in his every word. "You don't understand about this bill, Congressman," Reynolds told him, "Forty of our top educators will pass on the scholarship applicants and make certain no communists are involved." This gave Hoffman a new understanding of the soundness of the program, so that the Congressman himself moved to report the bill out of the House committee, much to the surprise of everyone. Within days it passed the House and Senate and was signed into law by President Truman on August 2, 1946. For two decades thousands of students have benefited from the vision of Senator Fulbright and from the astuteness of Walter Reynolds.

When the chairman of Foreign Relations and the President concur, the unity that results is a powerful positive force. So it was when peace phased out war in 1945 and Chairman Tom Connally found his finest hour in preparing the Senate to accept the United Nations Charter. One might have hoped for a more agreeable personality to do the job. The testy old Texan naturally wore a scowl most of the time and spoke with a biting tongue in sarcastic phrases that could cool friendships quickly. The next day he might win them back again in the cloakroom with one of his drawling, storytelling moods, for as a raconteur Connally was rivaled only by Senator Tom Heflin.

From the 1920's I remember a mild and genial young Congressman Connally who often came over from the House to visit with Senator Morris Sheppard. Even then Connally looked the part of an old-fashioned Senator. He kept his hair at that special length that left a slight curl to the ends below his wide-brimmed Western hat. With his string tie, Tom Connally was the walking image of the cartoonists' Senator. As he grew older and his health declined, his spicy humor gradually dried up into a vindictiveness that gave a sour taste to his last days. But at the time of the United Nations' development, Connally put aside personal differences to project the imperative need for an international organization.

Senator Connally's committee was as star-studded as any Foreign Relations group has ever been, having within it the operating core of the Senate. Leaders Barkley and White were both there. Walter F. George of Georgia could speak for his Finance Committee while New Dealer Robert Wagner of New York could answer for his Banking and Currency Committee. Gerald P. Nye, Young Bob LaFollette, and Minnesota's Henrik Shipstead represented the skeptical isolationists. If Hiram Johnson's failing health had permitted, the old warrior would have pursued his consistent stand for nonintervention that dated back to his support of Senators Borah and Lodge against the League of Nations in 1919.

In place of Borah and Johnson, the Republican minority on the Foreign Relations Committee had new leadership from Arthur Vandenberg of Michigan. His tolerant bipartisanship and his conversion to internationalism excited the country and earned for him the genuine title of statesman. Senator Vandenberg's positive leadership at a critical period raised him to the threshold of greatness. His one problem was that he began to believe in his own greatness.

It had not always been so. The Vandenberg who came to the Senate in 1927 was a newspaper editor fresh from Grand Rapids, obviously awed by Washington and grateful for any assistance anyone could give him. He gained importance as his ideas became

Jubilant over Senate support for the United Nations, Foreign Relations Chairman Tom Connally of Texas and Democratic Leader Alben Barkley of Kentucky share a prize story.—photo: UPI

The Harry Byrds of Virginia: Father and son made an effective team.—photo: Winchester (Virginia) Star

law, authoring Federal Bank Deposit Insurance which was credited to the New Deal. As his national stature grew, so did his opinion of himself until it could be stated that no one in the Capitol was more puffed out with his own importance than Arthur Vandenberg. His was a model case of that stultifying disease that might be called Washington-itis. It came through in his private conversation as well as his public speaking. The intonations of his broad accent varied up and down in a condescending sliding of tones which amounted to a sneer. The one remnant of his early unpretentiousness returned when he sat at a cloakroom typewriter, pecking away like a newspaperman.

Vandenberg was the only pompous Senator whom the discriminating press admired. Newsmen eagerly awaited his condescending smile and his cigar. Any news from Arthur Vandenberg was a valued story. When he presided over the Senate as President Pro Tem in the 80th Congress, correspondents leaned over the gallery rail to watch him draw elaborate kaleidoscopic doodles. I often went up to the Chair to ask him to autograph a doodle for one of his favorite newsmen. With an ostentatious air he complied, as convinced as the newsman that someday, possibly when he became President, they would become coveted collectors' items.

Arthur Vandenberg's fame rankled deeply with Tom Connally. Like two old roosters greeting the dawn of the United Nations, if one crowed, the other tried to outdo him. Connally with his lashing whine wanted it known that he, as Chairman of Foreign Relations, was running the show. His veins stood out and his face became purplish while Vandenberg preened himself on the Republican side. When the Senator from Michigan spoke, he took a heroic stance with an upraised arm, notes in his other hand; and with his chin scruched down in his collar, he threw out his voice in a deep-throated growl. In spite of his pomposity, Senators took their seats and listened to Vandenberg's ideas which were impressive.

In describing his hopes for the United Nations, Senator Vandenberg said:

"You cannot plant an acorn, Mr. President, and expect an oak from it the morning following; but you will never have an

oak unless you plant the acorn. In the San Francisco Charter we
undertake to plant the roots of peace. No one can say with
finality how they will flower, but this I know: Without roots
there will be no flowers. I prefer the chance rather than no
chance at all."

Congressional Record, 79th Congress, 1st Session, 1945, p. 6982.

It is greatly to their credit that two prima donnas like Senators Connally and Vandenberg made themselves work together
toward the goal of a United Nations that was acceptable to the
United States Senate. Warren Austin, Republican of Vermont,
played a valuable role so completely nonpartisan that President
Truman appointed him as our representative to the United Nations
in 1946.

The lesson of the League of Nations debacle of 1919 had
been learned. Instead of expecting the Senate to agree to the
completed Charter as Wilson had done, the Foreign Relations
Committee was closely consulted by the Roosevelt administration
at various stages. I saw sunny-faced Bob Shirley, the Committee's
confidential counsel, frequently on the Floor, now conferring with
one Senator, now clearing up a detail with another member. When
the day came for Vandenberg and Connally to leave for San
Francisco to help draw up the UN Charter, the Senate sent them
on their way with cheers and good wishes and welcomed them
back with a standing ovation. There was a spirit of "we" that I had
not seen in 1919.

When Senator Connally returned, he summarized the thinking
of a war-weary nation:

"The central idea of the Charter is that the comradeship of
war must be carried forward in a comradeship of peace. If we
have been able to fight side by side in killing and destroying,
why shall we not league together to save millions of human lives
and permit the peoples of the earth to rebuild their tortured
lands . . .

". . . Let us be among the architects of a structure more
marvelous than one built of steel and stone. Let us create a

temple of law and reason and justice and peace to serve the peoples of the world. The world charter for peace is knocking at the doors of the Senate. We shall not turn it away . . ."
Congressional Record, 79th Congress, 1st Session, 1945, p. 6878.

It was no surprise when the Senate agreed to the United Nations Charter with the only two votes against it cast by Bill Langer, the North Dakota maverick, and loyal isolationist Henrik Shipstead of Minnesota. The Foreign Relations Committee had done its work well. Later the leading roles were reversed twice when Vandenberg became chairman in the Republican 80th Congress and again when Connally returned in the Democratic 81st.

It took a man of the stature of Walter F. George of Georgia to rise to bipartisanship without fanfare. Though a Democrat, he backed President Eisenhower's foreign policies more forcefully than many longtime Republicans. Senator George was an accomplished legislator. Whether as Chairman of Finance or Foreign Relations, he commanded universal respect akin to Senator Borah on a plane few statesmen have attained.

Walter George came to Washington in 1922 after ten years on the Georgia bench. Even then he had the judicious steadiness that carried him through thirty-five years in the Senate. With the graciousness that was his hallmark, George waited two days of the session before taking his seat so that Mrs. Rebecca Latimer Felton could have the distinction of being the first woman in history to serve in the Senate, if only for two days. I well remember the lively little lady, at eighty-seven the oldest person to become a Senator in my time. Governor Hardwick of Georgia had appointed her the month before in recognition of her active public life which included six years as her husband's secretary when Congressman William Felton served in the House from 1875–81. Sedate, in a long black dress, Mrs. Felton sat in the back row, her sharp eyes never missing a trick. She seemed to enjoy her two days as a United States Senator thoroughly. Then Walter George took the oath of office that began his dedicated career in the Senate.

Even as one of the youngest Senators, Walter George always

Patriarchs Kenneth McKellar of Tennessee and Walter F. George of Georgia were Senate powers for over thirty years.—photo: UPI

The first woman senator, Rebecca Lattimore Felton of Georgia, was appointed in 1922.—photo: Underwood & Underwood

moved with proper Senatorial majesty like Oscar Underwood. In public and in private George retained his innate dignity. He was a tenant farmer's son who received the highest honors the Senate could bestow, including President Pro Tem, but none of it went to his head.

Senator George was a solid figure, both in body and mind, the essence of stability, strength, and sound judgment. He never rose to speak unless he had something important to say. Consequently the Chamber filled with Senators of various political persuasions, anxious to listen to his careful reasoning. George was one of those who weighed ideas as carefully as he weighed every phrase and emphasized every word. "Wurrrrrd" he would almost purr in the delicately soft accents of Georgia.

Whenever I approached him for the press, we went through the same dialogue. With a warm smile George said, "Do ya reeeeely think Iah ought to go, Rich-arrd? Iah haven't a thing wurth sayin' to him." "It will certainly help Joe, Senator," I answered, to which he slowly replied, "Well, Iah rec-kon so." Then he put his hands on the edge of his desk, pushed himself upward and with a sigh, always with a sigh, he moved in a courtly manner toward the President's Room. Joe Hall, AP's expert on finance, questioned the Senator at length and more often than not, Joe's story made the front pages of the nation's papers. Chairman George always had an abundance of news that was well "wurth sayin'."

Like Borah, issues rather than personalities dominated George's thinking. When Senator George joined those who fought against Franklin Roosevelt's court-packing plan, the President sought vainly to purge him in the next election. A lesser man would have been anti-Roosevelt from that moment on; but instead, George joined Majority Leader Barkley in leading the President's fight for Lend-Lease in 1941.

A noninterventionist at heart, Senator George was a realist who had accepted our international role by World War II and went on to make history as President Eisenhower's cooperative Chairman of Foreign Relations. The 1955 resolution authorizing troops,

if necessary, to defend Formosa passed overwhelmingly because
Chairman George gave it his full support. The President showed
his gratitude by appointing George his special ambassador to
NATO upon the Senator's retirement. Led by Vandenberg, Austin,
and George, the Senate achieved a bipartisanship in foreign policy
undreamed of in 1919.

   If modern legislation seems complex with intricate tax structures and precarious budgets, it is nothing to the shuddering agony
of living through an old tariff bill. Before the advent of reciprocal
trade agreements in 1934, Congress had to consider each item in
the tariff, one by one. It took thirteen months to pass the Ford-
ney-McCumber Act in 1921–22, while eight years later it required
an extra session to raise restrictions to a record high with the
Smoot-Hawley Act, the last of the big tariff bills. Cordell Hull's
reciprocal trade agreements meant that no more would the Senate
have to agonize item by item. No longer would we hear the voice
of Reading Clerk "Uncle" John Crockett rolling off a thousand
times the exact amount of ad valorum duty on each article. A
wearisome age was ended, and few mourned its passing.
   A tariff bill did have amusing sides. The back of the Chamber
took on the flavor of a church bazaar, complete with tables displaying every sort of item manufactured in the United States—
from rubber balls to bolts and nuts. The Senators acted the part of
dignified hucksters. They picked up an article made in their state,
describing at length its cost and economic virtues. A Senator might
be holding a large baby doll while he explained why the entire
economy depended on surrounding it with a protective tariff wall.
If he became too spirited and waved the doll around a bit, it might
come forth with a forlorn "Maaaaa-maaaaa" which would bring
down the house or in this case the Senate. When the day's session
was over, pages liked to shatter the silence of the Chamber by
seeing which doll cried the loudest. There were also cuckoo clocks
on display. It was a source of great regret to me that not one ever
struck the hour. Toward the end of the thirteen months' debate, a
sharp cuckoo or two would have been particularly appropriate.

The hero of the Smoot-Hawley Tariff was Reed Smoot of Utah, Chairman of the Finance Committee. Gravely serious, always working, he floor-managed the entire bill by personally overseeing action on each of the one thousand amendments. The highly respected Senator Smoot walked with the straight back of unbending propriety, befitting one of the Twelve Apostles of the Mormon Church. In debate he could become vigorous, even riled, but in daily conversation I found him to have a benign, soft-spoken way that was mildness itself.

Unwittingly, Senator Smoot provided the means for one of the best shows ever staged on the Floor. It began when Bronson Cutting, a Progressive Republican from New Mexico, took exception to the censorship that prohibited the importation of certain books on moral grounds. A dapper Easterner who had gone West for his health, Cutting was prim in his high collar and a precise Harvard accent. He ably presented the intellectual's view of literary censorship.

Senator Smoot with righteous indignation answered him by bringing on the Floor a stack of prohibited books so that Senators could see for themselves how much they needed the hand of the censor. Smoot did not foresee what a hilarious Pandora's box he was opening. Senators reacted by swarming to the Republican side of the aisle like birds to a feeding station. With a scowling, ponderous air a Senator lowered his chin and devoured one page after another, the next one more rapidly than the last. Sneaking a muffled laugh behind his hand to keep a semblance of dignity, he said "Oooooh!" or "Aaaaah!" or "How awful!" and read on with doubled enthusiasm. When a Senator denounced a book, several others rushed over to check his judgment. The more dreadful the book, the more legislators were waiting to read it. After a period of avid academic inquiry, Smoot won his point, while every other Senator enjoyed the day.

Congressional investigations are big news. The spotlight they turn on an area of national life can uncover corruption or focus attention on misgovernment, health hazards, and monopolies against the public good. They often lead to positive, corrective legislation.

Potentially all investigations are dynamite. No one knows at the beginning who will be affected: what party, what union, what business, what individual reputation. In the course of uncovering information, an investigation can destroy whatever it finds, so that it is extremely important that the spotlight be used judiciously.

Within the framework of the Senate rules, the chairman sets the climate for his investigation. More than any one factor, his personality determines how the spotlight will be used. One need look no further than the Government Operations Committee and its Permanent Investigations Subcommittee to find two classic examples of the power of a chairman to decide what will be investigated and how. John McClellan of Arkansas and Joseph McCarthy of Wisconsin have directed the same committee down different roads to totally divergent goals.

Senator Joseph R. McCarthy dramatically illustrated the power a committee chairman can hold; not only over the Senate, but also over the lives of individual citizens throughout the country. Within the Senate family Joseph McCarthy was the problem child of his decade, if not of the century. Others could be contained and perhaps babied along with little known about them outside the Senate; but McCarthy, basking in international notoriety, seemed for years to be the tail that wagged the dog.

When Joseph McCarthy entered the Senate from Wisconsin in 1947, replacing Young Bob LaFollette, an epoch in American politics automatically ended. For the first time in forty-one years a LaFollette did not sit in the Chamber. For a while McCarthy was known only as the man who had defeated LaFollette, but before he moved very far into his ten years in the Senate, he had blasted his own niche in history by adding a new "ism" to the country's vocabulary, "McCarthy-ism." It ignored some of our oldest legal traditions, reversing the concept that a man is innocent until proven guilty.

Any description of McCarthy, the man or his methods, cannot escape being politically subjective. Presumably McCarthy considered himself a crusader for the supreme cause of saving his country from communism; in his eyes he was fighting fire with fire. His most bitter antagonists charged that he was a self-serving witch hunter, while his most charitable critics termed him a misguided zealot. The fact remains that his actions affected the country's psychological health for many years.

The august Senate Chamber, which enveloped him with the shelter of Senatorial immunity guaranteed by the Constitution, became the major platform from which he staged his crusades. Later the televised hearings of McCarthy's Permanent Investigations Subcommittee of the Government Operations Committee magnified his entire performance into a national sideshow. Senator McCarthy took the Floor periodically to drop a much heralded explosive charge. Intoning with the abrasive quality of a duet rendered by a grindstone and a deep bass tuba, he spoke at the pace of a pile driver. Each blow was accented by a clenched fist with eyes glowering under his heavy eyebrows.

The Press Gallery would fill with newsmen, pencils in hand, waiting breathlessly for the bombshell to explode. The blast would come as he recited group after group of "known Communists." After this scattering of shrapnel, the mopping up operations would continue for months in a vain search for proof. McCarthy became the country's expert in creating smoke without fire. The real communists could lose themselves under his fireless smoke screen while confused citizens turned on each other, triggered by McCarthy's hate and smear tactics.

Senator Joe, as he liked to be called, had the kind of rough personality that gave rise to bombastic methods. He was a rugged man who had struggled to make his own way early in life. Stocky in build like the boxer he had been, McCarthy had a bull neck and a determined square jaw that seemed to be looking for trouble. He was always surrounded by a tense air of expectancy which made one wonder what was coming next. Like the central figure in a cloak-and-dagger drama, he would stride through the Lobby and into the Chamber looking as he must have when he climbed into the ring in earlier days. When he would cross the Chamber and go among the desks, McCarthy had a habit of grinning and tapping Senators on the shoulder as he passed. But other than among his close friends, the response was very cool, limited to a polite nod or a forced smile from his colleagues.

The Senator from Wisconsin was most certainly good copy for the Washington correspondents who got along well with him. They would josh and laugh together, typical of the newsmen who in their craft deal with everyone and must be able to acclimate themselves to every situation. As I would bring McCarthy out to see the correspondents or ask him questions, I found it hard to realize that he was one of the country's most controversial figures. He would give one's arm a little squeeze and flash a broad natural grin that seemed to be truly affable. The man who could charge mercilessly at his target as he led his committee into excess upon excess was also capable of cordiality.

In 1950, early in McCarthy's rampage, Margaret Chase Smith courageously spoke out against his tactics in her "Declaration of Conscience" in which she said, "As a United States Senator, I am not proud of the way in which the Senate has been made a publicity platform for irresponsible sensationalism . . . I am not proud of the way we smear outsiders from the Floor of the Senate and hide behind the cloak of Congressional immunity . . ." Senator Smith was joined by six Republican colleagues: George Aiken, Wayne Morse, Charles Tobey, Irving Ives, Edward Thye, and Robert C. Hendrickson. McCarthy contemptuously called the group, "Snow White and the Six Dwarfs."

For four years the Senator from Wisconsin continued to lash out in all directions. After attacking the State Department he feuded with Senators William Benton of Connecticut and Millard Tydings of Maryland, and ultimately he declared war on the Army. In maverick style he aimed as well at his own party. The Senate watched with growing apprehension, raising its respectable eyebrows at this offensive colleague who somehow belonged to them in name though not in spirit.

Finally in the summer of 1954 the festering issue came to a head. Senator Ralph W. Flanders of Vermont rose on the Floor to charge Chairman McCarthy with personal contempt of the United States Senate. When McCarthy turned his vilification on the committee appointed to investigate him, he felt the ranks close against him and the mighty prestige of the Senate brought to bear upon him alone. An extra session was called in November of that year specifically to consider the charges against him. McCarthy's was the fifth censure case in history to come before the Senate. Censure is an official reprimand far less serious than impeachment; it does not involve removal from office. The McCarthy resolution even used the term condemn rather than censure, but the effect was the same.

The censureship session wrote the end to the McCarthy era in the Senate and the nation. It seemed to deal him a mortal blow, depriving him of most of his power and influence. Like a ghost town after the mines had been worked out and only the saloon remained open, Senator McCarthy sat at his desk a piteous specter with a bloated face. The glower was gone and in its place there was a vacant look of one who had lost sight of the prey he could no longer stalk. In this inebriated state, with failing health his steps became ever slower until in 1957 he died of cirrhosis of the liver.

As though to challenge the Senate's verdict of censure, Mrs. McCarthy exercised the privilege that any Senator's family can claim, but few do, of requesting a state funeral. It left the Senate with no alternative but to honor in death the man they had reprimanded in life. As he lay in state in the Chamber, no charges or countercharges were heard, only the solemn pageantry of the funeral that drew the final curtain over the tumult of McCarthy's stormy career.

When John McClellan took over the Government Operations Committee from McCarthy in the 82nd Congress of 1955, there was a complete shift from the realm of melodramatic fiction to the solid, factual world of professional investigation. Chairman McClellan does not subject the Senate to rumor or throw names around as did McCarthy. He begins with facts carefully assembled and checked by his hardworking staff who stay well within the bounds of good legislative procedure. When John McClellan takes the Floor to report the findings of his committee, he may shout in the old style if sufficiently aroused, but he will present his case with well-documented thoroughness in the tradition of Thomas J. Walsh, Gerald P. Nye, Charles Tobey, and Estes Kefauver.

Senator McClellan began his investigative career as prosecuting attorney of his home county in Arkansas before coming to the Senate in 1943. Investigation is the field in which he excels and prosecutor is the role he knows best. Through the past decade he has demonstrated his ability to probe fairly and properly into crime and labor-business racketeering. When he believes a witness is telling the truth, McClellan's patience is enduring, but he can be as severe as an avenging angel when confronted with a disrespectful witness.

Against the sensational nature of investigations, Senator McClellan himself is staid. Hard-hitting but basically uncolorful, he absorbs little of the limelight in contrast to Senator McCarthy who played to the grandstands and gloried in the spotlight's strongest rays. In McClellan's hands the committee is the means of offering Congress and the public information about a problem and legislation to correct it. McCarthy never reached a constructive stage. He was mired by personal involvement in the pursuit of shadows. His downfall established the fact that a vulnerable investigator destroys himself.

Senator McClellan with his indominitable perseverance has restored the prestige of Senate investigations which were at an all-time low in the McCarthy days. The best tributes to his fairness have come from Republican minority members, led by Karl Mundt of South Dakota, who have said in effect, "If John McClellan is running the investigation, we'll agree to it. We know it will be a fair one!" Senator McClellan has proven, as many chairmen have, that under judicious direction a Congressional inquiry can embody a maximum of truth seeking and a minimum of sensation.

Any committee of Congress has an element of drama about it, but some excel in talent, interest, and dedication to a cause. Such was the old Public Lands Committee which was a "Western fraternity" within the Senate as fully as its successor the Interior Committee is today.

The young Chairman of Public Lands in the 1920's was North Dakota's new Progressive Gerald P. Nye, who found himself presiding over the committee after only two years in the Senate. He owed his unusual good fortune to several older Senators who became jittery and abandoned the committee in the days of its investigation by Thomas J. Walsh of Montana during the Teapot Dome scandals. The ones who remained were busy with the chairmanship of other committees, which gave the vigorous young Nye uncommon power for a freshman. With a characteristic concern for the job to be done, Senator Nye did not seek the credit but often let others introduce legislation that he favored, utilizing the talents and prestige of his senior Senators.

Nye's committee had more than its share of colorful figures whose backgrounds had led them to discover the West firsthand. Wyoming's John B. Kendrick had driven a herd of cattle from Texas to Wyoming Territory where he settled to become a cattleman, governor, and Senator. Henry F. Ashurst, the most polished and eloquent product of the old West to come to Washington, had been born on the frontier in Winnemucca, Nevada, and when six moved to Arizona with his parents in a covered wagon.

Either of Nevada's two Senators could have stepped out of a Western novel. Eastern-born Tasker L. Oddie had been graduated from New York University Law School and had gone West to prospect for gold and silver. His peaches-and-cream complexion and kindly eyes blinking rapidly behind pince-nez hid a rugged outdoorsman who had struck it rich in the Tonopah and Goldfield districts of Nevada. In 1925, Oddie became the only Senator ever to join the National Park Service as an unpaid, mounted ranger in Yellowstone Park during his summer vacation.

Oddie's equally rich colleague from Nevada Key Pittman was

tall and slender with a sharp Barrymore profile and the stern, cold manner of a Basil Rathbone character. A Mississippi aristocrat, young Pittman had been lured to Alaska by the gold of the Klondike. In the Senate his suave, knowing air made Senator Pittman a favorite of the Democrats who elected him President Pro Tem in the 1930's.

Peter Norbeck of South Dakota introduced himself as "Pee-tah Nooor-beck" in the Scandinavian accent of his parents who had immigrated to Dakota Territory before he was born. A deep-well driller by trade, Norbeck's compelling desire was to preserve the rare beauty of the South Dakota Badlands as well as the Grand Teton Mountains of Wyoming. But it was not to be a simple undertaking.

Typical of the complicated procedure behind most of the bills passed by Congress, the story of the Grand Tetons involved the cooperation of many people. The initial vision of the Grand Teton National Park came from a far-sighted Director of the National Park Service Horace M. Albright, son of California pioneers. He had been with the Service since its creation under Stephen Mather. Director Albright's vision, Senator Norbeck's initiative, and Chairman Nye's blessing were not enough to put it over. It was necessary to persuade another member of the committee to join them. John B. Kendrick favored the idea but hesitated to act in the face of local opposition. Peter Norbeck found a way to prod Kendrick into action by introducing a bill authorizing the Kendrick National Park in Wyoming. To further stir up the Wyoming Senator, Norbeck introduced another bill to include the Badlands in a Teton National Park in South Dakota. All of this legislative maneuvering was too much for John B. Kendrick, who knew that any park called Teton should be in Wyoming. Horace Albright remembers when Kendrick said to the committee, "I don't think a national park should be named for an old cattleman like me until he is dead —a long time dead."

Consequently, Senator Kendrick introduced his own bill to authorize the Grand Teton National Park. In the meantime the Rockefeller family quietly did its part by buying over a million dollars worth of land to add to the park. It took two decades of controversy to iron out local difficulties and to secure the magnificent park of today. The original Wyoming objective was attained when the bill passed both Houses of Congress and was signed by President Coolidge on February 26, 1929. The last day of the session Peter Norbeck's Badlands National Monument in South Dakota became a reality as well.

To Senators and the public alike, the National Park Service has been one of the most popular arms of the government, one in which taxpayers can see and enjoy the results of their tax money. The "watchdog of the Treasury," Harry Byrd, Sr., maintained that the Park Service was the only agency that returned $1.20 tor every dollar spent. Byrd was one of the firmest friends of the parκs from his days as governor of Virginia when he helped establish the Shenandoah National Park. His favorite recreation was hiking up the Park's Old Rag Mountain with good friends like Shenandoah's Superintendent R. Taylor Hoskins. At those times politics were not mentioned and Nature held the floor.

With greater urgency than ever, many battles have been waged in the 1960's to save what is left of the country's unspoiled beauties, as Frank Moss secured Canyonlands National Park, and with partial success Paul Douglas fought to save the Indiana Dunes and Tom Kuchel the Redwoods. Padre Island National Seashore was won by Ralph Yarborough with the support of Interior Committee Chairman "Scoop" Jackson. The preserving of every area that is administered by the National Park Service has been the result of someone's vision and the perseverance of many who have worked to save our natural heritage, as the Park Service's motto declares, "for the benefit and enjoyment of the people forever."

Senators flying around the world are a common sight today. Twenty-six years ago in the bleakness of total war, five Senators made history as the first committee to circumnavigate the globe by air. In a four-motored Liberator transport, then the latest model of prop plane, they logged 37,000 miles in two months of hazardous travel during August and September, 1943. It was certainly no junket but a practical mission to acquire firsthand an understanding of conditions on each of the major war fronts. As Chairman Richard Russell of Georgia put it, the trip was worth more than months of committee hearings. It was also the most dramatic Senatorial encounter with the war.

The Senate bade farewell to the five colleagues with a definite grimness, for the dangers of war magnified the risks considerably. Two Senators had already died in plane crashes during peacetime, Bronson Cutting in 1935 and Ernest Lundeen in 1940. To this day they remain the only ones, a remarkable fact considering that practically every day Senators are flying somewhere. But in 1943 it seemed entirely possible that we would never again see the five brave Senators: Chairman Russell, at forty-six one of the youngest members; James Mead of New York, an affable friend of government employees; Albert B. Chandler of Kentucky, always known as "Happy" because of his perpetual good nature and broad grin; Owen Brewster, the serious Senator from Maine; and the youngest of all, forty-one-year-old Henry Cabot Lodge, Jr. As a longtime Army Reservist, Lodge had seen combat the year before in Libya with a tank unit assigned to the British Eighth Army. He was singularly well equipped to make the trip, both as a Senator and an Army major on a first-name basis with the military. Within the year he resigned his Senate seat to go on combat duty in Europe, becoming the first Senator to leave for war since the 1860's.

When the first Congressional committee goes into outer space or explores the ocean floor, it will be comparable in drama to the mid-war, round-the-world adventure of these five. Their return was a joyous occasion. They emanated tremendous pride in our armed services, doubt on a few points of operating the war, but above all, profound relief at their safe arrival home.

At first Chairman Russell, in deference to wartime security, reported to a closed Executive session; but so many misleading comments were leaked to the press that he told his entire story over again to a full Senate with packed galleries. An immense globe about six feet in diameter was brought into the Chamber,

The first Senate committee to go around the world investigated war fronts in 1943. With a military escort in England are Senators "Happy" Albert B. Chandler of Kentucky (looking up), Richard Russell of Georgia (front center) and Henry Cabot Lodge, Jr., of Massachusetts (waving).—photo: U.S. Army

The fact-finding trip called for roughing it, as Senators Lodge and Russell found in the South Pacific.—photo: U.S. Army

which made Russell's report a fascinating geography lesson.

While he dwelt chiefly on war conditions for our soldiers overseas, Russell did not leave out traumatic moments such as crossing the awesome ice cap of Greenland. Like characters in a spy drama, the Senators had taken off at midnight from a gigantic airport in southwest England, bound for Marrakesh, North Africa. The most hazardous experience of all was the 3,200-mile crossing of the Indian Ocean from Ceylon to Australia with nothing below but shark-infested waters held by the Japanese. Theirs was the first landplane to succeed in crossing the vastness of the Indian Ocean. By no means a lark, the trip presented the most rugged conditions any Senators had ever endured while serving on a committee. They slept in everything from palaces to pup tents and ate with heads of state as well as GI's.

Henry Cabot Lodge in his report waxed eloquent about the scenery of the South Pacific, describing the beauty of islands rich in green vegetation, rising from white coral reefs and set in a brilliantly colored sea. His years as a working member of the press had trained Lodge to observe the human scene. He gave poignant descriptions of the wounded as well as several stories of individual heroism. In praising the armed forces, he cited one example of particular interest in view of recent history:

> "I think of Lt. Jack Kennedy, of Massachusetts, son of our former Ambassador to Great Britain, whose PT boat was cut in two by a destroyer, who drifted for eighteen hours on the hull and finally reached a small island. Every night that young man would swim out to the channel, and, supported by his life preserver, would signal with a flashlight all through the night to attract the attention of an American boat. He finally succeeded in doing so, and thus, by means of his brave conduct, the other members of his crew were rescued."

Congressional Record, 78th Congress, 1st Session, 1943, p. 7924.

Little did Lodge know that he was giving a boost to the man who would defeat him for his Senate seat nine years later and eventually reach the presidency of the United States.

Richard Russell went on to become Chairman of the entire Armed Services Committee for fifteen years, making a lifetime study of the legislative process in general and our defense structure in particular. So thoroughly does Russell personify the instrument of state that when he settles down with natural poise in his chair by the center aisle, he looks as though he is about to take quill pen in hand and ratify the Constitution. Now, the Senate dean, Senator Russell has filled many key positions in Congress, but none so colorful and exciting as his leadership of the first committee to go around the world.

The people of a state grant vast powers to a fellow citizen by electing him to the Senate. Those powers can be multiplied into dominance if the Senator has the aggressive bent of a Boies Penrose, a Kenneth McKellar, a Styles Bridges, or a Robert Kerr. That Senator Kerr was a self-made, oil multimillionaire made his thrust in the Senate all the more formidable. His wealth gave him a commanding confidence, while his intellect gave him an advantage that he never hesitated to use with effrontery. His huge skull narrowed into a gable that, far from limiting his mental capacity, was like a storage attic. Bob Kerr was impartial in his disdain for anyone who was not as brilliant as he. He would scowl and snort at Senators and newsmen alike with an impatient, "Why! Don't you know . . ." His brusqueness often cut to the heart of a problem, laying bare a solution in line with his interests.

The Senator from Oklahoma did not take time for the niceties of human relationships. Literally throwing his weight around, he would lunge into the Chamber like a football tackle. His shoulders were constantly shifting. With raised eyebrows he glared menacingly about him as if to detect anyone who might be in disagreement. When Senator Kerr came to see the press, he usually stopped short of the President's Room, preferring a quick interview in the anteroom where everyone could hear. Tall to begin with, the Senator would draw himself up and look down, literally and figuratively, on the newsman. There would be a rare condescending smile, but he usually glared over his glasses as he parried the questions shrewdly. Let a newsman question him unduly during an interview and Kerr would slam the back of his hand on a paper and thunder out an answer that could be heard down the hall.

Very few disagreed openly with the Senator from Oklahoma. Kerr was the heavy artillery of any debate in which he participated. When he roared out his withering sarcasm everyone in the line of fire quaked, everyone except John Pastore. Like David facing Goliath, the spirited little Senator from Rhode Island would stand his ground, bare his teeth, and make the towering bulk of Kerr shudder in frustration.

The first Senator of Italian descent, Pastore is a continually serious man with heavy eyebrows that go up and down in concert with his trim mustache. Off the Floor his manner is deliberate and calm, providing the leadership to the Joint Committee on Atomic Energy that secured the test ban and nuclear nonproliferation treaties. But when confronted with Bob Kerr's arrogance in debate, all of Pastore's fighting instincts would arise.

The two were on friendly terms most of the time, even working together to enact the Communications Satellite Act in 1962. Two years earlier, however, they had a memorable confrontation during the debate on a bill that would have placed community antenna systems under the Federal Communications Commission. The debate revealed more about the David and Goliath personalities of the two Senators than about the issues.

"Mr. Kerr: . . . I say to my good friend, who knows more, he thinks, than anybody else on earth, that if he will read a little, or find out a little, he will know more even than he now thinks he knows."

"Mr. Pastore: "Is the Senator through?"

"Mr. Kerr: "I do not know whether I am."

"Mr. Pastore: Will the Senator harken for a moment?

"Mr. Kerr: I do not know what that means.

"Mr. Pastore: It means to listen.

"Mr. Kerr: Yes.

"Mr. Pastore: When we listen, we learn.

"Mr. Kerr: I do not know about both of us . . . (adding later) . . . The Senator does not know what he is talking about.

"Mr. Pastore: The Senator said that yesterday. I do know what I am talking about. The difficulty with the Senator from Oklahoma is whenever he cannot run anyone into the ground he gets a little intemperate."

Congressional Record, 86th Congress, 2nd Session, 1960, pp. 10425 ff.

Senator Kerr apologized at one point and then they went at it again. Later that afternoon after holding Kerr at bay for two days, Pastore lost his battle by one vote, 38 to 39, and the bill was sent back to committee.

Senator Kerr was generous with his millions. In giving to charitable causes, he knew not only the power but also the satisfaction that comes from well-placed, unlimited funds. But Bob Kerr was not the type to hide his light under a bushel. His pride in being born in a fourteen-foot log cabin led him to erect one in the lobby of a Chicago hotel during the Democratic Convention of 1952. Kerr may well have been the last politician to be born in a cabin; these days a genuine log cabin is hard to find.

Loyal to many interests, Senator Kerr was the spokesman for the oil industry. He was also the big wheel of the billboard lobby and was able to neutralize every advertising restriction on the new interstate highway system. The Public Works Committee under Kerr's heavy hand killed Richard Neuberger's bill which would have prohibited all billboards on the new network. In a rough-and-tumble Floor fight over the 1958 Highway Bill, Senator Kerr was almost successful in his attempt to knock out even the meager incentive to states who voluntarily limited outdoor advertising. No other Senator in history has left as many monuments to his memory. Each of the 71,000 billboards strewn from coast to coast on the interstate highway system is a memorial to Robert Kerr.

The Senator lived hard by his own code. He was a giant

bulldozer who drove himself in high gear to a fatal heart attack in 1963. The power of a Senator in the hands of someone like Robert S. Kerr has few limits.

Progress at the Senate originates in cooperation between committee chairmen, Leaders, colleagues of the same party, and like-minded members of the opposite party; but one example of teamwork stands out above all the rest. Colorado's two Senators through the 1940's and into the 1950's outdid Senate tradition by cooperating with one another at every turn. While Senator Ed Johnson was a moderate Democrat and Senator Eugene Millikin a conservative Republican, the welfare of Colorado and the nation was the first consideration of both.

They went so far as to join forces with the four Congressmen from Colorado, two Republicans and two Democrats, in order to form a joint office to handle Colorado problems. Unique in Congressional history, the office continued for five years until Ed Johnson retired from the Senate in 1955. If one telephoned its administrator Ed Keating, who had been Johnson's administrative assistant before serving in World War II, he would answer in his careful, methodical manner, "This office represents Senators Millikin and Johnson and the Congressmen from Colorado." However the two Senators might differ in their votes on the Senate Floor, when it came to something for the good of Colorado, they went down the line together.

The Air Force Academy at Colorado Springs is one monument among several that proved the value of their teamwork. Every state in the union would have liked to capture such a prize. Colorado's legislators won it through five years of groundwork, combining the efforts of many people, including Governor Dan Thornton and the state legislature who saw to it that the site was purchased and donated to the federal government. During the Truman administration Senator Ed Johnson, as Chairman of the Commerce Committee, had an inside track. When Eisenhower became President and the Republicans took control of Congress, Finance Committee Chairman Millikin had easy access to the White House where the final choice of Colorado Springs was made in 1954. Members of the President's party have the advantage of advance information from the Executive, but neither Millikin or Johnson sought to outflank the other by releasing advance news. They worked as a team and Colorado was the winner.

These two who could put politics aside were rare men. Senator Millikin, a lawyer with a massive bald head that Barnie Nover of the *Denver Post* once called "the noblest dome in Washington," was one of the crack Floor debaters of all time. He looked and sounded like a bass viol. With the only voice deeper than that of Everett Dirksen, his resonant words would roll out effortlessly like the rich tones of a hi-fi speaker. During the tax bill debate of 1954 when the Democrats were predicting economic disaster, Millikin chided them for their pessimism with merriment in his eyes. In a resounding basso profundo he declared that what the country needed was not "dooooom and gloooom but zooooom and booooom!" Senator Millikin stands beside Walter F. George as one of the most brilliant chairmen of the Finance Committee.

Senator "Big Ed" Johnson had the reflective way of a grandfatherly rancher. His huge head with hair brushed straight back gave him a roughhewn bearing, but his pensive scowl meant only that he was thinking carefully, seeking to be fair. Never has the Senate known a more natural, gentle personality.

Senator Johnson's chairmanship of the Commerce Committee climaxed a grass-roots career in commerce, including eight years as a railroad worker, a try at homesteading, and a successful milling and produce business. He served as one of Colorado's most popular governors, both before coming to Washington and after he retired from the Senate. As a result, his knowledge of American life was basic and his common sense monumental. While Johnson believed in limited government like Burton K. Wheeler before him, he did use his chairmanship to protect the consumer public. He strengthened the regulatory agencies such as the Interstate Commerce Commission, all of which he treated as agents of Congress rather than as servants of the Executive. Johnson personified the spirit of the hardworking, no-nonsense homesteader with a simple but eloquent way of convincing those around him, while his agreeable colleague Millikin, by sheer brilliance, could out argue anyone. Together they were an unbeatable team for Colorado as well as the nation.

The chairmanship of a committee is a blank check to be filled out by the personality of the Senator who holds the job. Within limits, he commands as much power as he is inclined to exercise, and his committee usually accomplishes only what he considers important. His values and his *modus operandi* are the key to much that happens at the Senate.

J. William Fulbright, the dissenting scholar.—Photo: Muto Brothers

Carl Hayden, dean of Congressional deans—photo: Muto Brothers

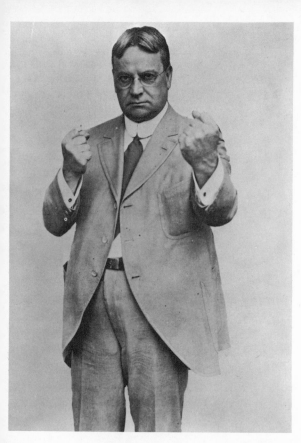

"And in this corner is" California's fighting Progressive, Senator Hiram Johnson.—photo: Underwood & Underwood

The Bob LaFollettes of Wisconsin, father and son, battled for Progressive reforms.—photo: Underwood & Underwood

MAVERICKS

The dissenting mavericks of the Senate have been those who could not be branded as party regulars, whose actions have not been predictable within the framework of either Democratic or Republican policies. They stand out with the bold relief of individual landmarks. As a group they have been among the most colorful and dramatic, the most articulate and unique of all Senators. By nature mavericks are aggressive, vigorous individuals who tenaciously hold to goals that may not be realized in their lifetimes, or ever. Ardently self-reliant, they usually savor their lonely journey as evidence of their "sole" fidelity to the truth. They have been the noncomforming personalities who have added to the United States Senate the free voice of dissent.

Contrary as it may have been to their natures, the mavericks of the early part of the century were organized under the Progressive label and even gained representation in the White House with Theodore Roosevelt. Most of these men were elected as nominal

245

Republicans, but this did not inhibit them. They were known as Insurgents in the Senate and were led, as far as any group of independents would submit to leadership, by an oratorical colossus from Wisconsin Robert M. LaFollette.

To a little page boy listening wide-eyed from the rostrum, the lone fighting figure of the senior Bob LaFollette loomed as a giant in every way but height. At such close range I was fascinated by his finger gestures and his voice that often trembled with fervor. As he took the Floor in debate, his eyes flashed with determination. He thrust his arms forward with the palms of his hands outstretched, all fingers working to and fro in a beckoning motion. Then as he reached a high point in an impassioned plea, he thrust both hands through his leonine pompadour in a crowning gesture of climax. LaFollette's voice, issuing from deep within his barrel chest, was always rich in emotion. His skillful blending of profound feeling with the reality of hard facts was that rare quality that made him an oratorical genius. His passionate pleadings so gripped me that I was filled with foreboding. He made it seem that if the Senate did not follow LaFollette, our country would soon near the end of the road.

Evidently Fighting Bob had the same electrifying effect wherever he went throughout the nation. In Wisconsin he established a political dynasty that endured for forty-one years. He was first Congressman, then Governor, and ultimately Senator for the rest of his life. His son "Young Bob" succeeded him as Senator and another son Phil was Governor of the state. A cousin Charles LaFollette served as a member of Congress from Indiana.

Throughout the country LaFollette's powerful lungs rang out as the leading voice of the people against the interests of special privilege. The LaFollette Seamen's Act of 1915 is the only law that bears his name, but it testifies to his persistent championship of labor. This dedication to social reforms for "the people" was the hallmark of the Progressive, the unifying force that held together such independent fighters as LaFollette, Hiram Johnson, George W. Norris, William E. Borah, Burton K. Wheeler, Gerald P. Nye, Smith W. Brookhart, and Clarence C. Dill.

Fighting Bob may have been one of our most flamboyant orators but his everyday demeanor was marked by a quiet courtesy. Life was serious business to him as it was to all the Progressives, but they did lunch together at a special table reserved for them in the Senators' private dining room. LaFollette was never part of the cloakroom camaraderie for, like most mavericks, he had neither the time nor the inclination for anything that might distract him from his crusading mission in life. The senior LaFollette was a self-contained visionary with his head in the clouds, leading the Spartan life of a solitary crusader.

I well recall this aging warrior's last battle when he ran for President in 1924 on the Progressive ticket. Together with his vigorous young running mate Burton K. Wheeler, another born maverick who happened to be a Democrat, LaFollette challenged the regular party candidates Calvin Coolidge and John W. Davis. Publicity for the campaign was managed by a young newsman Ernest Gruening, who went on to become Governor of Alaska and to serve as one of its first Senators. The almost five million ballots cast for the Progressives was an impressive sixteen percent of the vote, and it became the nation's farewell tribute to Bob LaFollette, Sr., who died the following year. In 1959 his place in history was recognized when Senator John Kennedy's committee chose him as one of the "Five Greats" whose likenesses now adorn the walls of the Senate Reception Room.

To recapture the fighting spirit of Bob LaFollette, one can visit the old House Chamber that is known as Statuary Hall. There among a circle of other stone figures he is seated in his Senate chair, leaning forward with his hands on the armrests, looking exactly as I have seen him many times. The sculpture portrays lips that are about to move, eyes that have an uncanny intensity, and arms that are poised to raise him from the chair. So vivid is this work of art that in the softly lighted Statuary Hall it is not difficult to imagine Senator LaFollette leaping from his chair into the Well of the Senate to begin a new crusade.

The son of a famous man should not have to rise or fall upon comparison with his father. Young Bob LaFollette taken on his own was a remarkably vital person, always more youthful than his years. He was completely at home in the Senate, having grown up in Washington during his father's tumultuous career. When poor health forced him to leave college, Young Bob became clerk of the Manufactures Committee. We observed the Senate sessions from the side of the Chamber while he commented to me on the scene before us, "The Senate needs to be better organized—too many committees and not enough clerks. We need a little less tradition and a lot more efficiency!"

When his father died in 1925, Young Bob was immediately elected to take his place, beginning the second stage in the four decades of the LaFollette era. For a while the differences between son and father were painfully evident. Though a sharp debater, Bob, Jr., was a rapid, mechanical speaker whose monotonously light voice and jerky motions left no doubt that he would never be an orator. Nevertheless he successfully maintained the Progressive link with the LaFollette name, working with his father's old colleagues—Borah, Norris, Nye, Hiram Johnson, and the rest.

Following the 1924 Progressive Party platform, Young Bob stayed in the vanguard by advocating public ownership of power, rails, and banks. In the 1930's this still put him left of the New Deal, a distinction he carefully maintained. To be worthy of his support, an idea had to originate with the LaFollettes.

His accomplishments in behalf of Labor would have pleased his father for the LaFollette-Wagner Labor Relations Act gave unions the cutting edge that management had always held. Young Bob's own specialty of parliamentary procedure led to the effective LaFollette-Monroney Reorganization of Congress of 1946, enacting into law the ideas he had shared with me a generation before.

Though he always sat on the Republican side, he was twice elected as a Progressive. His political undoing came in 1946 when he tried to return to the Republican label and lost the primary and thereby his Senate seat to Joseph McCarthy. Defeat was not the LaFollette way. Six years later he left his office in the National Press Building, where he had been an economic-research consultant, went home and shot himself. He was in his fifties at the time, but to most Senators and to me, he was and always would be "Young" Bob LaFollette.

One of the fiercely independent Senators of all time, Hiram Johnson of California was a founder of the Progressive Party. He ran with Teddy Roosevelt on the Bull Moose ticket in 1912. His gray hair meticulously parted in the middle and his stocky frame gave him the deceptive appearance of a placid Pooh bear. But the real Hiram Johnson sprang into debate like the original California bear in action, verbally ripping to shreds everyone in his path.

Typical of Progressives', Johnson's ideas were a mixture of conservatism abroad and liberalism at home. Fighting for Boulder Dam, now known as Hoover Dam, was one of his major projects. In foreign affairs Hiram Johnson was like a machine-gun implacement on the Senate Floor. Admant for nonintervention, he rose to shoot down any proposal that would involve us with other countries, be it the League of Nations or the World Court. In an unrelenting blast of his staccato delivery, the pitch of his voice never varied and he seemingly paused for breath only once an hour. Johnson's entire fusillade fascinated me, as his fists never stopped, sparks seemed to fly from his eyes, and his face contorted with snarls and growls. Though Hiram Johnson joined solidly with Senator Borah in blocking foreign alliances, Borah argued on principles while the fiery Johnson would have gladly consumed his opponents along with the issues in question. Yet even in his most vehement oratory, he maintained Senatorial dignity.

The fire-eater from California came within one word of being President of the United States. If he had said yes when the Republican Party offered him the vice presidential nomination in 1920, he would have become Chief Executive upon President Harding's death two years later. Instead of keeping cool with Coolidge, we might have been fighting fire with Hiram. He would have been another Teddy Roosevelt who could have stirred the nation into booming reforms that might have left no need for the New Deal. He would not have vetoed progressive measures like TVA and the McNary-Haugen Farm Bill as Coolidge did. But Hiram Johnson could no more go along with the conservative Harding or accept the apparently dead-end shelf of the vice presidency than he could agree to join the cabinet of Franklin Roosevelt in the 1930's. Fighting was his very life and he wanted to be in the thick of action on the Senate Floor.

At first I looked upon the combustible Hiram Johnson as someone to be handled discreetly with asbestos gloves. When the Roosevelt landslide made drastic changes in Senate personnel, Johnson found fewer and fewer staff members whom he knew. I became a valued old-timer at the age of twenty-four and he completely mellowed toward me, becoming one of my special friends. In 1940 I asked him to be the first to pose for my new movie camera. At first he refused to budge from his seat, thinking that as usual I had asked him to come out for the news photographers. When he understood what I wanted, Senator Johnson replied instantly, "Oh, the pictures are for *you,* Richard! I'll be able to come in five minutes."

Hiram Johnson awed anyone who did not know him, so that it was with some trepidation that Harry Frantz, chief of UPI's Latin American desk, first asked to interview him. The Senator beamed, however, when Harry reminded him that one summer at Lake Tahoe he had set pins for a first-rate bowler named Hiram Johnson. On such a casual basis lifetime friendships can begin.

Hiram Johnson's stroke mellowed him even more in his latter days, but it also banked his old fire. He would get up to speak in his stinging staccato, "Mis-teh—Pres-i-dent-," but after a few minutes of hitting his old stride with his fist hammering away, Johnson's eyes would become glassy and he would have to hesitate and his thoughts would come out slowly and painfully. His deskmate and pal through the years, Senator McNary would tense up in sympathy for his stricken colleague but was powerless to help him.

In 1945, Hiram Johnson's final illness took him to the Bethesda Naval Hospital from which the immovable old warrior sent word that if he could, he would return to cast his last vote against the United Nations Charter.

While many could disagree with Hiram Johnson's policies, particularly his lifelong antagonism for the Japanese, none could fail to admire his courage and his independence. Senator Johnson meant it when he once referred to his friendly but peppery little wife in his best Scottish twang, "Ya know, Mrs. Johnson is the only bahss [boss] I have!"

One of the freest men in American politics of this century has been Burton K. Wheeler of Montana. His disregard of party rules is legendary. Though a freshman Democratic Senator, he ran on the Progressive ticket with Bob LaFollette, Sr., in 1924. Within a few years Wheeler became an early booster of Franklin Roosevelt, yet he courageously broke with the powerful President to lead the opposition to the Supreme Court packing plan. In defiance of all political sanity Wheeler staked his career on the court fight and dealt Roosevelt his major defeat in Congress. Each of Wheeler's deliberate and independent stands netted him some enemies, but his self-reliance and perspective were such that he always managed to come out on top.

In 1923 the young upstart from Montana paced onto the Senate Floor, unawed by his surroundings, and proceeded to rock the Senate to its organizational roots by objecting to the proposed nomination of Albert B. Cummins of Iowa as Chairman of the Interstate Commerce Committee. He considered Cummins partial to the powerful rail interests. At first I found it unthinkable that anyone would upset the carefully packed applecart of the leadership and tie up the Senate for thirty long days. But the young Senator who tore into the Establishment was a needed breath of fresh air. To the helpless embarrassment of party leaders, Wheeler stopped the Cummins nomination, incidentally establishing himself as a force to be reckoned with.

Senator Wheeler's tall figure strode around the Chamber with the bold intensity of a man who knew exactly where he was going. With a sharp profile and watchful eye, he was like an eagle with wide-angle vision, always ready to dig in his talons where needed. There was no question that the Senator from Montana enjoyed blood. A born fighter with the shrewdness of a predatory animal, Wheeler, like Wayne Morse, was happiest in the thick of battle. In the same spirit with which his Montana colleague Thomas J. Walsh was uncovering the Teapot Dome scandals, Wheeler turned the spotlight on Attorney General Harry M. Daughtery and his banker brother Mal. Rather than face the charges of corruption, Daughtery resigned.

Burton K. Wheeler was always a headline-maker, but it took me many years to understand that he was not first of all a headline seeker. He had none of the Don Quixote about him, but chose his issues soundly, learned his facts thoroughly, and moved with cunning strategy. In this way Burt Wheeler reached his greatest height as leader of those Senators who opposed the Supreme Court packing. After pulling a coup by producing a letter from Chief Justice Charles Evans Hughes which opposed President Roosevelt's plan, Wheeler followed through in his hard-hitting style:

"I say the step proposed is one of the most dangerous ever suggested, and it will set the most dangerous precedent of which I can conceive. You can bring political pressure to bear upon me; you can say . . . that my privilege of appointing postmasters will not be accorded me; you can say that I will get no more projects for my State, worthy or unworthy; you can say what you please but . . . so far as I am concerned, I will vote against this proposal because it is morally wrong, morally unsound. It is a dangerous precedent; it is not liberal; it is reactionary; it gets us nowhere; it is an expedient; it is a stopgap and dictatorial, and, so far as I am concerned, if I am the only man in the Senate to do so, I shall vote against it."

Congressional Record, 75th Congress, 1st Session, 1937, p. 2823.

Senator Wheeler called everything as he saw it, mincing no words, and the press admired him accordingly. He met correspondents matter-of-factly, cigar in hand, and spoke between bared teeth, often wearing a satisfied grin that resembled Wayne Morse's perpetual look of the cat that had swallowed the canary. Among others, Chesly Manly of the *Chicago Tribune* listened to him eagerly, wanting to know, "What scrap have you got to tell us about now?"

Wheeler's twenty-three years' experience in the Senate tempered but never mellowed him. Typical of independent thinkers, Burt Wheeler kept his distance from back-room amiability. Once he told me, "You have to watch out for the boys in the cloakroom or first thing you know, you'll be taken in!" To my knowledge the unaffected Senator Wheeler was never taken in by anyone, including himself. He had none of the Congressional trappings of stuffy self-importance that are sometimes evident on Capitol Hill.

Wheeler's amazing effectiveness has come from his concentration on issues rather than on personalities. He has never made his maverick role an end in itself as Huey Long and Bill Langer did. If he could be an agitator when he felt the occasion demanded it, Senator Wheeler could also slave behind the scenes where no glory awaits. As Chairman of the Interstate Commerce Committee, he produced, among many pieces of legislation, the Food and Drug Act of 1938 and the intricate Transportation Act of 1940 in the spirit of a good Senate workhorse.

President Roosevelt paid him the supreme compliment of wanting him as a running mate for his third term despite their serious disagreements. But Wheeler refused in his most resolute stand of all. He could not compromise his strong antiwar views to support Roosevelt's sympathies for the Allies. Had he done so and later gone along with the fourth term, Burton K. Wheeler would have succeeded Roosevelt as President of the United States.

I once heard Wheeler's eloquent friend and classmate at the University of Michigan Senator Henry F. Ashurst sum up political freedom in the neat admonition, "Never dissolve the pearl of independence in the vinegar of obligation!" Burton K. Wheeler was an effective maverick who succeeded in pulling the Senate along with him, and always he lived by the code of the free man.

The one maverick who did not seem to relish the constant battle that an independent stand requires was George W. Norris of Nebraska. In his wistful way Norris would have preferred to live in harmony with everyone. Instead he chose the rugged path of the realist, struggling against formidable odds throughout his long career to see many of his ideas become law.

Everything about Norris was conservative except his political philosophy. He had the modest appearance of an old-fashioned country doctor, from his kindly expression to his plain, black bow ties. His way with the press was direct but easygoing and peaceable, accentuated by the dreamy look in his eyes.

Senator Norris' voice was neither heavy nor sharp, but he was a lively combatant in debate. Almost daily he would rise on the Floor to take the offensive against what he termed "the spider web of Wall Street," the innumerable interlocking directorates and industrial monopolies. Like all Progressives, he cast a suspicious eye on big business and put his trust in government as the protector of the people.

Norris, like Wheeler, chose his issues carefully and never let go until he had won a decisive victory. His Lame Duck Amendment to the Constitution took over ten years and six Congresses, but eventually he reduced to two months the interval between the November election and the inauguration of the President and convening of Congress.

Senator Norris fought a seven-year battle for the development of the resources of the Tennessee Valley, a part of the country in which he had no constituents. As I would pass his desk, the solitary Norris would be verbally traveling up and down the Tennessee River, now pausing at Muscle Shoals, now shooting it out with the Alabama Power Company, while Lister Hill was leading the fight in the House. After a succession of defeats, it all seemed

Senator Burton K. Wheeler, Montana maverick, called the shots as he saw them.—photo: Herbert French Collection, Library of Congress

Nebraska's Senator George W. Norris was a "peaceful" loner, the father of the Tennessee Valley Authority.—photo: Herbert French Collection, Library of Congress

William E. Borah of Idaho joined Majority Leader Henry Cabot Lodge, Sr., of Massachusetts, to defeat the League of Nations.—photo: Herbert French Collection, Library of Congress

destined to remain Norris' most cherished dream until President
Roosevelt waved the magic wand of the New Deal and the TVA
blossomed forth in the valley of the Tennessee. When I have
toured the colossal power system including Norris Dam, it recalls
those long afternoons at the Senate and the mild maverick from
Nebraska who never lost sight of his goals.

Along with other Progressives, Norris declared that party
labels are meaningless and party loyalty too often compromises a
man's conscience and his common sense. In his forty years in
Congress, George Norris evolved from a loyal young Republican
to a disillusioned independent Republican to an outright Independent, a label which enabled conservative Republican Kenneth
Wherry to defeat him in 1942.

While Progressives like Hiram Johnson and Young Bob La-
Follette backed Roosevelt to varying degrees, George Norris became an ardent disciple of FDR. After waging continuous war on
other administrations, Norris finally found in Roosevelt a President
who shared and implemented his own social philosophies. The
peace-loving independent was no longer an outsider, and he fell
victim to his own warnings about loyalty. The Nebraskan had
filibustered vigorously with the senior Bob LaFollette against our
entry into World War I, but Norris could not bring himself to join
the Progressives in opposing World War II before Pearl Harbor. It
would have meant deserting Roosevelt.

George Norris was unquestionably an earnest American,
thoroughly dedicated to solving problems, but he had one notable
blind spot. While no communist himself, Norris gave the Soviet
communists credit for an equally selfless dedication to the better-
ment of the Russian people. Somehow the great liberal chose to
ignore Stalin's ruthless blood purges. Sharp-faced Laurence Todd,
an American who represented the Telegraph Agency of the USSR,
came daily to interview Norris. While waiting for the Senator,
Todd lectured me, "You are a young man surrounded by reactionaries here, but some day you will see the light. Follow Senator
Norris. He points the way to the future!" Norris was definitely
taken in by his failure to comprehend the "state religion" of

atheism, the tyrannical control, and total imperialism that are the heart of the communist movement. But none of that cancels out the lifetime of combat that George Norris waged in order that others might live a better life.

No independent in the Progressive mold fought a more strenuous battle to keep the United States out of World War II than Gerald P. Nye of North Dakota. He was a product of LaFollette's Wisconsin where his father had given "Fighting Bob" the full support of his newspaper. As editor of his own small-town papers in Wisconsin, Iowa, and North Dakota, Nye learned firsthand the debilitating effect of the aftermath of World War I on the farmers of the Midwest. When the tall young newspaperman was appointed to the Senate in 1925 by the Governor of North Dakota, he came with a natural prejudice in favor of farmers and against foreign involvements, two tendencies which made him a readymade Progressive from the start.

Senator Nye caught the fighting spirit of men who had been the heroes of his youth and now became his mentors: Johnson, Borah, and Norris. I could tell that Hiram Johnson liked Nye immediately. He set about making the young man from the plains feel at home among the formidable legal and oratorical minds of the day. When Gerald Nye rose to give his maiden speech in opposition to our participation in the World Court, he looked around to find Hiram Johnson sitting beside him. "Go ahead, Boy," the stocky Californian said. "Don't let anyone stop you. I'll back you up if they do." Strengthened by that kind of support, the young Senator did a creditable job, secured his Senate seat at the next election and held it for twenty years.

Gerald Nye's springy step and firmly set jaw gave him the outward air of a fighter, but he tempered it always with an underlying, rawboned charm. Senators appreciated his deferential fairness that put the job to be done ahead of personal advantage. Newspapermen liked his candor, and Senatorial campaign investigations kept Nye in the center of activity for years and much in demand by the press.

The investigation that carried Gerald Nye to the high point of his career and placed him beside John McClellan among the foremost Senate investigators was his penetrating examination of the munitions industry in the 1930's during the New Deal Democratic majority. It began with Senators Borah and Nye reading into the *Record* an article from *Fortune* of March, 1934, entitled "Arms and the Men." Nye's carefully worded resolution calling for an investigation passed only upon threat of a filibuster. The resulting special committee paid an unprecedented tribute to the nominal Republican and independent by electing Nye chairman, one of the few times in Senate history that a minority member has chaired an important committee.

Gerald Nye's presentation of his committee's findings about the sordid background of World War I stands as one of the landmarks of the era. Though not a lawyer, Senator Nye gave one of the best documented cases I have heard brought before the Senate. Complete with dates and amounts of profits derived from both sides of a conflict, it was a story that rocked the nation. Nye's amassed facts converted public opinion to his conviction that the manufacturers of munitions conspired to promote conflict in general and World War I in particular. When the Neutrality Act of 1936 resulted, it seemed for a time that Nye and the Progressives might be able to keep the country on a hemispheric road and avoid involvement in the hates and fears of Europe. But their neutral road was suddenly bombed out of existence at Pearl Harbor.

On December 26, 1941, two weeks after the Japanese attack, a sturdy figure mounted the rostrum to address a grim and shaken Congress at a joint meeting in the Senate Chamber. The essence of John Bull himself, Winston Churchill came directly from the battle of Britain to give us the kind of shot in the arm that he had given his own people. The Prime Minister set a jovial mood of Anglo-American solidarity that had every member laughing from the start:

". . . I cannot help reflecting that if my father had been

American and my mother British, instead of the other way
around, I might have got here on my own."
Churchill's spirited eloquence gave a strength and purpose in the
midst of the crisis that was reflected in the face of every Senator.

"Sure I am that this day, now, we are the masters of our
fate; that the task which has been set for us is not above our
strength, and that its pangs and toils are not beyond our endurance. As long as we have faith in our cause and unconquerable
will power, salvation will not be denied us . . ."
The Prime Minister could not resist a historical might-have-been:

"Five or six years ago it would have been easy, without
shedding a drop of blood, for the United States and Great
Britain to have insisted on fulfillment of the disarmament
clauses of the treaties which Germany signed after the Great
War. That also would have been the opportunity for assuring to
Germans those raw materials which we declared in the Atlantic
Charter should not be denied to any nation, victor or van-
quished."
Congressional Record, 77th Congress, 1st Session, 1941, p. 10017–18.

It was as though years of history were telescoped into that
one moment. Like a giant mural spread before us were the past
debates on neutrality, munitions, the injustices of the Versailles
Treaty, and the warnings of Borah, Johnson, and Nye that had
echoed through the Chamber. Now that world had ended forever.

During the thunderous applause after his speech, I remembered the quiet day in the 1920's when a newsman identified a man
walking past us down a gallery corridor. "That's Winston Churchill
going there. Ever hear of him? He's the British Chancellor of the
Exchequer." From being a routine visitor, Churchill had become
the embodiment of Allied ideals.

As members came down to the Well to shake hands with the
Prime Minister, Senators Wheeler and Nye happened to be introduced to him at the same time. On hearing the names of America's
top isolationists, Churchill gave instant recognition. His eyes twin-

kled as he shook hands with them. He knew that, like it or not, everyone had to share the same boat now. Senator Nye later expressed his admiration for the British Prime Minister with the lament, "If we only had a leader who would look after our country's interests in the way that Churchill looks after Britain's!"

In retirement, Gerald P. Nye and Burton K. Wheeler are the remaining Progressives. While still consistent noninterventionists in foreign affairs, on domestic issues they find themselves out of tune with modern liberals. The independent mavericks of yesterday have become the conservatives of the political scene. Have they changed or has the country changed?

Basically, Progressives and modern liberals have shared one central goal through the years, to better the lot of ordinary people. Each has had a different emphasis. In the heyday of progressivism the greater part of the population lived on the farm where rural problems were foremost. Today the swelling city population has shifted the liberal focus to a set of urban problems. Progressives emphasized the regulatory powers of government rather than federal aid. They were concerned with fiscal responsibility in a fundamental way which rarely troubles modern liberals. Today when faced with a constitutional conflict between meeting human needs and the rights of states and individuals, liberals give first priority to solving the human need. Progressives like Wheeler and Nye revered the Constitution too much to tangle with its balance of powers, which led them into the fierce battle to prevent the packing of the Supreme Court. They were independents in the minority then; they find themselves in a conservative minority now. The political scene has changed.

The only wealthy maverick was multimillionaire James Couzens of Michigan, who made his fortune by organizing the Ford Motor Company as the partner of Henry Ford. When the precise and immaculately trim Couzens walked into the Senate in 1922, he looked like a Wall Street banker who could be expected to settle back in his Senate seat and preserve the status quo. But everything about James Couzens seemed to be at odds with the complacency of the 1920's. With his naturally antagonistic temperament, the rosy-cheeked Senator alienated almost every colleague. His moods alternated between fiery and more fiery, so that he was often touchy and irritated from a Floor fight.

Senator Couzens had a regard for little people and a skepticism of other rich men that must have harked back to his early days as a railroad-car checker. He never forgot what it was like to work hard for small wages, and he could not tolerate poverty. Couzens may well have been the most generous man to serve in the Senate, for his charities for the health of the children of Michigan went into the millions.

When he attacked the economic policies of the Coolidge and Hoover administrations, Couzens sounded like a Progressive, but he went farther than most to advocate government spending for relief as the depression deepened. Senator Couzens was in the vanguard of social thinking, originating the idea of youth camps which the Roosevelt administration later incorporated into the Civilian Conservation Corps. Even more than George Norris, Couzens became a Roosevelt supporter of the most ardent kind. He refused to become a Democrat, however, because he wanted to remain an outsider, free to criticize.

His outspoken criticism of his own Republican party made him excellent copy for the press. Jay Hayden of the *Detroit News* would meet the Senator daily in the President's Room and emerge with a fresh viewpoint on the problems uppermost in Couzens' active and independent mind. Prickly but fair, critical but constructive, Senator James Couzens walked a lonely road, isolated by a social conscience that would give him no peace as long as he saw people in need.

One maverick stood so uniquely alone as to defy all political traditions. Huey Long was a phenomenon, the equal of which has never been known, either in or out of the United States Senate. Like a character out of a lusty novel, the Senator from Louisiana could outbluster and outcuss the loudest of them, but he could also out think his opponents with lightning speed and with an occasional eloquence that few could match.

When Huey Long came to the Senate in 1932, his was no ordinary arrival. Long's unorthodox victories in Louisiana had held the nation wide-eyed during his four controversial years as governor. Was he the dangerous dictator that his bitter and vanquished enemies in the political and business worlds decried? Or was he an honest though unpolished strongman who was out to right the wrongs of our society? Other autocrats had built their showcases, from Augustus' Rome to Hitler's autobahns. But in our country none could rival Huey Long's rural roads that lifted the bayou people out of the mud for the first time in history, or his free bridges built of the finest material at the lowest cost. The towering state Capitol, where he was destined to be assassinated, stands as a monument to him, but Huey Long was most proud of the free school books he secured for public school children and Louisiana State University at Baton Rouge. Without race hatred, blood purges, or proven corruption, Long had brought these things about at the incredible pace that only autocracy allows. Years before he reached Washington, the Senate had heard trumpets both of praise and alarm for Huey Long. He was a national sensation.

Everyone wondered what effect he would have on the Senate. Would Washington mold him, as it had done so many others, or would he be the one to change the Senate? The suspense continued for ten months during which Huey Long delayed taking his Senate seat, remaining in Louisiana to complete his program as governor as the senior LaFollette had done in Wisconsin in 1906. I never doubted that the Louisianan would make a fascinating addition to the Senate, but only after he became a member did it become apparent how completely he was a law unto himself.

A new Senator usually enters with a modest hesitation as to where he should sit and what he should do when he is introduced and takes the oath of office. Huey Long strode in arrogantly as though he owned the Chamber. His every air said, "Move over, boys. The Kingfish is here!" He would burst in upon Senators he had never met before, introduce himself loudly, and call them by their first names, ruffling decorum right and left. The elders of the family, who were not about to move over, gave him a chilly reception. Hot-tempered Carter Glass tried to wither him with one consuming look after another, but Huey Long could not be withered. With an ego that made all others pale into insignificance, he seemed not to care what his fellow Senators thought of him.

Driven by the superhuman energies that propel all mavericks, Huey Long did everything fast with the gusto of the natural showman. He never stood still but bounced around, tossing his head as his son Russell does in the Senate today. While waving and shouting in quick, jumbled words, Long rushed at his opponent or slapped the open book on the desk before him wherein lay the facts. Many speakers who flail the air do so to cover up a lack of knowledge, but not Huey Long. He believed that high-volume bombast and buffoonery were essential to a good show and a lively performance. The galleries responded with appreciative laughter to the dismay of the presiding officer who would sharply demand order, reminding the visitors that the rules forbid a demonstration of any kind.

Huey would shout, "We want these people fed! We want these people clothed! We want homes for these people—and they won't even trade us the devil for a witch!" But he could also be eloquent. Words from a Senate speech became his epitaph carved on the statue at his grave in the Capitol grounds at Baton Rouge:

"I know the hearts of the people because I have not colored my own. I know when I am right in my own conscience. I know one language. Its simplicity gains pardon for my lack of letters. Fear will not change it. Persecution will not change it. It cannot be changed while people suffer."

In spite of the barriers his backwoods' vocabulary and bluster created for him, Long had a brilliant mind that a Harvard man might have envied. (He mastered Tulane University's three-year law course in eight months.) His phenomenal grasp of facts and his shrewd interpretations made him a deadly adversary. I cannot remember any Senator who got the better of Huey Long in a debate. He could quote statutes from memory, tossing them off in loose-jointed banter. Or he would snap for a page in the midst of a debate and send him for a volume from the Senate Library. When the page rushed in with the book, Long would flip instantly to the legal precedent he wanted and begin to quote it without a second's pause. It was impossible to top his legal arguments presented with such showmanship.

No one since the senior LaFollette had been more adept at the filibuster than Huey Long with his craving for notoriety plus his physical stamina and extraordinary mind. Before an all-night speech that lasted sixteen hours, the Senator from Louisiana confided in me that he suspected foul play in the cloakroom. He said that on previous occasions his drinking water had been doctored with a laxative. After Senator Long told me that I was the only person there whom he could trust not to slip anything in it, I agreed to keep him supplied with water throughout the night. Anything to protect the right of free speech in the Senate!

Roman holidays are missing from today's more serious Senate, but Huey Long created a spectacle almost every day. The Louisianan's favorite targets were two formidable colleagues from neighboring states, caustic Pat Harrison of Mississippi and Democratic Leader Joseph T. Robinson of Arkansas. Other Senators let them follow their abrasive ways unchallenged, but Huey Long baited and cornered them like snarling lions. While Robinson's face paled and flushed with rage, Long gleefully refuted his arguments and finished him off with dire predictions as to the Leader's dim future in Arkansas. Hot-tempered at best, the frustrated Robinson stood fuming with clenched fists. I half expected to see the Leader knock Long flat on the Floor of the Senate the way he had struck a prominent surgeon on the golf course of the Chevy Chase Club.

In the face of such militant disregard of the Senate's elder statesmen, it was not surprising that Huey Long never won great support for his legislative proposals. He did have friends among the independents, however, notably Senators Norris and Wheeler who admired his basic honesty and directness. Passionately eager to solve the social dilemmas of the depression, Long developed his "Share the Wealth" plan which would have limited annual personal income to one million dollars and inherited fortunes to five million. The government would spread the remainder among the impoverished by providing work projects. The simplicity and straightforwardness of Long's proposals were met with horror by moneyed interests who branded Long a rampant demogogue. Intellectuals scourned his evangelical fervor and rough manners, but the voters listened to a man who seemed to care about their needs.

Huey Long's growing national influence was proven in 1933 when he stumped Arkansas and almost single-handedly won the election for Mrs. Hattie Carraway. The soft-spoken, motherly widow had taken her husband's seat, as Huey Long's own wife would do after his assassination. But no one expected Mrs. Carraway to run in the next election, least of all her colleague Joe Robinson who declined to help her. Thanks to Huey Long, Senator Carraway became the first woman to be elected, not merely appointed, to the Senate. I never knew how much of Long's support was to help a lady in need and how much was to beat out Robinson on his home ground, but Long won on both counts.

Though originally a key Roosevelt supporter, Long soon broke with the new President, charging that the New Deal did not go far enough. In the Senate Huey Long was outvoted, but throughout the country, the Kingfish was rapidly becoming the only man who stood the slightest chance of successfully challenging Roosevelt for the presidency.

Long put the finishing touches on his invincibility by a most amazing feat. Without a tapering-off period, he stopped drinking and smoking in a single day. Abstinence did not quiet Huey down any, but it kept his mind clear at all times.

However, in September, 1935, after Congress had adjourned, Huey Long was assassinated as he walked through the Louisiana State Capitol building, despite his ever present bodyguards. At least one major radio network remained on the air for two twenty-four-hour periods to give bulletins from his bedside. Huey Long's secretary Earl Christenberry, who was with him at the last, told me that Long's dying words were, "What will my poor University boys do now?" Huey Long died as sensationally as he had lived. His three and a half years in the Senate were so dynamic that they added up to more activity than most persons' entire lifetime.

No public figure has had a more antagonistic press than Huey Long. While his relationships with newsmen were generally calm, I have watched him turn on correspondents whom he considered spokesmen of the enemy camp of big business. He would shout angrily while glaring at them and waving his hands.

At other times when the President's Room was empty, I saw a different side of Huey Long that the press did not see. In a moment of quiet tenderness his bombastic outer shell disappeared and Huey Long, the father, sat down with me and talked gently about his family in subdued, relaxed, and affectionate tones.

His son Russell was a high school student when I first saw him as he accompanied his widowed mother, then Senator Rose McConnell Long, to the unveiling of Huey Long's sculptured figure in Statuary Hall. By 1948 Russell Long came himself to represent Louisiana, marking a personal milestone for me. He was the first Senator who had been born after I came to the Senate.

During his two decades in the Senate, Russell Long has emulated the calmer, reasoning side that his father revealed only in private. Slowly, steadily, the son has done what the father could never achieve. Russell became part of the inner Senate circle, serving as Democratic Whip from 1965 to 1968. Identical to Huey in appearance and mannerisms, Russell Long can sound like his father in an occasional spirited debate. His legal arguments are quick and sharp, but no one, related or not, could be expected to match the phenomenon of Huey Long. And even if the father had lived long enough to gain seniority, he could never have joined the Establishment as his son has done. It would always have been the Senate and Huey Long.

Wayne L. Morse of Oregon was the only independent to bridge the span of years from the last of the Progressives to the

"The Kingfish", Senator Huey Long of Louisiana, was a rising political star before his assassination in 1935.—photo: USIA, National Archives

Maverick Wayne Morse of Oregon, the Senate's marathon debater, always wore a red rose before an all-night speech.

1960's. His narrow defeat in 1968 deprived the Senate of its only full-blown and indisputable maverick. Morse had the spirit of the old Progressives translated into the philosophy of modern liberalism. He was everything a loner should be: aggressive, tenacious, meticulous about ethics, not wedded to party labels, and self-sufficient to an extreme that made him prefer to be a minority.

However, when Wayne Morse became Chairman of the Subcommittee on Education in 1961, it made him the leading Senator, if not the biggest man in Congress, in the field of education. The lesson is clear. Give a maverick responsibility in a field to which he is dedicated and he will channel his energies into effective action. The Kennedy-Johnson administrations gave Morse the same opportunity for accomplishing his goals that Franklin Roosevelt's New Deal gave George Norris.

Senator Morse floor-managed every education bill in the 1960's during which period the federal government was given a major responsibility for the nation's schools. At first it was unbelievable to see Morse the "insider" acting for the majority and putting down the opposition himself. Few Senators wanted to tangle with his logic and parliamentary skill, and so his bills usually passed intact. At such moments he purred and beamed like a Cheshire cat, but he also had a sheepish grin that seemed to say, "I know, I know. It is out of character for me to be part of the Establishment. Tomorrow I shall be the gadfly again!"

True to form, Morse would lash the Johnson administration without mercy for what he called "McNamara's War in Viet Nam." Or he would deliver a lengthy sermon to his fellow Senators on their failure to set ethical standards comparable to his own high level. Or the Senator would champion the "forgotten" District of Columbia, long among his one-man crusades.

Wayne Morse took pleasure in being on the minority side of a question where he could continually use his energies in a good fight. I have never seen the Senator at any hour of the day or night in anything other than high gear. With a seemingly inexhaustible supply of adrenalin, he kept himself perpetually on battle alert, in a state which others reach only at a moment of crisis. Exemplary personal habits gave him the stamina to keep up his incredible pace, so that perhaps his physical makeup best explained why Senator Morse enjoyed the arena and sought the bloody center at all times.

As a mediator of labor disputes, the Senator had a national reputation for fairness and expertise. At the Senate he championed the cause of staff members if he felt an injustice had been done them, and he was ready with compliments when he thought they were deserved. But he never hesitated to take on his peers, no matter how powerful the adversary. Unfortunately, like Hiram Johnson, Senator Morse allowed himself to become vindictive and personally bitter. Almost every opponent was a sinister figure to him. Wayne Morse had the loner's basic distrust of those in power. He was an Old Testament prophet, warning the people of abounding corruption and impending doom. And like most prophets, he believed only in his own prophecies.

None of the mavericks let party labels influence their beliefs, but Morse was able to do what the others did not. He switched from one major party to another and made the voters like it. After coming to the Senate as a Republican, Morse declared himself an Independent in the Progressive tradition. He made much of being the sole member of America's Independent Party and chided his old colleagues, "I have never resigned from Abraham Lincoln," meaning that it was not he but the party that had left the fold.

In 1955 when the Senate was evenly divided between Republicans and Democrats, Morse's one vote held the balance of power. I have not known one Senator to have greater influence than Wayne Morse did at that instant. If he voted with the GOP, William Knowland would be Majority Leader, while if he voted Democratic, Lyndon Johnson would direct the Senate. It was a moment of poetic justice for the maverick spirit. Morse voted with the Democrats and lost no time in making practical gains, as the majority showed its appreciation by giving him choice committee assignments. Senator Morse cheerfully became a Democrat though he continued to criticize when he felt the party needed it. Elected twice under his new label, Morse proved that the electorate will support the man, rather than the party, if they believe in the man. Strom Thurmond was one of the few politicians to corroborate this when he was successfully elected as a Republican in South Carolina in 1964.

Born and reared in the LaFollettes' Wisconsin, Wayne Morse was much like Fighting Bob with his tone of righteous indignation, his sense of perpetual crisis, and his championship of the rights of labor. A compulsive speaker, Morse was the first Senator to surpass the filibuster record the elder LaFollette had held for forty-five years. Though not the moving orator Old Bob was, Morse could come up to his convincing logic in a running debate and match the LaFollettes ego for ego.

In his years as instructor of argumentation in the Universities of Wisconsin and Minnesota, and professor and dean of the Law School of the University of Oregon, Senator Morse accumulated an overwhelming oratorical arsenal. Logic was his basic tool and parallelism his ultimate weapon. During his long years as a feuding Republican, then a lone Independent, and finally an uneasy Democrat, the Senate learned the Morse method of argumentation.

Only after he had gained the influence that came with seniority and a compatible administration did Wayne Morse cease to treat the Senate to a daily "State of the Union Message." The Senator used to walk alone onto the Floor every evening about five o'clock. Like a college professor whose students had all cut class, he unburdened himself to an empty Chamber hour after hour, night after night, year after year. Lacking votes in those days, he tried to put across his ideas by sheer mass of evidence. Each evening Morse read for the record endless pages, thoroughly documented with statistics, which he had prepared with the aid of his loyal staff, including Administrative Assistant William Berg and Legislative Assistant Phyllis Rock.

As the hour grows late, other Senators with prepared speeches frequently read a paragraph here and there to the empty Chamber and the speech is printed in the *Congressional Record* as if it had been given in its entirety. But Wayne Morse made certain he would not be too brief by extemporizing with professor-like side discourses that bored into the subject and all adjacent ones. As he droned on and on into the night, his delivery became rasping and unvarying in its urgency. "Let me say, Mr. President, I think the American people are entitled to know . . ." remained his favorite preamble.

Monotonous George Malone of Nevada produced his own evening show in the 1950's, whining away for hours about the metallurgical problems he knew firsthand as a former mining engineer. The keen argumentation of Senator Morse was scintillating by comparison. Nevertheless, it was like a daily sentence to staff members whose evening plans had to depend on one variable: how long would Senator Morse hold forth? Wives knew by heart the sober lament, "I'm sorry to be late, but you will never guess who spoke four hours tonight!" The Senator occasionally apologized to the staff saying, "I can be exasperating. I know that!"

One memorable evening Senator Morse's captive audience got up and walked out, leaving him momentarily speechless for the first time in recorded history. Senator Daniel Brewster of Maryland, a freshman who had to serve his "KP" duty by presiding, was more than anxious to keep a dinner date. No Senator was available to relieve him by taking the Chair, and it was no comfort that Morse had barely begun. Even a California Senator could fly home during a Morse speech.

When the Senator from Oregon paused for a brief intake of air, Brewster interpreted it as his final gasp. In no time he pounded the gavel, pronounced, "The Senate stands adjourned," leaped out of the Chair and bounded out the Lobby door. Senator Brewster may have cleared the Capitol before Morse found his breath and could believe his eyes that the Chair stood empty. With ever-reddening face, he began to protest vociferously to the "Mr. President" who was no longer there. Wayne Morse went on for half an hour while official reporters wrote down every lucid word. Legally the presiding officer has no right to declare the Senate adjourned until a motion is made by a Senator from the Floor. Morse was well within his rights and knew it.

The following day Leader Mansfield was closeted with his

maverick Senator all morning in an effort to sooth his feelings. In the best family tradition Brewster apologized to the ruffled Morse, explaining that he thought the Senator from Oregon had finished. He might have known better. George Norris' "Spider Web of Wall Street" speech may have lasted for fifteen years, but Morse had been saying "In conclusion . . ." for two decades.

Wayne Morse did relax while discussing his prize Devon cattle with Senator Albert Gore of Tennessee or Floyd "Doc" Riddick, the Senate's Parliamentarian, both of whom raise the same breed. At other times I could be certain that Senator Morse was in a good mood when he raided the licorice drops in the desk next to his own. Reaching over to open the drawer, Morse poked among the papers until he uncovered the special candies of Senator Clinton Anderson of New Mexico, who seemed happy to provide this small pacifier and add to the well-being of the Senate.

What is the value of a maverick like Senator Morse whose extravagant speaking exasperated the most patient soul on Capitol Hill but whose legislative accomplishments often justified his excesses? The independence of Morse and of all the mavericks who preceded him freed them to be our national watchdogs. If everyone in Congress were a strict party man, there would be no one to check on and publicize the inadequacies and extremes of both parties. In the future I would hope that the Senate would always have a Wayne Morse by some name who would build a career out of sheer, even though ornery, independence.

Mavericks not only stand out from other Senators, but like the peaks of a mountain range, each one has been distinctive from the other. Remarkable as it may seem for an independent maverick to be a stabilizing force, Senator William Edgar Borah of Idaho was the balance wheel of his day for both liberals and conservatives, the one who could give them perspective. He was a national legend, the free and independent "Commonwealth of Borah" within the United States of America. He embodied so many of the qualities of statesmanship that to portray Senator Borah is to define the greatness and uniqueness of the Senate itself.

Borah had practically everything. He had the oratorical genius of a Bob LaFollette with none of the emotional extremes. He had the stamina of a Hiram Johnson but none of the personal vindictiveness. He possessed the sound judgment and courage of a Burton K. Wheeler. His encyclopedic mind was unsurpassed, even by a Huey Long or a Bob Taft. Charting his own course, Borah was controlled by no one. He matched his capacity for independent thought with intense work, well planned action, and a spirit of dedication completely beyond self-interest. Little wonder that during his thirty-three years in the Senate from 1907–40, Borah became a national institution.

Senator Borah's great round head was framed by thick, sweeping strands of hair that flowed down to but never over his collar. He resembled a pensive portrait of Beethoven, another lone thinker with flowing locks and ample jowls. To his admirers his mane of hair symbolized his spirit, earning for him the epithet Lion of Idaho. In debate he never needed to roar. His forceful voice carried over the Chamber by virtue of its resonant clarity of expression. Borah's command of the language came from his daily ritual of reading the classics aloud to himself, in his office or at home. While not a dramatist like LaFollette, Borah presented an awesome sight in the height of debate when he would stride forth among the desks as if charging his opponent. It required a stout heart as well as an agile mind to face Borah in debate. He would stand with arms akimbo, unruffled and intent. Punctuating his points with quick chopping gestures, Borah spoke with authority, always in command of his facts. With keen directness he amassed his original arguments from deep within his remarkable mind.

The Senate never failed to listen. When the word would go out through the Press Gallery, "Borah's got the Floor!" streams of newsmen would flood the Gallery and lean forward to catch every word. Simultaneously, the cloakrooms would empty as Senators took their seats to listen to the Lion of Idaho. Only Everett Dirksen can hold the attention of the Senate as Borah did. Dirksen excels as the expressive virtuoso who can enliven any debate. Borah's powerful presentation of his independent judgment was the definitive statement that gave proportion to the question at hand. To each man's words the Senate has given top priority. They have listened for different reasons, but they have listened.

Senator Borah's stand on any issue was his own and not necessarily that of his party or of his Progressive wing of the Republican Party. He followed no one, not even Teddy Roosevelt in the Bull Moose revolt of 1912. After opposing William Howard Taft's nomination, Borah remained within the Republican Party. But so often was he at odds with the political centers of power that only in 1936 did he seriously campaign for the Republican presidential nomination. Stubbornly refusing to accept any campaign contribution larger than $500, Senator Borah lost by financial default to Alf Landon. After his failure to head his party's ticket, I have heard him joke, "I'd much rather be Borah than President!"

He was so thoroughly independent that there was hardly a person with whom he did not differ at one time or another. I could never understand Senator Borah's vote against the Nineteenth Amendment for woman suffrage, because he favored *state* laws that allowed women to vote. Yet rarely has a Senator disagreed with so many and still held the respect of all the Senate, even when he was proven at times to be in error.

Borah had a strict code of ethics. Upon becoming a Senator, he severed all business and law connections in order to be a free man. This principle was so basic to his philosophy of government that he introduced a bill in the early 1930's to require all Senators to relinquish their law practices while serving in the Senate. It was not acceptable to the other members who argued, as did Huey Long, that outside funds were a financial necessity for life in Washington. By following a Spartan life, Borah managed to live on his Senatorial salary alone.

No matter how important he became to the nation, Borah always considered himself first the Senator from Idaho. He was born in Illinois, educated in Kansas, and was heading for the West

Coast to practice law when an unplanned stopover in Boise began a lifetime of devotion to Idaho and its people.

Peace for his country was the main concern of Senator Borah's life. Largely because of his influence, President Harding and Secretary of State Charles Evans Hughes called the Washington Disarmament Conference in 1921 to put limits on the naval arms race. Borah believed that world trade was the path of peace. His was the most powerful voice raised in the 1920's to advocate establishing normal diplomatic relations in order to trade with Russia. Expecting the communist revolution to moderate, Senator Borah perhaps underestimated the evangelical zeal and world scope of the communists. He concentrated instead on his conviction that a strong America could overcome any influence as long as she remained strong by staying clear of political entanglements with other nations.

The paradox of Borah was that he could be farthest out in the international field of trade with and recognition of Russia and at the same time present the most adamant opposition to the Versailles Treaty and the League of Nations. Borah was basically a liberal who considered the League a mere tool of power politics which would underwrite the empires of the world. On November 19, 1919, I remember when he rose to give extemporaneously what has been considered the greatest speech ever delivered in the United States Senate. The Senators in the packed Chamber were entranced as he unfolded his concept of democracy and contrasted it with the politics of Europe:

"Senators, even in an hour so big with expectancy we should not close our eyes to the fact that democracy is something more, vastly more, than a mere form of government by which society is restrained into free and orderly life. It is a moral entity, a spiritual force, as well. And these are things which live only and alone in the atmosphere of liberty. The foundation upon which democracy rests is faith in the moral instincts of the people. Its ballot boxes, the franchise, its laws, and constitutions are but the outward manifestations of the deeper and more essential thing—a continuing trust in the moral

purposes of the average man and woman. When this is lost or
forfeited, your outward forms, however democratic in terms
. . . are a mockery . . . These distinguishing virtues of a real
republic you can not commingle with the discordant and de-
structive forces of the Old World and still preserve them . . .

"When this league, this combination, is formed four great
powers representing the dominant people will rule one-half of
the inhabitants of the globe as subject peoples—rule by force,
and we shall be a party to the rule of force. There is no other
way by which you can keep people in subjection. You must
either give them independence, recognize their rights as nations
to live their own life and to set up their own form of government, or you must deny them these things by force . . .

"Can you hope for peace when love of country is disre-
garded in your scheme, when the spirit of nationality is rejected,
even scoffed at? . . . And this you call justice. This, you cry,
means peace. Peoples who have dreamed of independence,
struggled and been patient, sacrificed and been hopeful, peoples
who were told that through this peace conference they should
realize the aspirations of centuries, have again had their hopes
dashed to earth . . . No; your treaty means injustice. It means
slavery. It means war . . .

"Mr. President, I turn from this scheme based upon force
to another scheme, planned one hundred and forty-three years
ago in old Independence Hall, in the city of Philadelphia, based
upon liberty. I like it better. I have become so accustomed to
believe in it that it is difficult for me to reject it out of hand. I
have difficulty in subscribing to the new creed of oppression, the
creed of dominant and subject peoples . . ."
Congressional Record, 66th Congress, 1st Session, 1919, p. 8781 ff.

It is a rare speech that actually changes votes. After months
of growing opposition throughout the country, Borah's speech
turned the final tide against the League in the Senate. By arguing
on the highest plane and never stooping to personal invective in an

age when this was the norm, Senator Borah held the respect of
such a protagonist as Woodrow Wilson.

After they had sent back to Europe a defeated proposal for
our entry into the League of Nations, Borah visited Henry Cabot
Lodge at his summer home on the shore at Nahant, Massachusetts.
As the two colleagues looked out over the Atlantic Ocean, they
voiced their gratitude that the deep waters before them provided a
vast insulation, almost a week's separation from the political entanglements they had so carefully avoided by rejecting the League.
The globe-shrinking flights of the jet and space age were far in the
future in an era when world leadership by the United States would
become unavoidable. Senator Borah's values as a statesman were
applauded in his day but are deprecated by those who would judge
his stand in international affairs by present realities.

On domestic issues Borah was one of the foremost of the
Progressives. No Borah law can be found on the statute books but
that need not be the true yardstick by which to evaluate a Senator.
Much legislation has been named for lesser lawmakers whose
names have long been forgotten. During his long Senate career
Borah threw the weight of his oratory and prestige on the side of
genuinely liberal measures that guaranteed individual freedom.

Senator Borah took the lead in Congress in securing for the
people their right to vote for United States Senator, a reform that
had gradually gained momentum throughout the country. The
framers of the Constitution had provided for the House of Representatives to answer to the people directly but for the Senate to
represent the sovereign states with Senators chosen by state legisla-
tures. To Borah the state houses were too-ready tools of the special
interests and the Senators they chose too often the voices of
privilege. He set about making the Senate responsible directly to
the people by advancing an amendment to the Constitution.
Though his resolution failed to secure the necessary two-thirds
majority, a similar one passed later in 1911. While the direct
primary reform came about a few years before my time, its impact
has continued to shape the character of the Senate since the

Seventeenth Amendment was finally adopted in 1913. Like Carter Glass, some have argued that this change has been the ruination of the Senate, but one might assume that Glass had faith in the people of Virginia when they elected *him* for twenty-six years by popular vote. There can be little doubt that the Senate has been gradually more attuned to the voices of the electorate since the time of Progressives like LaFollette and Borah.

The newspaperman's Senator, Borah was the most available public figure and the most popular with the press of all the Senators I have known. Senator Borah was the only one who held a daily press conference in his office to which were invited any members of the press who cared to come, and cared they did. Again, Everett Dirksen runs a close second today, breaking tradition by holding his popular weekly press conference in the Press Gallery. The two men have been universally valued by the press in different ways. Borah's hold on the newspapermen was not in the warmth and charm of a Dirksen personality nor were his press conferences enlivened by the stream of humorous stories with which Senator Dirksen endears himself to his listeners. Borah, like Dirksen, could be counted on at all times as an excellent factual news source who took the newsmen into his confidence in a relationship of mutual respect.

When a newsman would question Borah, it was as though his story had been written for him by the end of the interview. No matter what was needed, Borah had it: background information, Sunday feature, spot news, or answers to an editor's query. More than any other Senator, newsmen sought out Borah to know the real meaning behind legislation, the cause, the cure, the effect of all types of issues, national and international. As Chairman of the Foreign Relations Committee from 1924–33 and ranking Republican member until his death, Borah always seemed to have more information and to speak with greater authority in that field than anyone else in the country, except the President. It was said that a letter from Senator Borah went farther in Russia, in those days before we had established diplomatic relations, than did one from the government.

Members of the press today who knew Borah, such as Gould Lincoln of the *Washington Star,* fairly glow at the mention of his name, shaking their heads at the wonder that such a man could exist at all. For his part, Borah's press conferences were a form of mental recreation. He could relax while parrying newsmen's questions that would have unnerved many another public figure. Though no egotist, he obviously enjoyed the adulation of the press and welcomed the stimulation of matching wits with some of the sharpest minds on Capitol Hill. Had there been television news conferences in his day, Borah would have been a star guest.

In conversation he was direct. We who knew him found him readily approachable, while a stranger must have thought him overly brusque. Senator Borah did not preface what he said by trivia, even in greeting people. I have noticed visitors go through the usual social amenities while Borah with polite impatience waited for them to get on with it. His whole manner said, "Now let's get to the point. What do you want to know and I'll tell you." The moment he came to see a newspaperman he would smile and shake hands, but immediately they dove into the business at hand.

Like everyone at the Capitol I had stood in awe of Senator Borah since my page days. I would approach him for newsmen as the living legend that he was, a presence who dwelt on a mental Mount Olympus not known to ordinary men. I was just another young employee to him until one day late in 1931 when he suddenly discovered my existence as an individual. Senator Borah was reading intently in the Marble Room while nearby I conversed quietly with a Senate official about the cross-country camping-trailer trip my mother and I had just completed. Curious to see how Senator Borah would react, I deliberately raised my voice to tell of an interesting experience we had had in Idaho. At the mention of his beloved home state, Senator Borah dropped his paper, whirled and demanded, "When were *you* in Idaho?"

From that moment we were friends. I had touched the sacred soil of Idaho, a revelation which transformed me at the age of twenty-two into an associate worth knowing and a friend with whom he cared to share experiences and judgments about the world. Senator Borah became my mentor, a giver of guidelines and gauges to go by in evaluating personalities. As he became a good friend rather than a formidable legend, I realized that his penetrating look was pensive rather than stern. He gave the impression that he was taking the measure of a person, either in debate or in conversation. In his thorough realism he was rarely fooled by people. Once he took exception to my wishful description of a nonpolitical leader as meaning well despite his ineptitudes. "No, he doesn't mean well," Senator Borah asserted. "I wouldn't trust a man who would compromise his basic principles merely to gain popularity." Most certainly Senator Borah never did.

He had the largest mouth I have ever seen. When he chuckled, his eyes would brighten and his huge mouth would bend into a smile that was completely disarming. His mouth would give other clues as to his inward thoughts, according to the Senator's spritely little wife. On one occasion when I chatted with "Little Borah" as she was known, she confided: "You know, Mr. Borah is so funny when he comes home. I open the door and he just stands there with his mouth wide open and stares at me for a few moments."

Through the years I think I discovered what might have been responsible for this curious idiosyncrasy. Senator Borah had such an exceptional mind himself that he was not swayed by the eloquence of the average Senatorial argument. Only one Senator could hold Borah spellbound. I saw him sit for at least an hour with his mouth literally hanging open while listening entranced to Huey Long. Borah could look straight through the Louisianan's bombast to his brilliant legal arguments, which alone would have held Borah had Long merely whispered his speech. Perhaps Huey Long and "Little Borah" were the only people in the world who could impress the Senator so much that his mouth would lose its moorings. Perhaps when his wife greeted him upon his arrival home, Borah was far more inspired by her presence than by any of the notable occurrences of the day.

Senator Borah drew great strength from nature. Some of our best discussions centered around our mutual interest in camping in Yellowstone, the Grand Tetons, and the surrounding high country of Idaho and Wyoming. While living in Washington he had to be content with riding horseback daily on the wooded trails of Rock Creek Park. President Coolidge was surprised to hear of the independent Borah's love for riding, remarking, "I always thought a rider had to go in the same direction as his horse!"

However the politicians may have chafed at his unique approaches to issues, to most people he was *the* Senator, as Everett Dirksen is *the* Senator today. Throughout the country those who could not name one other member of the Senate knew of William E. Borah and would ask me about him. His renown is clearly illustrated in a movie entitled *Ambassador Bill* starring Will Rogers. Cast in the title role of an American ambassador abroad, Rogers plays dinner host to a visiting Senator who, though drunk, insists on delivering a rambling speech to the assembled Europeans. Sitting beside him, Ambassador Bill pulls at the Senator's coat and tries to silence him by whispering frantically, "What would George Washington say? What would Abraham Lincoln say? What would *Senator Borah* say?" When I described this scene to Senator Borah, he delighted in the compliment from Hollywood.

Change comes gradually to the Senate which is a continuing body. With only one-third of its members facing the electorate at any given time, the continuity of the Senate is so well preserved that any alteration in membership caused by death, defeat, or retirement is never extreme. However, when Senator Borah died of a massive cerebral hemorrhage in January, 1940, the effect was as though a great part of the Senate had died. He was given the most impressive state funeral in Senate history. Whenever I pause at Senator Borah's statue in the main corridor of the Capitol, the Lion of Idaho seems to have taken the Floor again. It is as though I am once more facing one of the greatest Senators of all.

For if one Senator could symbolize the nature of the Senate as an institution of government, it would be William E. Borah. With his independence and stability, he did not become excited over the quick tides of public opinion as they ebb and flow any more than the Senate is swayed by every wind that blows. The proverbial dignity of the Senate was personified in Borah's sober, thoughtful demeanor just as the Senate's role as a free forum was fulfilled in his oratory. Borah's dissection of every problem and his judicious weighing of the monumental issues typified the Senate's thorough study of proposed legislation. Impulsive action based on rash decisions or deep prejudices would be foreign to the nature of both. This deliberate caution is what exasperates would-be reformers, and yet the real value of the Senate in our form of government is precisely this restraining hand that says, "Let us hear every opinion before we act." Some would say that Borah and the Senate have gone too slowly; few complain that the Senate has ever moved too fast. But whatever the momentary judgment may be, Borah was to the Senate what the Senate is to the government, an invaluable balance wheel.

THE MIGHTY

The saying was old when I was a boy, "All the great men are dead, Julius Caesar, George Washington, Abraham Lincoln, Robert E. Lee, and I am not feeling so well myself!" That kind of evaluation is not uncommon. Today we seriously lament, "The Senate is not what it used to be when Borah and La Follette were there; *they* were orators! Or Taft and George; *they* were legislators!"

I suspect that in the future when many of the present Senators are gone, we shall look back and wail, "If only we had men of the legislative acumen of George Aiken, Abraham Ribicoff, or Birch Bayh, the legal brilliance of Jacob Javits or Sam Ervin, the dedication of Karl Mundt, Alan Bible, or Ted Kennedy, the perspective of Fred Harris, Hugh Scott, or Gale McGee, the impartial judgment of John Sherman Cooper or Edmund Muskie, the leadership of Mike Mansfield and Everett Dirksen!"

What is it about the human mind that can see the past in a golden glow but does not have the perspective to recognize the best of our own time? Why are we so ready to believe the worst about those we send to represent us in Washington? A public figure usually has to leave office or die before his accomplishments are praised. While he is drudging away, knee-deep in the present and in need of encouragement, only his mistakes are recounted. Why are self-appointed critics so ready to write off the whole of Congress as inadequate when they themselves have probably never lifted a constructive finger in the public behalf?

283

Throughout half a century I have watched nine women and 549 men fill the role of a United States Senator. Year after year I have continued to marvel that such an extraordinary group can be assembled by the will of the people. The overall caliber of the Senate is one of the great achievements of our republic.

To be sure, almost any quality can be found within so large and powerful a group. There are ambitious men, fighting as in a jungle, jockeying for position, for headlines, for the presidency itself. There is the selfish side of the Senator who feels that the world must stop for him and that rules are for others to obey. There is the pompous side of those who take their official title of "The Honorable" too seriously; they are the ones who have been honored by the people.

But the truly striking quality of the Senate is the capacity of most of its members to adopt the broader vision, to care deeply about what happens to the country and the community of nations, to a minority, or to a single constituent who has little influence and many problems. I would hope that someone would always care as much about preserving natural resources as Frank Church and Ralph Yarborough, about solving the world's food problems as George McGovern, about auto safety as Walter Mondale, and about consumer labeling as Maurine Neuberger and Philip Hart. The quiet stories of hard work include the concern of Harrison "Pete" Williams for the migrant worker, Claiborne Pell's leadership in mass transportation, Joseph Montoya's success in securing the GI Bill of Rights for Viet Nam veterans, and Frank Lausche's legislation to regulate strip mining. The Senate has always had a majority of dedicated problem solvers.

Because Senators share a common concern about an issue does not mean that they will agree easily on one solution. When I came as a page with childlike faith in my elders, I found a scholar like Henry Cabot Lodge, Sr. opposing the equally penetrating mind of Oscar Underwood. A wait-and-see conservative like Jim Watson was continually at odds with an impatient liberal like James Couzens. Many times I have seen men of equal wisdom and sincerity on opposite sides of an argument. Truth is obviously too vast an entity to be limited to one philosophy, one party, or one man's mind. No one will have all the answers. Careful compromise is the wise course, the essence of the Senate way.

Though more slowly than the world has changed, the Senate itself has changed, and a new age produces new ways. Many of the changes are superficial. Senators used to strive to be a breed apart, to look Senatorial and to speak in ringing oratory. Today's legislator in the plain business suit may be doing twice the job his more colorful predecessor did.

Other differences are basic. In the days of Borah, the Senate was first of all a deliberative body where oratory counted and Senators would gather every afternoon to weigh issues as they listened to one another debate. In those simpler days, Senators had more time to devote to less legislation. They came to Washington at the beginning of the session and usually did not go home until after adjournment. Very few constituents traveled to the Capitol to see them, while today the offices are flooded with visitors and a Senator's day is packed with interviews.

Now it is taken for granted that a session will last throughout most of the year, which means that a Senator must often fly home to meet his obligations or attend committee hearings held in the field. Sometimes so many are out of town on business that it is impossible to get a "live" quorum. The tedious "token" quorum has become customary. The bells ring, the clerk begins to call the roll, but as soon as a speaker shows up, the quorum is rescinded and the Senator gives his speech to an almost empty Chamber.

In this way the deliberative nature of the Senate is fast disappearing. Only at the climax of an important piece of legislation does the Chamber today take on the flavor of the "old days." When a final vote is nearing, a crowd of Senators will gather on the Floor to hear summation arguments and to vote amendments up or down. In general, the spellbinding oratory of old has been replaced by the speed-reading of committee reports and the *Congressional Record* while a Senator's staff briefs him on his way to or from the airport. There is less time to consider legislation of far greater complexity than the old-timers could have imagined. The job of

Senator has become as involved and fragmented as the government itself. To delve deeply into fundamental issues becomes increasingly difficult and yet, that is the real task of a United States Senator.

What will the Senate be like in the future? At the present moment, living among the youth of our land are the President, the Vice President, and Members of the Congress of the twenty-first century. What is ahead for them? Someday a Congressional committee may inspect Mars and presidential candidates may prove themselves in a journey to the moon. Whatever the state of civilization, young leaders will inevitably rise up in criticism, find themselves molded by the realities of their own world, become the old fogies to a new generation of critics, and in the end, the best of them will be lifted up on some pedestal of history by their children's children. Through it all, some will undoubtedly look back to our century and say with nostalgia, "All the great men are dead!"

No one generation has a monopoly on greatness. It may take different forms. It may not be broadcast or make headlines or be coated with glamor. But during my forty-seven years in the halls of the mighty, I have seen greatness continue to live. Thus it should always be as long as there is a United States Senate.

ROLL CALL OF 47 YEARS
1918–1965

KEY:

R: Republican   A: Appointed   r: resigned

D: Democrat   E: Elected   u: unsuccessful candidate for re-election

FL: Farmer-Laborite   AE: Appointed and subsequently elected

d: died in office

H: Member, House of Representatives   nc: not a candidate for reelection

Abel, Hazel H.	(R-Neb.)	E:1954 r
Adams, Alva B.	(D-Colo.)	A:1923–24 u; E:1933–41 d
Aiken, George D.	(R-Vt.)	E:1941.....
Allen, Henry J.	(R-Kan.)	A:1929–30 u
Allott, Gordon L.	(R-Colo.)	E:1955.....
Anderson, Clinton P.	(D-N.M.)	E:1949..... H:1941–45
Andrews, Charles O.	(D-Fla.)	E:1936–46 d
Ashurst, Henry F.	(D-Ariz.)	E:1912–41 u
Austin, Warren R.	(R-Vt.)	E:1931–46 r
Bachman, Nathan L.	(D-Tenn.)	AE:1933–37 d
Bailey, Josiah W.	(D-N.C.)	E:1931–46 d
Baird, David	(R-N.J.)	AE:1918–19 nc
Baird, David, Jr.	(R-N.J.)	A:1929–30 nc
Baldwin, Raymond E.	(R-Conn.)	E:1946–49 r
Ball, Joseph H.	(R-Minn.)	A:1940–42 nc; E:1943–49 u
Ball, L. Heisler	(R-Del.)	E:1903–05 nc; 1919–25 u H:1901–03

Bankhead, John H., Sr.	(D-Ala.)	AE:1907–20 d
		H:1887–1907
Bankhead, John H., 2nd	(D-Ala.)	E:1931–46 d
Barbour, W. Warren	(R-N.J.)	AE:1931–37 u;
		E:1938–43 d
Barkley, Alben W.	(D-Ky.)	E:1927–49 r;
		E:1955–56 d
		V.Pres.:1949–53
		H:1913–27
Barrett, Frank A.	(R-Wyo.)	E:1953–59 u
		H:1943–50
Bartlett, Edward L.	(D-Alaska)	E:1959–68d Dele-
		gate:1945–59
Bass, Ross	(D-Tenn.)	E:1964–67 u
		H:1955–64
Bayard, Thomas F.	(D-Del.)	E:1922–29 u
Bayh, Birch	(D-Ind.)	E:1963 . . . . .
Beall, J. Glenn	(R-Md.)	E:1953–65 u
		H:1943–53
Beckham, John C. W.	(D-Ky.)	E:1915–21 u
Bender, George H.	(R-Ohio)	E:1954–57 u
		H:1939–49;1951–54
Bénet, Christie	(D-S.C.)	A:1918 u
Bennett, Wallace F.	(R-Utah)	E:1951 . . . . .
Benson, Elmer A.	(FL-Minn.)	A:1935–36 nc
Benton, William	(D-Conn.)	AE:1949–53 u
Berry, George L.	(D-Tenn.)	A:1937–38 u
Bible, Alan H.	(D-Nev.)	E:1954 . . . . .
Bilbo, Theodore G.	(D-Miss.)	E:1935–47 d
Bingham, Hiram	(R-Conn.)	E:1924–33 u
Black, Hugo L.	(D-Ala.)	E:1927–37 r
		Supreme Court:
		1937 . . . . .
Blaine, John J.	(R-Wis.)	E:1927–33 u
Blakley, William A.	(D-Texas)	A:1957 nc;
		A:1961 u
Blease, Coleman L.	(D-S.C.)	E:1925–31 u
Boggs, J. Caleb	(R-Del.)	E:1961 . . . . .
		H:1947–53
Bone, Homer T.	(D-Wash.)	E:1933–44 r
Borah, William E.	(R-Idaho)	E:1907–40 d
Bottum, Joe H.	(R-S.D.)	A:1962–63 u
Bowring, Eva Kelly	(R-Neb.)	A:1954 nc
Brandegee, Frank B.	(R-Conn.)	E:1905–24 d
		H:1902–05

Bratton, Sam G.	(D-N.M.)	E:1925–33 r
Brewster, Daniel B.	(D-Md.)	E:1963–69 u
		H:1959–63
Brewster, Ralph Owen	(R-Maine)	E:1941–52 r
		H:1935–41
Bricker, John W.	(R-Ohio)	E:1947–59 u
Bridges, Styles	(R-N.H.)	E:1937–61 d
Briggs, Frank P.	(D-Mo.)	A:1945–47 u
Brock, William E.	(D-Tenn.)	AE:1929–31 nc
Brookhart, Smith W.	(R-Iowa)	E:1922–26; E:1927–
		33 u
Brooks, C. Wayland	(R-Ill.)	E:1940–49 u
Broughton, J. Melville	(D-N.C.)	E:1948–49 d
Broussard, Edwin S.	(D-La.)	E:1921–33 u
Brown, Ernest S.	(R-Nev.)	A:1954 u
Brown, Fred H.	(D-N.H.)	E:1933–39 u
Brown, Prentiss M.	(D-Mich.)	AE:1936–43 u
		H:1933–36
Bruce, William Cabell	(D-Md.)	E:1923–29 u
Brunsdale, Clarence N.	(R-N.D.)	A:1959–60 nc
Buck, C. Douglass	(R-Del.)	E:1943–49 u
Bulkley, Robert J.	(D-Ohio)	E:1930–39 u
		H:1911–15
Bulow, William J.	(D-S.D.)	E:1931–43 u
Bunker, Berkeley L.	(D-Nev.)	A:1940–42 u
		H:1945–47
Burch, Thomas G.	(D-Va.)	A:1946 nc H:1931–
		46
Burdick, Quentin N.	(D-N.D.)	E:1960.....
		H:1959–60
Burke, Edward R.	(D-Neb.)	E:1935–41 u
		H:1933–35
Burke, Thomas A.	(D-Ohio)	A:1953–54 u
Bursum, Holm O.	(R-N.M.)	AE:1921–25 u
Burton, Harold H.	(R-Ohio)	E:1941–45 r Su-
		preme Court:1945–
		58
Burton, Theodore E.	(R-Ohio)	E:1909–15 nc;
		E:1928–29 d
		H:1889–91;1895–
		1909;1921–28
Bush, Prescott S.	(R-Conn.)	E:1952–63 nc
Bushfield, Harlan J.	(R-S.D.)	E:1943–48 d
Butler, Hugh A.	(R-Neb.)	E:1941–54 d
Butler, John Marshall	(R-Md.)	E:1951–63 u

Butler, William M.	(R-Mass.)	A:1924–26 u
Byrd, Harry F., Sr.	(D-Va.)	AE:1933–65 r
Byrd, Harry F., Jr.	(D-Va.)	AE:1965.....
Byrd, Robert C.	(D-W.Va.)	E:1959.....
		H:1953–59
Byrnes, James F.	(D-S.C.)	E:1931–41 r
		H:1911–25
		Supreme Court:
		1941–42
Cain, Harry P.	(R-Wash.)	AE:1946–53 u
Calder, William M.	(R-N.Y.)	E:1917–23 u
		H:1905–15
Cameron, Ralph H.	(R-Ariz.)	E:1921–27 u Delegate:1909–12
Cannon, Howard W.	(D-Nev.)	E:1959.....
Capehart, Homer E.	(R-Ind.)	E:1945–63 u
Capper, Arthur	(R-Kan.)	E:1919–49 nc
Caraway, Hattie W.	(D-Ark.)	AE:1931–45 u
Caraway, Thaddeus H.	(D-Ark.)	E:1921–31 d
		H:1913–21
Carey, Robert D.	(R-Wyo.)	E:1930–37 u
Carlson, Frank	(R-Kan.)	E:1950–69 nc
		H:1935–47
Carroll, John A.	(D-Colo.)	E:1957–63 u
		H:1947–51
Carville, Edward P.	(D-Nev.)	A:1945–47 u
Case, Clifford P.	(R-N.J.)	E:1955.....
		H:1945–53
Case, Francis H.	(R-S.D.)	E:1951–62 d
		H:1937–51
Chamberlain, George	(D-Ore.)	E:1909–21 u
Chandler, Albert B.	(D-Ky.)	AE:1939–45 r
Chapman, Virgil M.	(D-Ky.)	E:1949–51 d
		H:1925–29;31–49
Chavez, Dennis	(D-N.M.)	AE:1935–62 d
		H:1931–35
Church, Frank F.	(D-Idaho)	E:1957.....
Clark, Bennett Champ	(D-Mo.)	AE:1933–45 u
Clark, D. Worth	(D-Idaho)	E:1939–45 u
		H:1935–39
Clark, Joseph S.	(D-Penn.)	E:1957–69 u
Clements, Earle C.	(D-Ky.)	E:1950–57 u
		H:1945–48
Cohen, John S.	(D-Ga.)	A:1932–33 nc

Colt, LeBaron B.	(R-R.I.)	E:1913–24 d
Comer, Braxton Bragg	(D-Ala.)	A:1920 nc
Connally, Tom	(D-Texas)	E:1929–53 nc
		H:1917–29
Coolidge, Marcus A.	(D-Mass.)	E:1931–37 nc
Cooper, John Sherman	(R-Ky.)	E:1946–49 u;
		E:1952–55 u;
		E:1956.....
Copeland, Royal S.	(D-N.Y.)	E:1923–38 d
Cordon, Guy	(R-Ore.)	AE:1944–55 u
Costigan, Edward P.	(D-Colo.)	E:1931–37 nc
Cotton, Norris	(R-N.H.)	E:1954.....
		H:1947–54
Couzens, James	(R-Mich.)	AE:1922–36 d
Crippa, Edward D.	(R-Wyo.)	A:1954 nc
Crow, William E.	(R-Penn.)	A:1921–22 d
Culberson, Charles A.	(D-Texas)	E:1899–1923 u
Cummins, Albert B.	(R-Iowa)	E:1908–26 d
Curtis, Carl T.	(R-Neb.)	AE:1955.....
		H:1939–54
Curtis, Charles	(R-Kan.)	E:1907–13 u;
		1915–29 r
		H:1893–1907
		V.Pres.:1929–33
Cutting, Bronson M.	(R-N.M.)	A:1927–28 nc;
		E:1929–35 d
Dale, Porter H.	(R-Vt.)	E:1923–33 d
		H:1915–23
Danaher, John A.	(R-Conn.)	E:1939–45 u
Daniel, Charles E.	(D-S.C.)	A:1954 nc
Daniel, Price M.	(D-Texas)	E:1953–57 r
Darby, Harry	(R-Kan.)	A:1949–50 nc
Davis, James J.	(R-Penn.)	E:1930–45 u
Deneen, Charles S.	(R-Ill.)	AE:1925–31 u
Dial, Nathaniel B.	(D-S.C.)	E:1919–25 u
Dickinson, Lester J.	(R-Iowa)	E:1931–37 u
		H:1919–31
Dieterich, William H.	(D-Ill.)	E:1933–39 nc
		H:1931–33
Dill, Clarence C.	(D-Wash.)	E:1923–35 nc
		H:1915–19
Dillingham, William P.	(R-Vt.)	E:1900–23 d
Dirksen, Everett M.	(R-Ill.)	E:1951.....
		H:1933–49

Dodd, Thomas J.	(D-Conn.)	E:1959.....
		H:1953–57
Dominick, Peter H.	(R-Colo.)	E:1963.....
		H:1961–63
Donahey, A. Victor	(D-Ohio)	E:1935–41 nc
Donnell, Forrest C.	(R-Mo.)	E:1945–51 u
Douglas, Paul H.	(D-Ill.)	E:1949–67 u
Downey, Sheridan	(D-Calif.)	E:1939–50 r
Doxey, Wall	(D-Miss.)	E:1941–43 u
		H:1929–41
Drew, Irving W.	(R-N.H.)	A:1918 nc
Duff, James H.	(R-Penn.)	E:1951–57 u
Duffy, F. Ryan	(D-Wis.)	E:1933–39 u
Dulles, John Foster	(R-N.Y.)	A:1949 u
DuPont, T. Coleman	(R-Del.)	A:1921–22 u;
		E:1925–28 r
Dworshak, Henry C.	(R-Idaho)	E:1946–49 u;
		AE:1949–62 d
		H:1939–46
Eastland, James O.	(D-Miss.)	A:1941 nc;
		E:1943.....
Ecton, Zales N.	(R-Mont.)	E:1947–53 u
Edge, Walter E.	(R-N.J.)	E:1919–29 r
Edmondson, J. Howard	(D-Okla.)	A:1963–64 u
Edwards, Edward I.	(D-N.J.)	E:1923–29 u
Elkins, Davis	(R-W.Va.)	A:1911 nc;
		E:1919–25 nc
Ellender, Allen J.	(D-La.)	E:1937.....
Engle, Clair	(D-Calif.)	E:1959–64 d
		H:1943–59
Erickson, John E.	(D-Mont.)	A:1933–34 u
Ernst, Richard P.	(R-Ky.)	E:1921–27 u
Ervin, Samuel J.	(D-N.C.)	AE:1954.....
		H:1946–47
Fall, Albert B.	(R-N.M.)	E:1912–21 r
Fannin, Paul J.	(R-Ariz.)	E:1965.....
Feazel, William C.	(D-La.)	A:1948 nc
Felton, Rebecca Latimer	(D-Ga.)	A:1922 nc
Ferguson, Homer	(R-Mich.)	E:1943–55 u
Fernald, Bert M.	(R-Maine)	E:1916–26 d
Ferris, Woodbridge N.	(D-Mich.)	E:1923–28 d
Fess, Simeon D.	(R-Ohio)	E:1923–35 u
		H:1913–23
Flanders, Ralph E.	(R-Vt.)	AE:1946–59 nc

Fletcher, Duncan U.	(D-Fla.)	AE:1909–36 d
Fong, Hiram L.	(R-Hawaii)	E:1959.....
France, Joseph I.	(R-Md.)	E:1917–23 u
Frazier, Lynn J.	(R-N.D.)	E:1923–41 u
Frear, J. Allen, Jr.	(D-Del.)	E:1949–61 u
Frelinghuysen, Joseph S.	(R-N.J.)	E:1917–23 u
Fulbright, J. William	(D-Ark.)	E:1945.....
		H:1943–45
Gay, Edward J.	(D-La.)	E:1918–21 nc
George, Walter F.	(D-Ga.)	E:1922–57 nc
Gerry, Peter Goelet	(D-R.I.)	E:1917–29 u;
		E:1935–47 nc
		H:1913–15
Gibson, Ernest Willard	(R-Vt.)	AE:1933–40 d
		H:1923–33
Gibson, Ernest William	(R-Vt.)	A:1940–41 nc
Gillett, Frederick H.	(R-Mass.)	E:1925–31 nc
		H:1893–1925
		Speaker:1919–25
Gillette, Guy M.	(D-Iowa)	E:1936–45 u;
		E:1949–55 u
		H:1933–36
Glass, Carter	(D-Va.)	AE:1920–46 d
		H:1902–18
Glenn, Otis F.	(R-Ill.)	E:1928–33 u
Goff, Guy D.	(R-W.Va.)	E:1925–31 nc
Goff, Nathan	(R-W.Va.)	E:1913–19 nc
		H:1883–89
Goldsborough, Phillips Lee	(R-Md.)	E:1929–35 nc
Goldwater, Barry M.	(R-Ariz.)	E:1953–65 nc;
		E:1969.....
Gooding, Frank R.	(R-Idaho)	AE:1921–28 d
Gore, Albert A.	(D-Tenn.)	E:1953.....
		H:1939–53
Gore, Thomas P.	(D-Okla.)	E:1907–21 u;
		1931–37 u
Gossett, Charles C.	(D-Idaho)	A:1945–47 u
Gould, Arthur R.	(R-Maine)	E:1926–31 nc
Graham, Frank P.	(D-N.C.)	A:1949–50 u
Grammer, Elijah S.	(R-Wash.)	A:1932–33 nc
Graves, Dixie Bibb	(D-Ala.)	A:1937–38 nc
Green, Theodore Francis	(D-R.I.)	E:1937–61 nc
Greene, Frank L.	(R-Vt.)	E:1923–30 d
		H:1912–23

Griswold, Dwight P.	(R-Neb.)	E:1952–54 d
Gronna, Asle J.	(R-N.D.)	E:1911–21 u
		H:1905–11
Gruening, Ernest	(D-Alaska)	E:1959–69 u
Grundy, Joseph R.	(R-Penn.)	A:1929–30 u
Guffey, Joseph F.	(D-Penn.)	E:1935–47 u
Guion, Walter	(D-La.)	A:1918 nc
Gurney, Chan	(R-S.D.)	E:1939–51 u
Hale, Frederick	(R-Maine)	E:1917–41 nc
Hall, Wilton E.	(D-S.C.)	A:1944–45 nc
Harding, Warren G.	(R-Ohio)	E:1915–21 r
		President;1921–
		23
Hardwick, Thomas W.	(D-Ga.)	E:1914–19 u
		H:1903–14
Harreld, John W.	(R-Okla.)	E:1921–27 u
		H:1919–21
Harris, Fred R.	(D-Okla.)	E:1964 . . . . .
Harris, William J.	(D-Ga.)	E:1919–32 d
Harrison, Pat	(D-Miss.)	E:1919–41 d
		H:1911–19
Hart, Philip A.	(D-Mich.)	E:1959 . . . . .
Hart, Thomas C.	(R-Conn.)	A:1945–46 nc
Hartke, R. Vance	(D-Ind.)	E:1959 . . . . .
Hastings, Daniel O.	(R-Del.)	AE:1928–37 u
Hatch, Carl A.	(D-N.M.)	AE:1933–49 nc
Hatfield, Henry D.	(R-W.Va.)	E:1929–35 u
Hawes, Harry B.	(D-Mo.)	E:1926–33 r
		H:1921–26
Hawkes, Albert W.	(R-N.J.)	E:1943–49 nc
Hayden, Carl	(D-Ariz.)	E:1927–69 nc
		H:1912–27
Hébert, Felix	(R-R.I.)	E:1929–35 u
Heflin, J. Thomas	(D-Ala.)	E:1920–31 u
		H:1904–20
Henderson, Charles B.	(D-Nev.)	AE:1918–21 u
Hendrickson, Robert C.	(R-N.J.)	E:1949–55 nc
Hennings, Thomas C.	(D-Mo.)	E:1951–60 d
		H:1935–40
Herring, Clyde L.	(D-Iowa)	E:1937–43 u
Hickenlooper, Bourke B.	(R-Iowa)	E:1945–69 nc
Hickey, John Joseph	(D-Wyo.)	A:1961–62 u
Hill, Lister	(D-Ala.)	AE:1938–69 nc
		H:1923–38

Hill, William L.	(D-Fla.)	A:1936 nc
Hitchcock, Gilbert M.	(D-Neb.)	E:1911–23 u
		H:1903–05;1907–11
Hitchcock, Herbert E.	(D-S.D.)	A:1936–38 u
Hoblitzell, John D.	(R-W.Va.)	A:1958 u
Hoey, Clyde R.	(D-N.C.)	E:1945–54 d
		H:1919–21
Holland, Spessard L.	(D-Fla.)	AE:1946.....
Hollis, Henry F.	(D-N.H.)	E:1913–19 nc
Holman, Rufus C.	(R-Ore.)	E:1939–45 u
Holt, Rush Dew	(D-W.Va.)	E:1935–41 u
Houston, Andrew Jackson	(D-Texas)	A:1941 d
Howell, Robert B.	(R-Neb.)	E:1923–33 d
Hruska, Roman Lee	(R-Neb.)	E:1954.....
		H:1953–54
Huffman, James W.	(D-Ohio)	A:1945–46 u
Hughes, James H.	(D-Del.)	E:1937–43 u
Hull, Cordell	(D-Tenn.)	E:1931–33 r
		H:1907–21;1923–31
Humphrey, Hubert H.	(D-Minn.)	E:1949–64 r
		V.Pres.:1965–69
Humphreys, Robert	(D-Ky.)	A:1956 nc
Hunt, Lester C.	(D-Wyo.)	E:1949–54 d
Inouye, Daniel K.	(D-Hawaii)	E:1963.....
		H:1959–63
Ives, Irving M.	(R-N.Y.)	E:1947–59 nc
Jackson, Henry M.	(D-Wash.)	E:1953.....
		H:1941–53
Jackson, Samuel D.	(D-Ind.)	A:1944 nc
Javits, Jacob K.	(R-N.Y.)	E:1957.....
		H:1947–54
Jenner, William E.	(R-Ind.)	E:1944–45 nc;
		E:1947–59 nc
Johnson, Edwin C.	(D-Colo.)	E:1937–55 nc
Johnson, Edwin S.	(D-S.D.)	E:1915–21 nc
Johnson, Hiram W.	(R-Calif.)	E:1917–45 d
Johnson, Lyndon B.	(D-Texas)	E:1949–61 r
		H:1937–49
		V.Pres.:1961–63
		Pres.:1963–69
Johnson, Magnus	(FL-Minn.)	E:1923–25 u
		H:1933–35
Johnston, Olin D.	(D-S.C.)	E:1945–65 d

Lenroot, Irvine L.	(R-Wis.)	E:1918–27 u
		H:1909–18
Lewis, J. Hamilton	(D-Ill.)	E:1913–19 u;
		1931–39 d
		H:1897–99
Locher, Cyrus	(D-Ohio)	A:1928 u
Lodge, Henry Cabot	(R-Mass.)	E:1893–1924 d
		H:1887–93
Lodge, Henry Cabot, Jr.	(R-Mass.)	E:1937–44 r;
		1947–53 u
Loftin, Scott M.	(D-Fla.)	A:1936 nc
Logan, Marvel Mills	(D-Ky.)	E:1931–39 d
Lonergan, Augustine	(D-Conn.)	E:1933–39 u
		H:1913–15;1917–21;
		1931–33
Long, Edward V.	(D-Mo.)	AE:1960–69 u
Long, Huey P.	(D-La.)	E:1932–35 d
Long, Oren E.	(D-Hawaii)	E:1959–62 d
Long, Rose McConnell	(D-La.)	AE:1936–37 nc
Long, Russell B.	(D-La.)	E:1948.....
Lucas, Scott W.	(D-Ill.)	E:1939–51 u
		H:1935–39
Lumpkin, Alva M.	(D-S.C.)	A:1941 d
Lundeen, Ernest	(FL-Minn.)	E:1937–40 d
		H:1917–19;1933–37
Lusk, Hall S.	(D-Ore.)	A:1960 nc
Magnuson, Warren G.	(D-Wash.)	AE:1944.....
		H:1937–44
Malone, George W.	(R-Nev.)	E:1947–59 u
Maloney, Francis T.	(D-Conn.)	E:1935–45 d
		H:1933–35
Mansfield, Mike	(D-Mont.)	E:1953.....
		H:1943–53
Martin, Edward	(R-Penn.)	E:1947–59 nc
Martin, George B.	(D-Ky.)	A:1918–19 nc
Martin, Thomas E.	(R-Iowa)	E:1955–61 nc
		H:1939–55
Martin, Thomas S.	(D-Va.)	E:1895–1919 d
Maybank, Burnet R.	(D-S.C.)	E:1941–54 d
Mayfield, Earle B.	(D-Texas)	E:1923–29 u
McAdoo, William Gibbs	(D-Calif.)	E:1933–38 r
McCarran, Patrick A.	(D-Nev.)	E:1933–54 d
McCarthy, Eugene J.	(D-Minn.)	E:1959.....
		H:1949–59

McCarthy, Joseph R.	(R-Wis.)	E:1947–57 d
McClellan, John L.	(D-Ark.)	E:1943.....
		H:1935–39
McCormick, Medill	(R-Ill.)	E:1919–25 d
		H:1917–19
McCulloch, Roscoe C.	(R-Ohio)	A:1929–30 u
		H:1915–21
McCumber, Porter J.	(R-N.D.)	E:1899–1923 u
McFarland, Ernest W.	(D-Ariz.)	E:1941–53 u
McGee, Gale W.	(D-Wyo.)	E:1959.....
McGill, George	(D-Kan.)	E:1930–39 u
McGovern, George S.	(D-S.D.)	E:1963.....
		H:1957–61
McGrath, J. Howard	(D-R.I.)	E:1947–49 r
McIntyre, Thomas J.	(D-N.H.)	E:1962.....
McKellar, Kenneth D.	(D-Tenn.)	E:1917–53 u
		H:1911–17
McKinley, William B.	(R-Ill.)	E:1921–26 d
		H:1905–13;1915–21
McLean, George P.	(R-Conn.)	E:1911–29 nc
McMahon, Brien	(D-Conn.)	E:1945–52 d
McMaster, William H.	(R-S.D.)	E:1925–31 u
McNamara, Patrick V.	(D-Mich.)	E:1955–66 d
McNary, Charles L.	(R-Ore.)	AE:1917–18;
		AE:1918–44 d
Mead, James M.	(D-N.Y.)	E:1938–47 nc
		H:1919–38
Means, Rice W.	(R-Colo.)	E:1924–27 u
Mechem, Edwin L.	(R-N.M.)	A:1962–64 u
Metcalf, Jesse H.	(R-R.I.)	E:1924–37 u
Metcalf, Lee	(D-Mont.)	E:1961.....
		H:1953–61
Miller, Jack R.	(R-Iowa)	E:1961.....
Miller, John E.	(D-Ark.)	E:1937–41 r
		H:1931–37
Millikin, Eugene D.	(R-Colo.)	AE:1941–57 nc
Milton, John G.	(D-N.J.)	A:1938 nc
Minton, Sherman	(D-Ind.)	E:1935–41 u
		Supreme Court: 1949–56
Mitchell, Hugh B.	(D-Wash.)	A:1945–46 u
		H:1949–53
Mondale, Walter F.	(D-FL-Minn.)	AE:1964.....

Monroney, A. S. Mike	(D-Okla.)	E:1951–69 u
		H:1939–51
Montoya, Joseph M.	(D-N.M.)	E:1964.....
		H:1957–64
Moody, Blair	(D-Mich.)	A:1951–52 u
Moore, Arthur Harry	(D-N.J.)	E:1935–38 r
Moore, Edward H.	(R-Okla.)	E:1943–49 nc
Morrison, Cameron A.	(D-N.C.)	A:1930–32 u
		H:1943–45
Morrow, Dwight W.	(R-N.J.)	E:1930–31 d
Morse, Wayne L.	(R-Ore.)	E:1945–57;
	(D-Ore.)	E:1957–69 u
Morton, Thruston B.	(R-Ky.)	E:1957–69 nc
		H:1947–53
Moses, George H.	(R-N.H.)	E:1918–33 u
Moses, John	(D-N.D.)	E:1945 d
Moss, Frank E.	(D-Utah)	E:1959.....
Mulkey, Frederick W.	(R-Ore.)	E:1918 r
Mundt, Karl E.	(R-S.D.)	AE:1948.....
		H:1939–48
Murdock, Abe	(D-Utah)	E:1941–47 u
		H:1933–41
Murphy, George L.	(R-Calif.)	E:1965.....
Murphy, Maurice J.	(R-N.H.)	A:1961–62 u
Murphy, Richard L.	(D-Iowa)	E:1933–36 d
Murray, James E.	(D-Mont.)	E:1934–61 nc
Muskie, Edmund S.	(D-Maine)	E:1959.....
Myers, Francis J.	(D-Penn.)	E:1945–51 u
		H:1939–45
Myers, Henry L.	(D-Mont.)	E:1911–23 nc
Neely, Matthew M.	(D-W.Va.)	E:1923–29 u;
		E:1931–41 r
		E:1949–58 d
		H:1913–21;1945–
		47
Nelson, Arthur E.	(R-Minn.)	E:1942–43 nc
Nelson, Gaylord	(D-Wis.)	E:1963.....
Nelson, Knute	(R-Minn.)	E:1895–23 d
		H:1883–89
Neuberger, Maurine B.	(D-Ore.)	E:1960–67 nc
Neuberger, Richard L.	(D-Ore.)	E:1955–60 d
New, Harry S.	(R-Ind.)	E:1917–23 u
Newberry, Truman H.	(R-Mich.)	E:1919–22 r
Nicholson, Samuel D.	(R-Colo.)	E:1921–23 d

Proxmire, William	(D-Wis.)	E:1957.....
Purtell, William A.	(R-Conn.)	A:1952 nc; E:1953–59 u
Pyle, Gladys	(R-S.D.)	E:1938–39 nc
Radcliffe, George L.	(D-Md.)	E:1935–47 u
Ralston, Samuel M.	(D-Ind.)	E:1923–25 d
Randolph, Jennings	(D-W.Va.)	E:1958..... H:1933–47
Ransdell, Joseph E.	(D-La.)	E:1913–31 u H:1899–1913
Rawson, Charles A.	(R-Iowa)	A:1922 nc
Reames, Alfred Evan	(D-Ore.)	A:1938 nc
Reed, Clyde M.	(R-Kan.)	E:1939–49 d
Reed, David Aiken	(R-Penn.)	AE:1922–35 u
Reed, James A.	(D-Mo.)	E:1911–29 nc
Revercomb, Chapman	(R-W.Va.)	E:1943–49 u; E:1956–59 u
Reynolds, Robert Rice	(D-N.C.)	E:1932–45 nc
Reynolds, Sam W.	(R-Neb.)	A:1954 nc
Ribicoff, Abraham A.	(D-Conn.)	E:1963..... H:1949–53
Robertson, A. Willis	(D-Va.)	E:1946–67 r H:1933–46
Robertson, Edward V.	(R-Wyo.)	E:1943–49 u
Robinson, Arthur R.	(R-Ind.)	AE:1925–35 u
Robinson, Joseph T.	(D-Ark.)	E:1913–37 d H:1903–13
Robsion, John M.	(R-Ky.)	A:1930 u H:1919–30;1935–48
Rosier, Joseph	(D-W.Va.)	A:1941–42 u
Russell, Donald	(D-S.C.)	A:1965–66 u
Russell, Richard B.	(D-Ga.)	E:1933.....
Sackett, Frederic M.	(R-Ky.)	E:1925–30 r
Salinger, Pierre	(D-Calif.)	A:1964 u
Saltonstall, Leverett	(R-Mass.)	E:1945–67 nc
Saulsbury, Willard	(D-Del.)	E:1913–19 u
Schall, Thomas D.	(R-Minn.)	E:1925–35 d H:1915–25
Schoeppel, Andrew F.	(R-Kan.)	E:1949–62 d
Schuyler, Karl C.	(R-Colo.)	E:1932–33 u
Schwartz, Harry	(D-Wyo.)	E:1937–43 u
Schwellenbach, Lewis B.	(D-Wash.)	E:1935–40 r
Scott, Hugh D.	(R-Penn.)	E:1959..... H:1941–45;1947–59

Scott, William Kerr	(D-N.C.)	E:1954–58 d
Scrugham, James G.	(D-Nev.)	E:1942–45 d
		H:1923–42
Seaton, Frederick A.	(R-Neb.)	A:1951–52 nc
Shafroth, John F.	(D-Colo.)	E:1913–19 u
		H:1895–1904
Sheppard, Morris	(D-Texas)	E:1913–41 d
		H:1902–13
Sherman, Lawrence Y.	(R-Ill.)	E:1913–21 nc
Shields, John K.	(D-Tenn.)	E:1913–25 u
Shipstead, Henrik	(FL-Minn.)	E:1923–41;
	(R-Minn.)	E:1941–47 u
Shortridge, Samuel M.	(R-Calif.)	E:1921–33 u
Shott, Hugh Ike	(R-W.Va.)	E:1942–43 nc
		H:1929–33
Simmons, Furnifold	(D-N.C.)	E:1901–31 u
		H:1887–89
Simpson, Milward L.	(R-Wyo.)	E:1962–67 nc
Slattery, James M.	(D-Ill.)	A:1939–40 u
Smathers, George A.	(D-Fla.)	E:1951–69 nc
		H:1947–51
Smathers, William H.	(D-N.J.)	E:1937–43 u
Smith, Benjamin A., II	(D-Mass.)	A:1960–62 nc
Smith, Ellison D.	(D-S.C.)	E:1909–44 d
Smith, Hoke	(D-Ga.)	E:1911–21 u
Smith, H. Alexander	(R-N.J.)	E:1944–59 nc
Smith, John Walter	(D-Md.)	E:1908–21 u
		H:1899–1900
Smith, Marcus A.	(D-Ariz.)	E:1912–21 u
		Delegate:1887–95;
		1897–99;1901–03;
		1905–09
Smith, Margaret Chase	(R-Maine)	E:1949.....
		H:1940–49
Smith, William Alden	(R-Mich.)	E:1907–19 nc
		H:1895–1907
Smith, Willis	(D-N.C.)	E:1950–53 d
Smoot, Reed	(R-Utah)	E:1903–33 u
Sparkman, John J.	(D-Ala.)	E:1946.....
		H:1937–46
Spencer, George Lloyd	(D-Ark.)	A:1941–43 nc
Spencer, Selden P.	(R-Mo.)	E:1918–25 d
Stanfield, Robert N.	(R-Ore.)	E:1921–27 u
Stanfill, William A.	(R-Ky.)	A:1945–46 nc

Stanley, A. Owsley	(D-Ky.)	E:1919–25 u
		H:1903–15
Steck, Daniel F.	(D-Iowa)	E:1926–31 u
Steiwer, Frederick	(R-Ore.)	E:1927–38 r
Stennis, John C.	(D-Miss.)	E:1947.....
Stephens, Hubert D.	(D-Miss.)	E:1923–35 u
		H:1911–21
Sterling, Thomas	(R-S.D.)	E:1913–25 u
Stewart, Tom	(D-Tenn.)	E:1939–49 u
Stewart, David W.	(R-Iowa)	AE:1926–27 nc
Sullivan, Patrick J.	(R-Wyo.)	A:1929–30 nc
Sutherland, Howard	(R-W.Va.)	E:1917–23 u
		H:1913–17
Swanson, Claude A.	(D-Va.)	AE:1910–33 r
		H:1893–1906
Symington, Stuart	(D-Mo.)	E:1953.....
Taft, Robert A.	(R-Ohio)	E:1939–53 d
Talmadge, Herman E.	(D-Ga.)	E:1957.....
Taylor, Glen H.	(D-Idaho)	E:1945–51 u
Thomas, Charles S.	(D-Colo.)	E:1913–21 u
Thomas, Elbert D.	(D-Utah)	E:1933–51 u
Thomas, John	(R-Idaho)	AE:1928–33 u;
		AE:1940–45 d
Thomas, J. W. Elmer	(D-Okla.)	E:1927–51 u
		H:1923–27
Thompson, William Henry	(D-Neb.)	A:1933–34 nc
Thompson, William Howard	(D-Kan.)	E:1913–19 u
Thurmond, J. Strom	(D-S.C.)	AE:1954–56 r;
		E:1956–64;
	(R-S.C.)	1964.....
Thye, Edward J.	(R-Minn.)	E:1947–59 u
Tobey, Charles W.	(R-N.H.)	E:1939–53 d
		H:1933–39
Tower, John G.	(R-Texas)	E:1961.....
Townsend, Charles E.	(R-Mich.)	E:1911–23 u
		H:1903–11
Townsend, John G.	(R-Del.)	E:1929–41 u
Trammell, Park	(D-Fla.)	E:1917–36 d
Truman, Harry S.	(D-Mo.)	E:1935–45 r
		V.Pres.:1945
		President:1945–53
Tunnell, James M.	(D-Del.)	E:1941–47 u
Tydings, Joseph D.	(D-Md.)	E:1965.....

Tydings, Millard E.	(D-Md.)	E:1927–51 u
		H:1923–27
Tyson, Lawrence D.	(D-Tenn.)	E:1925–29 d
Umstead, William B.	(D-N.C.)	A:1946–48 u
		H:1933–39
Underwood, Oscar W.	(D-Ala.)	E:1915–27 nc
		H:1895–96;
		1897–1915
Underwood, Thomas R.	(D-Ky.)	A:1951–52 u
		H:1949–51
Upton, Robert W.	(R-N.H.)	A:1953–54 u
Vandenberg, Arthur H.	(R-Mich.)	AE:1928–51 d
Van Nuys, Frederick	(D-Ind.)	E:1933–44 d
Vardaman, James K.	(D-Miss.)	E:1913–19 u
Wadsworth, James W., Jr.	(R-N.Y.)	E:1915–27 u
		H:1933–51
Wagner, Robert F.	(D-N.Y.)	E:1927–49 r
Walcott, Frederic C.	(R-Conn.)	E:1929–35 u
Wallgren, Monrad C.	(D-Wash.)	AE:1940–45 r
		H:1933–40
Walsh, Arthur	(D-N.J.)	A:1943–44 nc
Walsh, David I.	(D-Mass.)	E:1919–25 u;
		E:1926–47 u
Walsh, Thomas J.	(D-Mont.)	E:1913–33 d
Walters, Herbert S.	(D-Tenn.)	A:1963–64 nc
Warren, Francis E.	(R-Wyo.)	E:1890–93 nc;
		E:1895–1929 d
Waterman, Charles W.	(R-Colo.)	E:1927–32 d
Watkins, Arthur V.	(R-Utah)	E:1947–59 u
Watson, James E.	(R-Ind.)	E:1916–33 u
		H:1895–97;
		1899–1909
Watson, Thomas E.	(D-Ga.)	E:1921–22 d
		H:1891–93
Weeks, John Wingate	(R-Mass.)	E:1913–19 u
		H:1905–13
Weeks, Sinclair	(R-Mass.)	A:1944 nc
Welker, Herman	(R-Idaho)	E:1951–57 u
Weller, Ovington E.	(R-Md.)	E:1921–27 u
Wheeler, Burton K.	(D-Mont.)	E:1923–47 u
Wherry, Kenneth S.	(R-Neb.)	E:1943–51 d
White, Wallace H.	(R-Maine)	E:1931–49 nc
		H:1917–31
Wiley, Alexander	(R-Wis.)	E:1939–63 u

Wilfley, Xenophon P.	(D-Mo.)	A:1918 u
Williams, George H.	(R-Mo.)	A:1925–26 u
Williams, Harrison A.	(D-N.J.)	E:1959.....
		H:1953–57
Williams, John J.	(R-Del.)	E:1947.....
Williams, John Sharp	(D-Miss.)	E:1911–23 nc
		H:1893–1909
Williamson, Ben M.	(D-Ky.)	E:1930–31 nc
Willis, Frank B.	(R-Ohio)	E:1921–28 d
		H:1911–15
Willis, Raymond E.	(R-Ind.)	E:1941–47 nc
Wilson, George A.	(R-Iowa)	E:1943–49 u
Withers, Garrett L.	(D-Ky.)	A:1949–50 nc
		H:1952–53
Wofford, Thomas A.	(D-S.C.)	A:1956 nc
Yarborough, Ralph W.	(D-Tex.)	E:1957.....
Young, Milton R.	(R-N.D.)	AE:1945.....
Young, Stephen M.	(D-Ohio)	E:1959.....
		H:1933–37;1941–43;
		1949–51

CONGRESS	PRESIDENT	VICE PRESIDENT	PRESIDENT PRO TEM
65th: 1917–19	Woodrow Wilson	Thomas R. Marshall	Willard Saulsbury
66th: 1919–21	"	"	Albert B. Cummins
67th: 1921–23	Warren G. Harding	Calvin Coolidge	"
68th: 1923–25	Calvin Coolidge	—	"
69th: 1925–27	"	Charles G. Dawes	George H. Moses
70th: 1927–29	"	"	"
71st: 1929–31	Herbert Hoover	Charles Curtis	"
72nd: 1931–33	"	"	"
73rd: 1933–34	Franklin D. Roosevelt	John Nance Garner	Key Pittman
74th: 1935–36	"	"	"
75th: 1937–38	"	"	"
76th: 1939–41	"	"	" William H. King
77th: 1941–42	"	Henry A. Wallace	Pat Harrison Carter Glass
78th: 1943–44	"	"	"
79th: 1945–46	" Harry S. Truman	Harry S. Truman —	Kenneth McKellar
80th: 1947–48	"	—	Arthur Vandenberg
81st: 1949–51	"	Alben W. Barkley	Kenneth McKellar
82nd: 1951–52	"	"	"
83rd: 1953–54	Dwight D. Eisenhower	Richard M. Nixon	Styles Bridges
84th: 1955–56	"	"	Walter F. George
85th: 1957–58	"	"	Carl Hayden
86th: 1959–60	"	"	"
87th: 1961–62	John F. Kennedy	Lyndon B. Johnson	"
88th: 1963–64	" Lyndon B. Johnson	—	"
89th: 1965–66	"	Hubert H. Humphrey	"
90th: 1967–68	"	"	"
91st: 1969–70	Richard M. Nixon	Spiro T. Agnew	Richard B. Russell

LEADERS

SPEAKER OF THE HOUSE	DEMOCRATIC LEADER	REPUBLICAN LEADER
Champ Clark	* Thomas S. Martin	Henry Cabot Lodge, Sr.
Frederick H. Gillett	Gilbert M. Hitchcock Oscar W. Underwood	* "
"	"	* "
"	Joseph T. Robinson	* " Charles Curtis
Nicholas Longworth	"	* "
"	"	* "
"	"	* James E. Watson
John Nance Garner	"	* "
Henry T. Rainey	* "	Charles L. McNary
Joseph W. Byrns William B. Bankhead	* "	"
"	* Alben W. Barkley	"
" Sam Rayburn	* "	"
"	* "	"
"	* "	" Wallace H. White
"	* "	"
Joseph W. Martin	"	* "
Sam Rayburn	* Scott W. Lucas	Kenneth Wherry
"	* Ernest W. McFarland	" Styles Bridges
Joseph W. Martin	Lyndon B. Johnson	* Robert A. Taft * William F. Knowland
Sam Rayburn	* "	"
"	* "	"
"	* "	Everett M. Dirksen
" John W. McCormack	* Mike Mansfield	"
"	* "	"
"	* "	"
"	* "	"
"	* "	"

* —Majority Leader

INDEX